SUPER LEARNING TECHNIQUE (SLT) AND CREATIVE THINKING

SUPER LEARNING TECHNIQUE (SLT) AND CREATIVE THINKING

DR. PRAMOD KUMAR PRUSTY

Ph.D., D.Litt. (Education)

Former Senior Lecturer in Education
Harakamaya College of Education
Gangtok, Sikkim
District Welfare Officer and DPC, SSA
Jagatsinghpur, Orissa.

Foreword by

PROF. (DR.) JAGANNATH MOHANTY

Former UGC Emeritus Fellow
Ravenshaw Autonomous College, Cuttack
and Former Prof. of Education and
Retd. Principal, Radhanath IASE
Cuttack, Orissa

DEEP & DEEP PUBLICATIONS PVT. LTD.
F-159, Rajouri Garden, New Delhi - 110 027

SUPER LEARNING TECHNIQUE (SLT)
AND CREATIVE THINKING

ISBN 978-81-8450-257-2

Printed in India at MAYUR ENTERPRISES
WZ Plot No. 3, Gujjar Market, Tihar Village, New Delhi - 110 018

Published by DEEP & DEEP PUBLICATIONS PVT. LTD.,
F-159, Rajouri Garden, New Delhi - 110 027 • Phone : 25435369, 25440916
E-mail : ddpubs@gmail.com • ddpbooks@yahoo.co.in
Showroom :
2/13, Ansari Road, Daryaganj, New Delhi - 110 002 • Telefax : 23245122

CONTENTS

FOREWORD

Yoga and meditation is the holy heritage of Indian culture. It is clearly explained in our Vedas and Upanisadas and Gita. Patanjali's "Yoga Sutra" is accepted as a milestone in compiling the literture of yoga in one form. All these principles are also found in meditation procedure of Jain and Buddhist cults. Though this tradition happens to be adopted by modern yogis of 19th and 20th century like Swami Vivekanand, Sri Aurobindha, Swami Nigamanand, Sri Sivanand and at present it is popularised by Swami Satyanand, Swami Ramdev, Shri Shri Ravishanker by its scientific interpretations, till now, we have failed to explore all its merits for utilization in our day-to- day life.

In the field of Indian education, implication of yoga and mediation is still awaiting a systematic curricular design and implementation. Under such circumstances the research of Georgi Lozanov, the Bulgarian doctor has ushered a new era in the field of education in developing super learning on the basis of Indian Raja Yoga and some principles of Bulgarian Yogic culture. Being interested in Lozanove's contribution many educationists, psychologists, military and defence personnel have used super learning in their field of work and have reported their success stories. But the land where Yoga originated is still in the form of theoretical speculation.

The research study entitled "Effect of Super Learning Technique [SLT] on Development of Creative Thinking" conducted by Dr. Pramod Kumar Prusty, an educationist and administrator has broken that inertia. This study is first of its kind in India which experimentally studied the effect of Yoga and mediation, i.e Super Learning Technique [SLT] in the classroom environment. It tried to scientifically and objectively justify the effect of super learning on students' creative thinking and academic achievement. The study gave a new direction to the educational system by establishing the fact through experiment that yoga and meditation, the basis of super learning, can be brought into classroom and subjects can be well-taught through it within the time frame of a class or period. It does not hamper the learning rather it is proved to be beneficial in developing students' achievement and creative thinking.

From 2008-09, Department of Higher Education, Government of Orissa, have introduced yoga as a compulsory subject at +2 level. In this context, it can be said that introduction of yoga and meditation will be more fruitfull if our curriculum, methods of teaching and teachers' training will be redesigned in that respect. Researchers of various discipline should come forward and conduct further study in classroom to extend its generalization. Tryst must be made at Government and non-Government levels to concretize the scientific approach of super learning so that in future it will be the basis of designing any courses of study, methods of teaching, evaluation procedure and overall influence the primary or pre-primary levels of education.

It is hoped that super learning will be helpful in enlightening the untapped area of human learning and personality if the suggestions of the auther will be sincerely implemented.

PROF. JAGANNATH MOHANTY

ACKNOWLEDGEMENTS

The individual has tremendous quantum of power. As accepted by the psychologists, a most advanced person at best utilized 1/10th of his mental power leaving 90% of his power unutilized. Psychologists, educationists and scientists are always endeavouring to explore such untapped power. Super learning is a means to achieve that it has incorporated some of the Bulgarian yogic principles with Indian Raja Yoga. People of different disciplines of the world have used it and have expressed its effectiveness. Its experimental use specially in the field of education though are many in foreign lands, this study is first of its kind in India. Being the land of origin of yoga and meditation, it is irony that till now we were in that philosophical set-up. However, this study showed that we can bring our yoga and meditation into class-room to energize the dormated brain cells of learners and enhance their creative thinking and scholastic achievement. It helps in synchronizing right and left hemispheric functions by transmitting more oxygen into brain cells thereby activate all sections to make the learner able for any sort of work. Thus, the study showed a new direction to researchers to verify the effectiveness of super learning in other fields of work.

It is a great pleasure for the author to express his deep sense of gratitude to Prof. (Dr.) J. Mohanty, Emeritus Fellow, Professor of Education and Retd. Principal Radhanath IASE, Cuttack, Orissa, only for whose valuable advice, scholarly and rhetoric guidance, this work could have seen the light of the day. The author deems it a privilege to work under him, who is the embodiment of all the features of friend, philosopher and guide.

The author expresses his deepest gratitude to Prof. (Dr.) R.C. Das, Ex-Vice-Chancellor, Berhampur University and Retd. Professor of Education, NCERT, New Delhi, who has been a ceaseless source of his inspiration. The author felt fortunate of being a research scholar under Prof. Das for his Ph.D. Degree and of experiencing the characteristics of a true teacher within him. In completion of this piece of research work, his contribution was unparallel. Influence of his personality on the life of the investigator was so profound that the researcher felt that mere words would be insufficient to show thankfulness to him.

The author expresses his indebtedness to Prof. B.K. Passi, Former Professor of Education, Devi Ahilya Viswavidyalaya, Indore who wrote the first research paper in India on super learning which made the investigator anxious to conduct the research study on this new topic. Further, postal-guidance which were provided by Professor Passi on different phases of this work were most valuable in making the study qualitative one. Therefore, the author expresses his deep sense of gratitude to Prof. Passi.

The source of inspiration and means of problem-solution for the research work were Dr. M.M. Mohanty, Former Director, SIEMAT, Orissa, Prof. S. L. Jena, Director, TE and SCERT, Orissa, Dr. P.L. Mohapatra, H.O.D., Education, B.J.B. College, Bhubaneswar, Dr. P.K.S. Ray, Principal, Harakamaya College of Education, Gangtok, Sikkim, Dr. G.C. Pradhan, Lecturer in Education, Nirmala Institute of Education, Panaji, Goa to whom the author feels very much grateful.

The Headmaster, staff members and students of University High School, Vani Vihar, Bhubaneswar were praiseworthy for tendering their valuable time and resource for the experiment.

The researcher also feels grateful to the authors and writers whose literature and websites helped in giving final touch to this work.

Whatever thanks the author gives to his family members, who succumbed varied troubles during the study, would be negligible. So he only expresses his love and pleasure for their stand by.

DR. PRAMOD KUMAR PRUSTY

1 SUPER LEARNING
Concept and Process

1.1 Super Learning—A Conceptual Analysis

1.2 Multidimensional Approach of Super Learning

1.3 Instructional Strategy of Super Learning

1.4 Yoga, Meditation and Super Learning—
A Comparative Analysis

1.5 Super Learning in Indian Schools—A Retrospection

1.6 Super Learning and Issues Relating Creative Thinking

SUPER LEARNING
Concept and Process

1.1 SUPER LEARNING—A CONCEPTUAL ANALYSIS

Learning is instinctive to the organism. Man and animal, both learn from their respective environment either automatically or in systematic process. So learning is regarded as a process by which behaviour is originated (Kingsley and Garry, 1957). It is very much systemic and scientific by nature. Although learning is organismic, it always depends on experiences (Smith, 1966).

When learning occurs automatically, person experiences change with no choice. But when the person systematizes the scientific process of learning for achievement of certain goal (Pressey, Robinson and Horrocks, 1967) or for overcoming the obstacles and to adjust to situations (Crow and Crow, 1973), he or she intends to reap maximum benefit from the process. For the acquisition of optimum success the person always seeks after most profitable process in consideration to his own interest, environment and potentiality. Thorndike's trail and error learning, Pavlov's classical conditioning, Skinner's operant learning and Kholer's insightful learning are not equally effective for all types of people. Similarly, every individual can not elicit same result from Gagne's hierarchical learning, Bloom's Mastery learning or Ausubel's meaningful learning. It is because of the variation that exist in inter and intra-individual characteristics.

Under these circumstances, Super Learning, by its very concept, acts as a super process of enhancing the learning ability by making the individual learn "how to learn". It never wants to follow other learning methods, rather it tries to enable individual "to know thyself". Basically, super learning is a process of revitalizing the inherent potentialities so that the individual's learning abilities will increase in manifold. Since there are various behavioural attributes of the personality, super learning acts as a subliminal message that encourages and energizes the person to perform in the best way. Therefore, Ostrander and Schroeder (1997) stated the super learning as "a technique of energizing the lethargic accessories of human organism as a hot cup of coffee brings back mental smartness and physical boldness."

After the thorough test of the effectiveness of this technique, the US government has accepted it as "Super Food" which can make people a startling 25% smarter. It's success in increasing intelligence, creative thinking, developing memory, concentration, mastering skills and relieving stress from psycho-physical systems. All these techniques are not directly related to day-to-day performance refinement, rather the process makes the man ever fit with all round well-manifestation of personality attributes through which the person can be a best performer.

"Vitamin E supplements can combat forgetfulness by preventing damage in human brain caused by free radicals and different metabolism", says US researcher Peter Zandi, neurologist of John Hopkins Bloomberg School of Public Health from his experiment conducted on 4500 forgetful people. He also states that such Vitamin E, as antioxidant, protects lens from hazardous effect of different metabolites and free radicals, checks heart disease by fighting against oxidation of bas cholesterol which blocks coronary artery, prevents untoward cell death and fight anemia through preventing premature death of the red cells. Unlike the action of Vitamin E, which rejuvenates the organs and mechanisms of human body by ioning out the inhibiting factors, Super learning helps in energizing the fundamental organismic constituents. The most significant aspect of super learning is that it helps in bringing more oxygen to the brain through breath holding games which increases IQ by five to 10 points in intelligence test scores. It also helps in creating and supplying amino-acid that is high power fuel for the whole brain development. (Garreet, 1967)

Conceptually, super learning refers to an accelerated form of learning. But an in-depth analysis of the effect of super learning signifies it as a means or technique of discovering and rediscovering the inherent power of different organs or faculties of human organism, so that the person will be rejuvenated with force of fruitful living. Alongwith, it presupposes a thorough technique of upgrading the performance of various faculties. Meaningfulness of the learning matter, no doubt, exerts significant impact on the learning of the individual (Ausubel, 1967). When meaningfulness of learning matter develops at high degree, learning goes on speedily, because it creates a stronger motivation drive in the individual. In contrast to the rate of learning in meaningful discovery, mastery learning concept of Bloom (1956) demands better result provided that the learner has acquired mastery over the previous learning. But most surprisingly, the super learning technique provide a different opinion on mastery, synonymous to Freud's concept-relating conscious, sub-conscious and unconsciousness. It states innumerable possibilities and unmeasurable abilities (approximately 9/10th) those are there in the unconscious level of the individual, which, generally remain undiscovered. So, Freud stressed on various technique of primary process for bringing out the unconscious level thoughts and abilities for all round development of the individual. Such primary process is referred by Arieti (1926) as primodial which deals with processes and forms. It consists of metamorphical thinking, day dreaming and intuitive and imagery thinking while Maslow (1957) speaks that thought are the outcome of interaction between primary and secondary processes. Kubie (1964) called it as "preconscious" deeds and Cannon described it as "extra-conscious work" (Rathenberg and Hausman, 1976). Like Freud's psychoanalysis super learning gives maximum importance on the development of individual's hidden potentialities. But, in exception, it capitalizes on the functional abilities of various personality attributes. Thorndike's multifactor theory of intelligence (1914) and Guilford's structure of intellect (1967), describes about 150 factors of intellect under three basic divisions, such as, contents products and operation, Likewise Lozanov's super learning has clearly identified that the fundamental faculties of human personality are the bases of the individual and intends to energize and reactivates those for all round success.

Thus Lozanov's super learning is bio-psychic to its core of action and basically tries to nurture the basic faculties of human personality, so that the person will be ever fit for any sort of spectacular performance. In most particular manner, "such technique," as defined by Passi and Prabhu (1996), "is to tap the reserves of the mind and an easy, relaxed way of learning that speeds up learning ten or more times." This accelerated learning conserves human energy to learn effectively without stress and tension. When it is said that learning is organismic, the very word "organismic" is quite related to the intra-*cum*-inter individual variations. Although such variations are factored by nature, maximum of them are either due to uncultivation of the powers stored before or uncongenial support characterized by mistaken and unaware practices predominated by cultural taboo, scientific fallacies and reliance on miraculous auto-exposition. All these anti-evolutionary factors never help in developing brilliance among organismic characteristics, rather those act as development—prone spurts for the organism. As such, individual organism has now become foreign to its own attributes. Some stress more on body than on mind and some others go in reverse. Even, amidst the psychologists who deal with mind and mental abilities of the organism, some stress on the effect of right hemisphere, where others give importance on the left hemisphere. But, the mind functions actively when it is at balance with the left brain, right brain and the body (Passi and Prabhu, 1997). It is because no activity of an organism is the product of only either psychic or physical exercise. As depicted by James's functionalism (Woodworth, 1948) and its scientific and objective analysis, the function of mind should be studied in relation to environmental adjustment. Likewise, Watsonian behaviourism stresses on scientific study of observable behaviour, mostly the overt activities of the organism. But, an analytic speculation shows that each behavioural disposition is preceded by some cerebral or mental activity, which we cannot see. Although, we cannot see those, we cannot also deny the fact of mentalistic functions as stated by Wundt and Titchener (Woolman, 1988).

Accordingly, Freud (1971) analyzed the function of unconsciousness and its influence over sub-consciousness and consciousness. Thus, a critical speculation of all the factors of human behaviour shows its origin out of psychological, physiological and environmental interactions. As changeability is the glaring feature of these fundamental factors, so the behaviour is explained as dynamic. Under such circumstances, super learning speaks of body-mind relaxation and use of music to make the super learning and super achievement more fruitful, it is clearly evident that the whole-brain functions better when it is made stress-free and relaxed. If the origin of stress and tension in the organism, which is totally cerebral or nervous-system-related, in many extent, is related to the environment or external events, then its control and minimizing process, i.e., by the use of music, etc., can also be attributed to environmental element. Thus, super learning is a process of bringing a harmonious bend among the psychophysical and environmental attributes so that the learning machine will be most functional.

With clear and concrete realization of all these considerations, Lozanov, through his super learning technique, has tried to hit on the individual's extraordinary mental abilities, which is the cynosure of the multidimensional energization. After several thorough scientific longitudinal studies, he claims that super memory is a natural human ability. Every individual is endowed with it. Each individual can develop super memory power, if he will use the appropriate learning technique. So, Lozanov conducted extensive and in-depth studies on the ancient system of relaxation, most specially on yoga from India and Bulgaria, and developed the super learning technique on the following assumptions (Passi and Prabhu, 1997).

1. The human mind has limitless capacities. It is almost infinite. Human ability to learn and remember is also limitless, but each of us conditioned by our culture, is blind to this culture.
2. Learning is effective when it is global, i.e., when body and mind work in harmony.
3. Learning under stress and tension is not only painful, but leads to quick forgetting. When the mind is stress free, learning becomes most effective.

In whole-brain synchronization, super learning also develops the activity of brain wave levels. Brain wave levels are quantifications of the electric charges emitted by the brain and measured by an electroencephalogram and expressed in terms of herts (hz). From among four major brain levels : Delta level (Hz 0.5-4) indicates deeper state of sleep; Theta level (Hz 4-8) refers to the state of drowsiness and dreaming; Beta level (Hz 14-22) is a state of outward action occurred due to concentrated mental activity, problem-solving, anxiety and apprehension; Alpha level (Hz 8-14) is a state of relaxed wakefulness. Here, the brain is actively engaged in specific mental and emotional activity. The mind is still, alert and inward-focused.

In the normal life situation, individual functions at Beta level. In this level, when a person concentrates continuously on a problem or issue, stress or tension increases within the individual. An increase in stress and tension decreases efficiency and leads to breakdown in the person concerned. To overcome such breakdown and to increase efficiency, one has to control the stress and rein the tension. To have it, a perfect harmony among left brain, right brain and body is required. Such balance brings a paradigm shift of stress-ridden Beta brain wave level to Alpha level, i.e., a relaxed state of mind, which is capable of accomplishing all miracles. In Super Learning Technique (SLT), learning takes place when the mind is in Alpha level. As explained by Passi and Prabhu (1997), in Alpha level the mind is alert, and perceptive awareness builds up and through expanded awareness one can control and select the expected perception. There is also a link, build up between conscious and unconscious mind. Such link produces a third state which becomes super conscious and which retrieves whatever one perceives. Thus super learning seems very much similar to the concept of super mind of Sri Aurobindo, which gives rise to the general man to super man (The Divine Life, 1964).

The Latin etymological derivation of the word education, which is related to "educere", refers to 'bring out' or 'draw out'. The very meaning indicates that the educand is full up with great possibilities which are to be digged out. That is what super learning system is designed to do. Accordingly, Socrates the great philosopher-teacher and his best disciple Plato operated on the principle that we all have innate genius and connected to infinite knowledge. Lozanov, through super learning, has tried to ignite those. It is explained by Brain Hamilton's memory with his home made tapes and special music as "In just two weeks of super learning I went from B minus to A's". Al Boothby, a college teacher in Sacramento school district leading many classes through imaginative exercises and helping many learners in being sucessful, discovered super learning as drawing out what is already there and igniting innate ability that can turn F's into A's more handily than suffing students" (Ostrander and Schroeder, 1997).

So, what educationist-philosopher Pestalozzi says of education—"natural, harmonious and progressive development of man's innate power", is made possible through super learning. It, as education does, coordinates the function of body, mind and sprit for any sort of activity so that the performance would be quite exhilarating. It makes the sense organs super sensitive which is analogous to Sri Aurobindo's strategy of developing mind (Manas) to super mind (Ati Manas). So, from own training experience, Boothby said, "through super learning one can learn anything he wants to learn". Super learning may operate automatically by collecting information from outward magnetic field which is belived by layman as miracle. But, actually as told by Hanilton, "super learning can sometimes work automatically" (Held, 1984). It, thus, sensitizes the receptiveness of cells, senses and inner self of the person. It awakens the sub-conscious and un-conscious layers of the mind (Freud, 1936).

Relating importance of levels of mind, the eminent medical hypnotist Milton Erickson states "your conscious mind is very intelligent and your sub-conscious is a hell of a lot smarter.

Super learning draws much of its voltage from that smart and shadowy power house—the subliminal memory. As Lozanov speaks, unlike all traditional education accelerated system address both conscious and unconsciouss mind (Loafland, 1992). Thus, super learning approaches for a better body mind make-up. It stimulates more areas of brain than all traditional learning do. As explained by Dr. Monique Le Poncin, "super learning acts as the mental toxin for strategic mobolity and development of brain cells through relaxation, visualization and imaginative rehearsals (Prichard, A. and Taylor, J., 1980). It is related to hypermnesia as it deals with the super memory. In Lozanov's style, super learning allows the growth of world class memory. It was a breakthrough in Communist Soviet during eighties under the scientific name of hypermnesia—the fascinating opposition of amnesia.

Like libido or life instinct (Eros) that is analogous to surat (Thakur, 1926) Super Learning has a significant parlance in exploring development of a full-fledged personality (Freud, 1936). For such divergent performance of super learning in different levels and walks of human personality, it has acquired various names, such as, Optimal learning, Power learning, Sound Learning, Inner Track Learning, Project Renaissance, Super Study. The analysis on psycho-philosophical bases of super learning exemplifies its much relevance to transpersonal psychology, which is one of the latest approaches prevalent in contemporary psychology and stresses on extraordinary overall excellence. It's high stress on the ignition of sensori perception to extrasensori and pre-cognitive perfection shows its relevance to theoretical speculation of parapsychology, suggestopedia, sorphology and hypermnesia.

1.2 MULTIDIMENSIONAL APPROACH OF SUPER LEARNING

John B. Watson (1926), father of Behaviourism—the most applauded theory of psychology, once asserted "give me a dozen healthy infants, well up in and I will guarantee to take any one at random and train him to become any type of specialist I might select-doctor, lawyer, artists, merchant chief and yes even beggar man and thief, regardless of his talents, penchants, tendencies, abilities, vocations and race of his ancestors". The former French dictator Napoleon Bonaparte once stated, "give me good mothers, I will give you a good nation". The above two statements are not synonymous. The former stresses on the impact of favourable environment and latter on hereditary propensities in moulding the individual's personality. But relating the impact of super learning the personal experience reported by Christian Drapeau, a Canadian neurologist, states, "I was a North American Tae know Do champion. I have a master's degree in neurology and neurosurgery, have composed music, studied and published books on philosophy, written another on nutrition. I am engaged in full time research and am making an in-depth study of religion. I am now twenty-seven years old. It was the super learning teachnique that allowed me to do what I conceive of as great work upon myself. What I had done all on my own".

Further, in explaining the secrecy of his success, Drapeau says, "I have always been interested in the fantastic faculties of the brain. I have always had, as long as I can remember, a certainty that man has the potential to do watever he wants and that his limits are those he decides to set for himself.

Thus, understanding own potentiality is the matter of great concern. Knowing, understanding and realizing own self, now, is at stake. What about one's perception on others brilliance? In today's society, stress and strain have not engulfed these adolescents only, as psychologists of the globe have been sounding loudly. People of all age levels and of every position are entangled with lack of self-confidence. In this post-modern age knowledge explodes unabatedly. Exchanging socio-economic and politico-religious conditions made the materialistic individual most busy and tension-ridden. Peace and tranquility has become foreign to people, thereby their personal, professional and social life lose glamour and pleasure. Unsatiated wants putting individual in maladjusted position, which, in many cases, has been aggravated to frustration. Under such hallow and colourless life, individual is searching for solace through resolving problems and by attending spectacular success. In the field of business, economy, social life, and family life and even in the issues of national and international importance, such struggle for existence is quite evident. And, in turn, the most adept one comes out fittest for survival. Why maximum fail? Are not they endowed with all potentials? Are they unaware of the ways and means of their struggle? Both the apprehensions are sure for the failures. Maximum are either of withdrawing tendencies or have feeling of impotency—the result of "foreign to own self".

Diagnosing the secrets of such chaotic personality embrrassment in the individual, Georgy Lozanov, the Bulgarian doctor has developed Super Learning as an absolute panacea. Siv Khera, the management specialist says, "You Can Win". Going miles ahead, Lozanov's super learnig always proposes "You Would Win", for substitution of any sort of hunches. It is because learning is super in it's assumption and approach. It is always positive and affirmative for comformity. The philosophy behind it is that accepts each individual entity as the cynosure of all potential energy, which can be, converted to any form—electrical, mechanical, sound, light, etc. as per the need of the holder. That is why, hundred years ago, William James calculated, "we use only about five percent of our innate abilities" (Ostrnder & Schroeder, 1997), which goes with Freud's statement, "all the activities individual performs is only one-tenth of his unconscious level." Relating such discovered talent, Dr. Raymond Abrezol, who has trained hundreds of Olympic stars, states, "It is more like three percent. Few of us use even five percent of our capacity". So, think of what amount is still strange for us !

Relating the magnitude of super learning, George Leonard, the writer-educator, says, "the ultimate creative capacity of the brain may be for all practical purposes, infinite" (Leonard, 1979). Gail Heidenhein, Director of Delphin, a German business training company, says, "again and again teachers, trainers and learners say that courses (super learning) have changed their lives." The Californian teacher Bruce Tylor, while expressing his experience speaks, "after thirty years of teaching, I knew, there had to be a better way. Super learning has changed my life for the better and that of my students too".

Ivan Barzakov of Bulgaria, who, in spite of all heavy hurdles natural and physical, swam the Adriatic sea successfully even not being afraid of the great earthquake in Trieste and emergence of treacherous Yugoslavian marshes speaks, "I had the kernels of the mental technology. I had to use the mental technology to block memories of death" (Ostrander, 1979). The aftermath of his mysterious and successful expedition into sea instigated Brazakov and his American wife Pamela Rand to lead optimal learning system in Novato, California to nurture kernels of mental technology into full-blown techniques to help others. Expressing his realization on the super learning Brazakov says, ". . . it creates a feeling of enormous potential of human beings, the excitement of our capacities. With this technique, I know, we could touch a profound source within us".

Super Learning, as a branch of parapsychology, always uses new technique to learn language in a month (Croucher, 1981). It is also used as suggestology-an electric bag of technique of alternative medicine to cure the sick and psychotics. In the field of education and learning also, such suggestopedia is used as a healing technique for students those suffer from didactogenic syndrome-sickness caused by poor teaching methods. The society for Accelerative Learning and Teaching (SALT), founded by Dr. Doland Schuster at Amoes in late 1970s and Society for Effective and Affective Learning (SEAL) of England have performed its works for professionals, learners, etc. In this regard, Gail Heidenhain, Business trainer of Delphin Co. reported that learners, teachers and trainers say again and again that Super Learning has changed their lifes." Dr. Lee Pulos, CEO of life long Communications, says, "it added to my creative thinking by lessening self-doubt and fear of failure.

Likewise, the researchers on super learning all over the world have acquired experimental knowledge relating its effectiveness on language learning, education of pre-school children, learning science, computer, high tech, mathematics, grammer, etc. As told by Ostrander and Schroeder (2001), it is found effective for businessmen and students having learning disabilities and multiple handicaps. Mind/body mental training programme for ultimate fitness of mind training secrets, used by Russian cosmonauts and European Olympic stars opened the new dimensions of mind power, health and physical skills. "Use them for mental physical wellness, sports and public performance from acting to guitar playing", says Ostrander (1995). Super learning has also full spectrum mind programmes to develop self-esteem, stress control, pain control, photographic memory and focused concentration. Special programmes for children proved to be boon to parents, teachers and youngsters in speed learning, overcoming blocks and awaking potentials. Relating the multi-dimensional impact of super learning, Dr. Bernie Siegel (2000) says, "it is full of breakthroughs in the use of sound, brain patterns, nutrients, imagery and much more to open potential plus to super learn almost anything and excel at work, school, sports and the arts". The research finding of M. Robinson of Newport Beach, California speaks, "by using baroque music of super learning, memory improved by 26% and learning improved by 24%" (*Iowa State University SALT Journal*, 2002).

John White says that the super learning is a powerful path to change through new dimensions of memory. According to him, "it connects with expanded realms of memory to turbo charge intelligence and memory, creates wellness-physical, mental, spiritual to rebalance life conditions, attract prosperity to find fulfilling work and relationship and releases exhilarating potentials." It gives new ways to beat intelligence robbing, diseases and disabilities and is a miracle memory builder. Psychologists accept memory as the center of expressing multiple potentialities, which brings many changes in person's body, mind and banishes illness. Super learning, thus, heals mind-body and releases new abilities super to travel the inner information highway and communicates with expanded memory to unsnarl memory traffic jams as a pass to its creative power to build new behaviours and draw wealth, success and serenity into individuals' life.

Spring (1992), in the book "Diamond Fire", stated the astonishing frontiers of memory that can be revealed by super learning technique. The frontier circumscribes followings:

- Under water birthing which reveals better birth equals better life and how recovering own memories of birth and life in the womb can bring new health and happiness.
- Spies and memory power-The chilling super power race to super memory powers and memory weapons. discovering of mind damaging electro-magnetic energy

fields and how to protect yourself with memory pollution busters.

- Memory survives death—the latest scientific evidence of how memory lives outside the body and brain. It helps one to communicate electronically with the dead.
- Worldwide explosion of Remembering—which changes life by recovering memories of pre-birth even the memories of earth's past (cosmic memories).

Thus, as told by Geller, "super learning is a great psychic discovery". Hugh Lynn Cayce, Director of Edgar Cayce Association, says, "Super learning is one of the most exciting books on psychic research." which, according to USA Psychic Magazine, "will stimulate and intrigue every imagination". The unprecedented photos, films and videos, released by Ostrander and Schroeder, are psychic breakthroughs. The films explain the actual activities of Russian psychic superstars, who used to move objects at a distance by psychokinetic power as of the Czech scientists who can turn on lights or machines with the psychic power of their eyes. The audio-videos also show the try out of a Russian psychologist's programme for developing psycho-kinetic (PK) abilities with photos of psychotronic generators—the devices that harness psychic force and put it to work (www.super learning. com.) The super learning relaxation session with stress easing 60 beat baroque music accompained by beautiful, colourful swirl of human aura, gives way to a new frontier of healing. Super learning also gives amazing evidence of animal telepathy.

Super learning has also created a tramendous impact on the society which trembles with war and horror (The Iron Curtain Lifted Order : Psychic Discoveries, 2001). The ultra-secret KGB UFO files of Schroeder and Ostrander (1979) state, "here is stratling revelation of how Soviet scientists succeeded in harnessing psychic weapons which were used in Espinose, politics, the military, even sports and more surprisingly to combat UFO's that were swarming and landing all over Russia" (The ESP papers : Soviet Scientists Speak Out PSYCHIC DISCOVERIES—The CD ROM Item #188). Thus speaking of the multidimensional approach of super learning 60 beat music, Robinson (2002) says that it can help you to activate super memory, speed up learning, put conscious and subconscious into communication, improve concentration, recharge health lower blood pressure; overcome fatigue; induce alert relaxation and to synchronize brain hemispheres and body rhythm to more efficient patterns. Super learning(r) (r) music Vol. I and all music Vol. II speaks of tension dissolution and inner awareness open up as you start to tap unused capabilities. "With this music", says Ostrander (Super Learning (r) All music Vol. III), "you can learn facts, figures, languages ultra-rapidly. You can heighten guided imagery and visualization exercises for any topic. You are in the ideal state to do mental training for sports and creative performance." The LARGO-TAPE, prepared by Dr. Charles Schmid (www.superlearning.com) acts as a means of stress reduction and helps in good listening and learning.

Likewise, there are numerous empirical evidences reported by educationists and psychologists relating many-sided effectiveness of super learning mechanisms. Allyn Pichard found it most effective in learning mathematics, vocabulary and in remedial reading in an accelerated speed (Super learning (r) Arithmetic/Mathmatics/vocabulary, 2003). Janale a Hoffman's "The Dolphin Song" has also proved beneficial for children's (of two to 10 years age group) all round development. Eli Boy (Maximizing Performance Tape #602) state that super learning can maximize performance for jobs, sports or whatever you put your talents to. It can also help in learning the lanugage at laser speed, which acts as a passport to more friends, widen horizon and to develop social and business assets (*Walls Street Journal's Editorial*, www.superlearning.com). Discussing on the effect of super learning on multi-dimensional development of the individual, Sheila Ostrander (1997) says, "Super learning speed, empower memory, language pharses are rhythmically paced and backed. You will save time, money and effort with it. It adds fun and pleasure to any vocation or business trip, easy travel stress, opens the door to rewarding foreign contracts and contacts, confidently handles every day travel situations—meals, changing money, shopping, registering at hotel, sight-seeing, emergencies, finding your way by train, plane, bus or car."

Besides developing language learning, super learning is also very much helpful in bringing complete stress control and in disolving IQ-hampring anxities. "It has a tremendous impact on developing the potentialities of MDs, hard driving managers, trades people, housewives", says Dr. Raymond Abrezol (Harmoney = Health, 2000). He has also found the impact of Sophrology, which is alomst same to super learning, in various types of sport stars, health issues, right-left brain functions. As told by Dr Doe Lang (1984), "it helps the doctors, teachers, scholars, artists, actresses in their respective fields". It also gives the tool to help people deal with anger in a non-toxic way before it explodes. Arthur Bernard's dream incubation and problem-solving is a new approach of super learning which helps in solving problems through dream incubation renaissance. Such activity energizes the individual potential and helps him in solving problems of varied nature, relating health, business relationship, personal hangs up, etc. (Bernard, 2000). Super learning increases creative learning ability, and sportiveness by emptying out absolete sub-conscious programmes and fill your deep mind with positive, healthy and motivating impulses. Accordingly Fryling in his stressfree learning and super performance exemplified the effectiveness of super learning in dissolving the learning blocks and in taking control of inner ability to super learn and accomplish through putting roots down deep into the source of vitality and getting energy and balance needed to do the best (Stressfree learning and Super performance TAPE, Side A & B #732). It enhances self-esteem and success and gives strength to overcome most trumatic events.

Beyond learning data and skill and passing examination there is another way—the core technique of accelerated learning, which can expand one's success in the new workforce. It develop the whole person (Ostrander and Schroeder, 1997). As told by Hartley (1985), Super learning has become "a corporate culture", through which people-to-people approach is strengthened. Researches of Jenny Vanderplank, Wallace (1989) and Lang (1984) reveal that experience of colour, smell, touch, etc. acquired by respective sense organs increases the capacities of memory and retention, when those get facilitated by super learning. Satub (1955), who had made sereval experiments on effectiveness of different colours, scents and odours (aromatherapy) added to various learning tasks concluded that unlike other senses, smell speeds directly to the brain. It has a quick trigger to summon peak performance. Thus, Super Learning Technique teaches the art of learning. It uses mind maps (visualization) as the means of attaining super-state. In this connection, the resarch work of Mieer and Caskey (1997) on the effectiveness of full-bodied imagery in learning scored 12 percent better in long-term retention. Paivo and Desrocheres (1971) experimented imagery and rote memory techniques on students at University of Western Ontorio and found that imagery as trains for visualisation of unlearn and already learnt things, boosts memory three times higher than repeatition. It is because about 80% of one's brain is involved, at least to some degree in visual processing. More than any other sense, visualizing engages the whole brain and so can tocuh the whole body (Ostrander and Schroeder, 1997). Such immagery activities, with modern technological intervention, has been changed to mnemonics, i.e., imagery through technology. Mnemonics resonate mental energies. Besides all these success stories, Super Learning is not free from physical and non-physical learning blocks like, innate deficiency, logical blocks, emotional blocks, ethical blocks, etc. Cultivating strong self-concept through affirmation, understanding and locking the blocks and by using suggestions, imaginative scenarios and confirming experiences were to be practised to dissolve the blocks and to bring super success (Ostrander and Schroeder, 1994). At many times, failure and negetive remarks strengthen learning putting challenges before the learners. It strengthens and enlightens the "golden rooms"—the whole brain, which is formed with right and left hemispheres.

The overall analysis shows that super learning has multi-sided effect on individual's life. In personal, professional and social situations, it plays a vital role. The business, commerce, sports, music, art, politics, teaching, managment and in all other fields, super learning exerts a monumental impact of bringing accelerated change. Basically, it is an imaginative and behavioural exercise, which gives the know-how and technique to individual for the best performance. It is very much clear from the statement of Christian Drapeau, who says, "again and again teachers, trainers and learners say the courses have changed their lives". William James says, "we bungle our way through life as if only half awake. Super learning (r) provided the fuel for awakening and synchronizing yourself with success consciousness". In most concrete manner, Pulos states the experimental findings to show the effect of super learning while he says that by using it, Can Edison's passing rate for their Electrical Cable Splicing course soared 70%, Kodak's of Electronics jumped 21%, Travelers Insurance for new computer system jumped 53% (David Meir Center for Accelerated Learning, Winconsin, 1986).

1.3 INSTRUCTIONAL STRATEGY OF SUPER LEARNING

The multidimensional approach of super learning and its excellent results experienced by its beneficiaries demand a lucid explanation of its strategic plans and programmes. Basically, super learning is accepted as a technique of knowing own-self and activating the inactive parts of body-mind components of the individual. So, the know-how of this super- approach is very much important.

Since super learning has manysided use for persons of varied problems, its technique changes as per the nature and content of the problem or the individual. Besides a slight change in dealing with the specific problem from super learning point, all the basic assumptions, principles and procedures remain same for all occasions. Lozanov, the founder of super learning technique, has accepted human mind as the storehouse of all possibilities. The development and success of the individual, so, lies in the maximum utilization of that inherent mental capacity. Super learning, in this direction, is easy, relaxed and amusing way which taps the reserves of the mind and speeds up the learning of the individual. The mind of delta level, beta level and theta level can be developed to alpha level which resembles as a sponge that absorbs and retains everything. This technique tries to make the mind ever-alert and perceptive by linking conscious and unconscious to produce super-consciousness.

Though super learning guarantees development of super memory and mind power, still, it is not accepted as super natural or an activity of memories or miracle. It is very much psychological and scientific in its approach and is based in sound principles and rationale. Since, super learning accepts human mind as the cynosure of all powers and possibilities, its technique provides a relaxed body-mind state, which paves the way for super-activity in repetitive field. So, "super learning" in general, "is any system of accelerated learning that releases stress, maximizes memory and potentials, works on both conscious and unconscious levels, enhances the whole personality globally, improves health and creativity and is enjoyable." (Ostrander & Schroeder, 1996).

Most objectively, super learning uses the following techniques to enhance the mind-body potentialities. The major techniques include psychological relaxation and visualization, to dissolve stress and help you reach the optimal mind-body state to superlearn; 60 beat baroque music that releases stress and anchors memory; presentation of course data without and with baroque music. Taking all the above points into consideration, Lozanov's super learning states two phases for its technical operation. The Phase I is called mind calming session and phase II is called the memory session. The activities relating the two phases are discussed as follows.

Phase I—The Mind Calming Session

As the terminology shows, the phase I aims at bringing calm, peace and tranquility to the mind of the individual. Such an attempt makes it clear that the people of present day's society are full of tension, stress, frustration and emotional imbalances. When the individual is mentally disturbed and there is maximum neurological tension, no conducive thought will emerge from the brain cells and thereby the attempt of developing the mind from Beta level to Alpha level becomes a day-dream.

Hypertension and high job stress raise levels of hormones called cortisols released by adrenal glands. All these cause irreversible diseases like strokes, sudden cardiac arrest, heart attacks, renal damage, dementia, blindness and peripheral vascular diseases. Headaches, migrainess, peptic ulcer, chronic fatigue, sleep disorders, palpitations are the syndromes of stressful life. Excessive tension in central nervous system produces wired sensations in all parts of the body. Irritability, impatience, bad-temper, lack of interest in work, disclination for bodily exertion, craving for alcohol or drugs, depression, dyspepsia, quick palplitation of heart and headache are accompanied by symptoms of tension and stress, which impaire efficiency and happiness, So, it is told that if you hold the pen firmly, the tension extends as far as the shoulder. However, diverse and alarming the symptoms may be, there is only one solution : putting the nerves back to normal, from their over-stretched condition. Long-time continuation of any stressful condition is disastrous for the being. The nervous system which is stretched to straining point over a long period becomes unable to perform its normal work. The central nervous system seems as a piece of elastic. This gives useful service for a considerable time. If it is kept at full tension, it soon becomes limp and useless. A constant feeling of mental fatigue produces restlessness and inability to relax or sleep. These, in turn, quickly accentuate the tiredness, thereby a vicious circle comes to exist to break which seems impossible and needs a lot of mental effort and nervous energy. In the field of business, industry, management, administration, family life, professional and occupational fields, everywhere the life is tension-ridden. Materialistic attitude, cut-throat competition, selfishness, untrustworthiness and moral degradation have also made the climate so. All such problem desynchronise the mind-body performance of the individuals and thereby they get enervated in their learning condition.

To be relaxed from these strains and stresses maximum people of todays society, most specifically the youngsters, are hooked on to synthetic drugs, designer drugs or lifestyle drugs, Rave parties (an abbrevation of Raw and Virtual Energy), where sex, drugs and now trance are buzzwords. These drugs are the latest inclusions in the substance abusers' diet. Such chemical compositions as $C_{11}H_{15}$ No_2 and $C_{13}H_{16}$ CINO, which should have been restricted to the chemistry lab, are today doing the rounds of rave parties, the world over. India, too, is fast becoming a part of such glóbal phenomenon. Farm house parties in the far flung suburbs of Dehli, Mumbai and Kolkata with infected mushrooms (A well-known trance group) playing in the back ground provide an ideal platform for these drugs (*The Telegraph*, weekend, March 13, 2004). Our young generations, those are losing their self-confidence and feeling frustrated enough, are attending late night parties at farmhouses or bungalows with designer cocktails and trance music in the background, synthetic drugs are the surest passage to a fun-filled night. They say, "the ambience at a rave party is completely psychedelic. The party starts at 2 am and goes on till 7 am. The fast paced music and shot of ecstacy energizes the entire environment" (*On a High*, weekend, March 13, 2004). The life of people has become so much frustrated that, unlike their counterparts in the early 80s, the new lot of drug users have discarded the once popular marijuana, heroin, brown sugar and ganja for the more expensive designer drugs : Ecstacy, Lysergic Asid Diethylamide (LSD), Methylene Dioxymethamphetamine (MDMA), Speed, Smack, Crank and Chalk to get side of low self-esteem and to cope with stressed-out life. Chemically, these drugs release endorphins and help reinforce a positive attitude in the confused and euphoria seeking youth-until, of course, the high wears off. Drug hallucinogenic and stimulant properties transform an otherwise shy guy to a 'dude'. A person on this drug will do everything in superlatives. The most surprising research finding is that the women outnumber men in the use of synthetic drugs.

But, the medical science speaks that these drugs create a false perception within the users. They get psychologically so addicted to drugs that people those are using these drugs realise a false bio-chemical effect through physical abnormality. The National Institute on Drug Abuse, an US based NGO reports that abusing MDMA can result in long-term perhaps permanent problems with learning and memory due to damage in brain cells. Other effects include confusion, depression, elevation of anxiety, hallucination, blurred vision, impulsive behaviour and selective impairment of some working memory and attention processes, even the dreaded death. Its use may cause paralysis, dehydration or heat stroke. Dr Rajan adds, "Drugs like LSD and MDMA directly affect the brain stem and create auditory hallucinations or verbal disorientation. A slight overdose or one toxic chemical may jeopardise the entire central nervous system. Basically, these drugs never solve problems but takes the person away from the problem-making him think a high when he feels low and helps the person to escape from the reality (*Ranjo Mathais*, weekend, 13th March 2004.)" Thus these tension ridden people, when use drugs, get more psycho-physical imbalance in affermath.

The same thing is evident in our school environment in the age of globalization, our educational institutions have turned into knowledge markets. Stringent competition in the employment sectors has made the students and their aspiring parents much more concerned to snatch away the opportunity by dint of their academic brilliance. Teachers are also trying to satisfy the parental need and give high stress on mark-oriented teaching, which is far away from actual behavioural modification. Heavy load of course contents, examination phobia, pressure for more percentage and maximum stress on rote learning are making our learners more sensitive and tense. They see and feel unsecured because their learning is becoming tasteless, demotivating, drudgery, redundant and generic. Instead of creating an atmosphere of joyful learning, today's schools have become a centre of boredom and painful feelings. Only for these, our system fails to reap the quality products as per expectation. The entire system of teaching and learning results in intellectual stagnation, disinterest and emotional problems among students (Passi and Prabhu, 1997).

In comparison with the emerging problems of stress and strain among the student community, the existing mathetics have proved fruitless in extracting expected results. Even though the present method of teaching and learning capitalizes on child-centred approach, the cost-effectiveness of such methods, no way proves satisfactory. Moreover, while teachers and parents are in dire need of making learning burdenless and students desperately desire to learn with joy and merry, the methods applied by our teachers in that direction have been resulted in didactogenic syndrome (Lozanov, 1979) yielding less effect in making learning less stressful and more enjoyable. Herbert Spencer so says, "It is time to preach the gospel of relaxation." In real sense, such gospel is vital, imperative and urgent on today more than ever. To get this Kipling suggests, "Keep your head, when all about you are losing theirs". Likewise when the cardiovascular experts report, "Three minutes of rearing laughter is worth many more minutes of aerobic exercise and Diller (1997) says "I'd rather have the laugh!" to release stress to make man superactive, at that time

Lozanov's stress on four major steps of mind calming proved very successful for stressfree and joyful learning.

Step 1 : Relaxation

Basically, relaxation refers to slowing down one's body rhythms while keeping your mind alert. As stated by Ostrander and Schroeder (1996), super learning brings to the individual such state of relaxation in four easy steps, such as, releasing all stress and tension in the body, calming and refreshing individual's mind, releasing worries and anxieties, reexperiencing a success point in one's own life to let the positive emotions of joy and accomplishment flow through the person into current learning situation and breathing in patterns that increase oxygen flow to the brain and help in synchronizing hemispheres. Thus, it is clear that before doing something, with expectation of perfect result, one should bring his body-mind relaxation. Although the so called proverb "sound body creates sound mind" is true to some extent, the reverse influence alongwith the impact of environment can never be undermined. Thus, a relaxed body-mind state in flexible environment is the basis of creating 'set' in the learner for super learning activities.

There are various means of oiling our stiffed body for making it relaxed and putting off the jams of the mind. Although all stress creates body-mind tension in the organism, in actual sense, the stress—either physical or psychological or environmental, varies in its degree and nature concerning the individual. According to the source and nature of stress, stress reduction techniques also varies. One must remember that neither healing nor psychotherapy and meditation is a cure or solution, each has its appropriate place and each person must go on his own unique way in his quest for freedom (Mirchandani, 2003). Generally, stress-busting mechanisms come from what counsellors call the "Rational you". The "Rational you" thinks its way through life's events, evaluating the degree of safety *versus* danger involved (Gill and Viswakarma, 2004). A list of what Hollywood and Bollywood stars do to cope with stress (Gill and Viswakarma, 2004) is given below, which indicates that likewise the varied nature of stress, persons have their specific approach to deal with that (Beat it, Fitness, *The Telegraph*, 16th Feb. 2004).

"..... goes in for Mexican yam the tension-relieving hormone-balancing supplement".

(Kate Winslet)

".... retreats the ranch she owns in Texas—enjoying the sunset and watching the grass grow".

(Sandra Bullock)

"...... Yoga is her answer to keeping focussed and relaxed".

(Madonna)

"...... Works out for up to two hours a day."

(Dame Moore)

"..... and all this does bring about a lot of stress and solution is staying happy. Whenever I am busy, I just try to stay happy".

(Shilpa Shetty)

".... I practise yoga and meditation to relieve stress....... I believe that when your body is healthy, your mind is relaxed".

(Priyanka Chopra)

".....I play some kind of sports to keep me stress-free. And rugby is a good stress-buster".

(Rahul Bose)

"..... When I feel dejected, I just switch on old Hindi songs...... sometimes I take long walks by myself".

(Jackie Shroff)

"Meditating exercise, sports, listening to music-good stress-busters".

(Urmila Matondkar)

For overcoming such problems Khanna (2004) gives following tips: "Relax your mind and body completely, just as you would allow an overheated engine to cool. The body has wonderful powers of recuperation and ten to twenty minutes can suffice to restore the nervous tansion to normal. Short breaks at intervals—five or ten minuets complete rest in the middle of the morning a short nap after lunch, are productive for normalizing nervous tension, covering the eyes with palms is not only effective in closing the mind to external things, but also soothing to the eyes. But if you are highly-strung, you need more powerful breaks." By consciously inhibiting these miner tensions, allowing legs to hang limphy while writing at a desk, planning of work, intelligent and correct use of time, to be conscious but not over-sensitive, self-analysis, performing job with smirk and willing heart, Lowering eyelids and consciously forcing the eyes into a smile, working hard but not beyond natural limit of endurance, avoiding over-fatigue, thinking thrice before blaming the work itself, taking reasonable care in planning leisure time to build up own reserves of energy, developing capacity of self-control, open-air exercise, developing good hobbies—singing, writing, reading, drawing, painting, music, taking adequate rest, watching television and power shut-offs for less time, not concentrating too much on result of activity, talking to own-self, developing sense of humour are very much stabilizing in making tension-ridden persons easy and carefree (Relax And Be successful, Personality and you, Competition Master, Vol. 45, No. 9, April 2004).

Smita Bhatia, in her article "the art of living well" states, "Pampering yourself at day spasm, meditating at home, practising yoga or just listening to music—chose your favorite de-stress method" (Weekend, *The Telegraph*, 14th February, 2004). She also gives some other tips of eliminating stress from body, mind and managing the stressful environment to stressfree congenial environment. She suggests the following tips.

- Treat yourself to some fresh flowers. Keep them on your desk at work or on your right stand at home. The smell of flowers can do wonders for mind, body and soul.
- Light aromatic candles in your house. Don't stave them just for special occasions, Candles are one of life's affordable luxuries.
- A luxurious bath is sure to relax and rejuvenate you. Add some aromatherapy oils, lots of bubble bath and sit back and relax. Spare a day to do some of the things you realy want to-browse in an antique shop, take a nap in your backyard hammock or catch an afternoon matinee.
- Treat yourself to a body or facial scrub, an aromatic bubble bath, a body wrap and pedicure. When you feel good, you feel good all over.

- Take spa vacation or just treat yourself to a day in at the neighbourhood day spa.
- Follow a fitness routine. When you look good, Join a gymnasium.

Stress is given in everybody's life whether you are a homebody or a busy professional on the tort. High levels of stress can result from serious situations such as recovering from an illness, facing up to danger or simply by being stuck in a traffic jam or working at a computer. Therefore, the famous aromatheraphy expert Blosson Kochhar says, " you are probably living with stress if your work requires you to meet several deadliness each week." (Weekend, *The Telegraph*, 14 February, 2004)

For a stress-prove life, Bhatia (2004) suggests, "settle your body into a yoga asana, learn tai chi or slip into meditation mode. Or go all out to pamper your senses with a blissfully delicious hot chocolate wrap, a papaya detox body scrub and a facial steeped with the goodness of fragrant roses. Then settle down to listen to a CD of your favorite music. Rejuvenating your body and soul is today's mantra as everybody scrumbles to counter the effects of stress and modern-day living induces. De-stressing is a buzzword as everyone looks to discover the perfect antidote to their busy lives. Just take your pick of any of the following: a royal Thai massage, a rejuvenator package at spa, a Swedish massage or even a bio face-lift. You can join a fitness centre, pamper yourself at a day spa or at a beauty salon, relish great tasting health foods and juices, enjoy a favorite sport or take up a new one."

But yoga guru Usha Chengappa (2004) says "pampering yourself is no longer considered decadent or forbidden pleasure. It is a way to preserve your sanity in an insanely paced world." Stress occurs in everyday life and in every where—in homebody and in busy professional. It occurs because our thoughts produce electrical impulses, which can be measured in both amplitude and frequency. Emotional thoughts can contribute much greater amplitude to the electrical energy produced by the brain. Hence, the more powerful the thought, the greater is the electrical stimulation of the body's muscular system. Therefore, to relax such psycho-physical stiffness, the famous Clinical psychologist Dr. Avdesh Sharma syas, "Think positive is the answer, then feeling good is one of the simplest solutions."

Comparatively, the super learning technique advocates an advanced process of relaxing the body-mind and environmental conditions so that the potential energy will be developed in the organism which will produce more and more kinetic, electrical and kinesthetic energies to enable the individual to do everything in best manner. Here, relaxation may be practised using different methods, such as muscle relaxation, meditation, simple exercise, etc. Lozanov gives a clear description of the wave of relaxation for dissolving stress and bringing body-mind set-up for effective learning, Accordingly, Ostrander and Schroeder give the following tips for relaxation.

"Stand or sit. Tense your muscles gently and briefly, starting with your toes and legs, upper legs, lower back and abdomen, upper torso, shoulders, chest, arms and face. Feel your whole body tense from toes to head. Hold the tension for a couple of seconds. Then let a wave of warm relaxation flow down through your body starting with your head. Let it roll over your body starting with your head. Let it roll over your neck, arms, shoulders, back, abdomen, legs and feet. Let the wave roll away strain and fatigue. Note where you are carrying or storing tension in your body or where muscles are tight or knotted. Let the wave of relaxation roll over them, feel the tension in your muscles wash away with each wave. Now tense and relax your whole body with a wave of relaxation. Do this two or three times. Add a few neck rolls to improve circulation to your head. Feel completely relaxed as you sit or lie down and move into the following exercise" (Super Learning—2000, 1997).

Here, the authors capitalize upon the sensitization of each part of the body and going on feeling and realizing them; Then supplying the wave of relaxation from head to feet and also in reverse direction. Such activities actually relaxes the cells and tissues of the mind-body, thereby any tightness and knots, exist there, get cleared and relaxed. Finally, the individual becomes stressfree and sets for doing any activities with 100% success. Therefore, Thakur (2004) in his book "Yoga for Stress Relief", states that pranayam, bandha, mudra, kriya, asana and finally meditaiton as the primary essentials of meditation-the means of making person stress-free. Accordingly Jack Cornfield, the famous American Buddhist meditation teacher and author of the book, "A path with a Heart", states "many of the American and Asian students ware deeply wounded, neurotic, frightened, grieving and often used spiritual practice to hide and avoid problematic parts of themselves. The meditation practice with its emphasis on concentration and detachment, often provided a way to hide, a way actually separate the mind from difficult areas of heart and body" (Life positive, page 100-101, March 2003). The yoga and meditation teachers, like super learning process, are in tryst of finding out the causes of stress and strain, so that the fruitful attempt can be made to release such tensions. So, transpersonal psychoanalysis and psychotherapy recognizes this and practitioners are trained in western psychotherapy, eastern meditation and other healing techniques in order to be able to appropriately address the needs of a person. (Mirchandani, 2003). Expressing own experience in bringing up mind-body relaxation, Shameen Akthar, the famous journalist-turned yoga teacher says, "each time you do yoga with mandatory mindfulness, you are affecting a dialogue with each of your body cells . . . all your cells collude to make you superbly healthy" (Life Positive, page 70-71, June 2003). Really, Yoga is the jump of the mind, helping one to take the leap between a life time of shifting conditionings to liberating peace. Even in its simplest Kriya (Cleansing action), Yoga is geared towards halting the natural movement of mind. It is an instrument that brings out the full contours of minds by unearthing all that is within the individual (Akthar, 2003). Therefore, the yogic practices can bring a harmonization between psyche and physique of the being and it is the prime process of making, the person stressfree, as told by Murti (Fitness, *The Telegraph,* 8th March, 2004). But an amalgamated view exemplifies that the relaxation technique of super learning hits on the actual problem which generates tension. It is also very much flexible in its approach and ultra-modern in its techniques. As experimented in various fields by different researchers, it has proved its much effectiveness in making the person stressfree and enabling him to achieve the ends in such profitable manner.

Step 2 : Visualization

Visualization refers to getting rid of worry, anxiety and fear of failure which gives one's abilities to shine. It is a stage of imagining a beautiful spot or incident, visualizing a calm and peaceful scene, which is soothing to the mind and have the capacity to release worries and pressure. In actual sence, relaxation combined with visualization has better effect (Passi and Prabhu, 1997). Visualization is always to be done in the present tense. It is a process of creating a mind set of tranquility and safety and thereby eliminating all sorts of obsessions and distractions from the individual and energizing the self for objective action.

Getting the stress out of learning from kindergaten to job retraining is fundamental to super learning and its sister systems. This technique has some powerful, proven and classical progarammes that can give the liberating ability to bring a healthier body-mind state of the individual. The tapes of Swiss Sophrologist Raymond Abrezol which includes two classics—autogenics and progressive relaxations fare well in enhancing learning in manifold. These programmes are also recommended by Eli Bay, one of the top corporate stress control trainers in Canada. In this regard, the contribution of Dr. Vera Fryling, one of the most popular autogenics experts in USA, is worth noting. He combined autogenic with super learning to produce an effective process of relaxation and visualization.

The breathing exercise is accepted as a cost-free mind enhancer. For its invisibility and portability, its usability extends from examination room to business meetings or to any locations. Resarches of Rivera (1996) show that the genius get that way from having good oxygen supply to the brain which enhances intelligence, creativity and originality through synchronization of two hemispheres. But he says, such breathing exercises, if would be done when the challenges faced by the person in the shape of examination, critical meeting, etc., always produces better results. The Gold-Blue energy breathing—the colour breathing exercise, is also accepted as a 'worry buster', which can charge up the energies when a person feels enervated and tired and thereby aids concentration and visualization (Ostrander and Schroeder, 1997), The process of such Gold-Blue Energy Breathing states as follows:

"Lie down in a comfortables spot with your head pointing north, feet south, Put your hands, palms up, at your sides. Take a slow, deep breath through your nose and visualize sunshined—yellow energy pouring through the top of your head and traveling through your body and out the soles of your feet. As you slowly and evenly breathe out, picture cool blue energy coming up through the soles of your feet, slowly moving though your body and going out through the top of your head. Continue to breathe in yellow; out blue for ten to fifteen minutes. You will start to feel a tingling energy current pulsing through your body with each in-and-out focus attention and concentration more easily (Super Learning, 2000).

In making visualization more profitable through relaxation, one may take up "sound bath" which clears away braindrain noise and sound pollution. For it, one has to select the tape or disc of a fovourite relaxation music. The person has to lie down in comfortable position and turn on the said music. Taking several deep breaths the practitioner has to allow the flow of the music through body to wash away all junk noise and sounds that have pounded all the day. The person has to be emmersed in the music. Here one has to imagine how the body cells dancing and moving alongwith vibration of the sound or music. Such music, no doubt, will energize and relax the person and by taking more slow deep breaths as the music ends, the tensions get releaxed and new visualization comes up automatically.

Likewise, "Shower of Power" is another exercise of bringing clear and profitable visualization in the individual. In this process, the person, while, is under a shower, has to imagine that he is standing under a golden water fall of pure and tingling energy. Under such condition one has to feel the golden energy flowing through the arms and legs, soaking unto every cell, which would make one feel that the entire body is filled with pure and vibrant energy. With water cascading over the body, the person will visualize the washing away of all tensions, worries and will feel refreshed, recharged with enthusiasm, and confidence and affirmation of achieving the desired things.

"Progressive Relaxation" is another recommended means of visualization and relaxation. it is found more effective in driving out the muscular tension and bodily stress. Its process of exercise speaks as follows:

> "Get comfortable in a quiet place. Do a few neck rolls to improve circulation to your head. Drop your chin to your chest and roll your head in a full circle to the right and to the left."
>
> "Sit on a chair, if you prefer, lie down on a couch or on the floor. Loosen any tight clothing. Make yourself very comfortable. Scan your bones and muscles and let the weight of them sink into the chair or floor."
>
> "Close your eyes. Take a slow deep breath. Exhale. As you exhale, feel tension beginning to float away. Say yourself, 'Relax'. Take a second slow deep breath and an exhaling, feel tension being carried away as your breath flows away. Relax. Take a third slow, even, deep breath. Exhale. Imagine tension leaving your muscles. Say to your self, 'Relax'."
>
> "Feel pleasant and relaxing feeling spreading over your entire body. It is a comfortable, pleasant sensation. Note how good it feels to be completely relaxed. Mentaly scan your entire body from head to toe and also in reverse by tensing up every mucle, hold it, relax it."

Here, when the individual progresses in relaxing his/her body regions and muscular system, he/she should enjoy the pleasant feeling of such relaxation flowing through head to toes and back up again. Such pleasant feeling is to be enjoyed and experienced by the person to uptimum. Such activity enables the individual to feel alert, refreshed, energized, free of tension and helps in obtaining concentration (Ostrander, 1983)

Accordingly Bay's (1983) 'Scan-and-Relax' process is very much analogous to progressive relaxation in-stead of tensing up muscles, It only scans them for tension and releases that tension. It makes person feel or visualize goodness through scanning, relaxing, unwinding and letting everything go.

A.G. Odessky's 'Autogenics' is also a widespread exercise of stress release and body-mind harmony. It, as a psychological gymnastics for creating psychological fitness, is found effective for dancers, athelets, teachers, actors, cosmonauts, businessmen and technocrats. For practice, it recommends the comfortable positions—sitting back, lying down, sitting up, to relax the body-mind state for a positive and calm visualization.

In 'sitting back' position one has to relax in a recliner or an easy chair with head resting against the back. Arms are to be either on the armrests or on own thighs. Legs and feet should not be crossed but be comfortably positioned with feet turned slighty outward. Eyes should be closed.

In 'laying down' position the person has to lay down on back on a couch bed or soft rug. A pillow be put under the head. The arms should be slightly bent at elbows, palms should be kept down besides the body, legs should be relaxed, apart and feet pointing slightly to the sides, not straight up. The eyes should be closed.

And in 'sitting up', the person is advised to sit on a chair or stool and let the head hang slightly forward. Let the arms and hands rest loosely on to the thaighs. He/she has to position the legs comfortably, feet pointed slightly outward and eyes closed.

With all these positions, the person should visualize the calm and pleasant environment all around. This thought, would, no doubt, add some encouraging psychological boost for bringing coolness in person's mind. Such activity is very much analogous to the "Cool Forehead" of step-VI of warm up activity which brings realization of coolness in the person. But the second level autogenics adds imaginative exercise to the six steps of visualization such as heaviness, warmth, calm heart breathing, stomach and cool forehead, which is also found more effective in this regard. The ancient oriental discipline of Qi Gong of China or Ki Gong of Japan to add power of gravity to develop 'chi energy' for better and effective visualization. Such chi energy opens abilities, enhances sports prowess, heals, balances, energizes and protects. It is accepted as the secret of longivity and a way to open the reserves of the mind. Likewise, the Basis of Japanese Martial art of 'aikido' is regarded as the means of developing mind-body harmony. Such effects have been realised by the persons of China and Hawai through the Qi Gong Clinics established by Chinese government and Ki Training Centres opened by the Hawai Department of Education. The process stresses on the impact of gravity point which is situated below navel. It is the centre of infinite spheres of the universe. With technical exercise, the tryst is made to develop every expected talent from the gravity point and even to radiate that energy through hands. But for a better visualization Schroeder and Ostrander (1997) have stated the following tips for doing the exercise:

- Avoid logical questioning and speculation. Simply concentrate on your topic and tune out any distractions.
- When doing visualizations or imagingtion, engage every sense. Visualize the colours, forms, shapes, textures, tastes and sounds as much detail as possible.
- For maximum effect and to conserve energy, it is recommended that whenever possible you do the exercises in a seated position, facing forward with your spine straight. Proper alignment is important so as not to block the flow of energy along the spine. Keep your hands resting on each other (palms up on your lap).
- Do a full-bodied visualization. Until you have trained your subconscious, it might mistake your visualizations for daydreams. A physical stimulus, however, impresses your sub-conscious with a greater sense of reality. Same light physical exercise such as a few jumping jacks or briefly running on the spot just before you start your visualization helps till your sub-conscious that you mean business. After a number of repetitions of this combination, you should be able to drop the physical stimulus and accumulate your super-charge by breathing and visualization alone, under any circumstance and in any location.
- Right timing is important, It is especially good to do creative visualization at night just before sleeping or in the morning just after waking. These are the times when mind and body are often deeply relaxed and receptive. A brief relaxation and visualization done at mid day will relax and renew you and help your day to flow more smoothly.
- Such visualization makes the individual aware of the sub-conscious mind which is the storehouse of

innumerable possibilties. A person, only then becomes the director of his/her destiny, when he/she recognizes, sees and becomes aware of such sub-conscious level and their activities. And the researchers and psychologists of super learning have given hints on some general postural techniques and then imagination/visualization with the help of multimedia programmes—either over phone, video cassettes. All are agreed with a general postural position, i.e., "taking a comfortable position. Close the eyes and raise them slightly upword. Breathe slowly and deeply through the nose. Take deep breath and exhale slowly, feel a wave of warm relaxation flowing gradualy over the entire body from the toes to head." After such relaxation, visualization is to be practised with imagery activities or through the audio or video cassettes. The cassette may contain the Kaleidoscope of Colours "to improve performance, memory lane garden and pleasant life video series" to eliminate bad, terrifying and agonizing memories which couses environmental pollution. "The Possible you" which speaks of imagining a lush of forest, park or garden surrounded by beauty of nature those are helpful in creating memories of the "future you" and recognize the inner natural environment, a familiar place where one can feel completely at ease, safe and protected.

In order to enhance concentration and to build an effective visualization "Mind design" is also used. When using this mind design "Prosperity Tree", the pattern can be "charged up" with sound to make it more effective. This prosperity pattern can be charged up by saying the word 'AUM', while looking at it or visualizing it. (See Figure 1.1.)

This Prosperity pattern, which is adopted from Indian texts by Lozanov, has to be enlarged and fixed on a wall as one has to focus his/her inner attention on it. By doing it the pattern invokes a state of consciouness focused on prosperity. As concentration strengthened, creative ideas emerge out which is very much helpful in manifesting the desired goal.

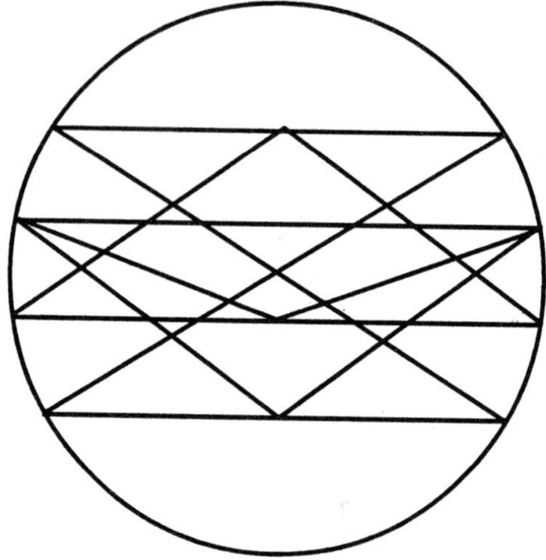

Fig. 1.1. The Prosperity Pattern

For practice of such prosperity pattern, Ostrander and Schroeder (1997) have stated the following points, where some alteration of the Indian meditative practices are clearly evident.

1. Sit in a chair about three feet away from the pattern.
2. Get into a relaxed state by your preferred method.
3. Close your eyes and imagine a black screen in your mind.
4. Look at the prosperity pattern and gaze at it for two mninutes.
5. Move your eyes to the wall and gaze at image of prosperity pattern.
6. Close your eyes and try to see the pattern on the screen of your mind.

Similar concentration exercise can be used to strengthen and develop photographic memory of different geometric and engineering patterns. Accordingly a "Prosperity Tree" can be imagined or visualized at a relaxed state. And for the relaxation, one has to close the eyes after assuming a comfortable position. Then through slow, deep and even breath he/she has to feel and roll the wave over the body from the head to toes washing away all wories and tensions which leads to realization of a relaxed state. Through "Prosperity Tree" one becomes aware of the infinite abudance of nature and the universe and links with source of infinite supply. Likewise the gradual step up of the imagination of such prosperity tree, the person, if wants to return, should walk slowly away from the tree taking several deep breaths. The person will feel the cool air flowing through him.

A critical analysis shows that the entire process of visualization depends on a mind, body relaxation. But the procedures of obtaining the mind-body relaxation recommended by super learning is primarily based on the Indian Yoga. But some modifications have been made in it looking at the western cultural environment. Overall, it is clear that the general meditating position—assuming a comfortable position closing the eyes, taking slow, deep, even breaths and feeling the wave of relaxation roll over the self from the head to toes and in reverse for releasing tension. By chanting of Aum also brings mind body relaxation and takes the individual to visualize or imagine a peaceful and calm state from which the possible potentialities will emerge out. Thus visualization is the stage of preparing the soil for breeding of all ideas and actions.

Step 3 : Affirmation

One of the basic assumptions of super learning is to accept the individual as full of all possibilities and also abilitiess to take up every activity for successful completion. But, the matter of inconvenience is failure in identification and recognition of those hidden capacities. Out of many potentials, those are within us and waiting to surface, we have become successful to bring out only 5 percent level through our emotion of Joy. Stress ridden life has supressed the leftout 95 percent potentials. Man, now, is stranger to his own self. Such "low self-concept" making the person enervated and mentally weak to stand up sraight. Therefore, it is imperative to understand one's own self first. "Knowing Thyself", the corner stone of the capacity building, will make the person aware of own potentialities and will recognize own capacities, so that the vison would be achieved lucidly. Before becoming master to guide the potentialites in appropriate direction, the person should be well conversant with the psycho-physical tools, conditions and their effectiveness to uptimum.

In the field of learning also, such self-concept or personal cenfidence counts much. As the effectiveness of learning situation mostly depends on the mental set and motivation of the learner concerned, development of self-concept, which acts as the precondition of creation of a sound and intended mental set and well guided motivation, considered as a steping stone of the learning paradigm. Now with endorphin-powered super learning which capitalisd on exhilaration for acceleration. Only stress free joyful learning is accepted as the key to opening the remaining 95 percent of hidden potentials. It is not only concerned to Thorndike's pleasure principle in the Law of Effect in learning (Mangal, 2003) but also now experimented in the laboratories. Neuroscientist Dr. Arych Routtenberg of North Western University (1997) has found that pleasure producing endorphins are also centre of memory consolidation. James (2000) has also found endorphins triggered by electrostimulation which made the general rats super learning Rats bringing high marks on IQ, memory, maze tests and doubled their learning. It is clearly evident that joy-its by products, neurotransmitters enhance learning and memory (Ostrander and Schroeder, 1997). For letting the positive feelings suffuse the personality, super learning, after proper relaxation, and visualisation, creates the positive mind set through trigerring intelligence-boosting endorphines.

Eventually, as it is realized and experienced that creating self-confidence through affirmation is a must for acclerating super learning, that pre-condition should be formed with guided plans. After visualization of a calm and peaceful state in relaxed position, positive self-concept, self-confidence and a conquering mental set has to be developed by speaking of affirmative statements. Affirmation should always be in positive statements, pleasurable form and in present tense. It accepts negative thoughts and memories as short-circuit ability. Refering to the importance of such positive attititude Ostrander (1996) says that joy of learning or feeling good about yourself is a plus for any sort of breakthrough in the brainmind science. That is why, the psychologists of Stanford University are of view that learning of things occurs better in good mood than the depressed one. Accordingly, Marilyn King (1996), the organiser of Applied Olympic Thinking, advocates, "once a negetive self-fulfilling prophecy begins to be replaced by a new script, a new film loop-watch out". Boothby (1996), who accepted positive thinking as the key to succes, mastered his problem cases in ten Portuguese words very quickly by infusing positive self-concept through verbal reinforcements such as, "you can learn", "you can do it easily," etc. Therefore, feeling competent, energetic, adequate and empowered are life-giving and change-bringing states (Ostrander and Schroeder, 1996). Any sort of negative thought, feeling inadequate, unworthy and enervated drain away the vitality of the person. So, affirmation is a means to acquire mental and emotional well-being to step away from minus states into plus states. And, at many times, memorisation or summoning of good memories and pleasurable occurances, success-stories of self and others develops the levels of self-esteem and makes the person more adequate and healthier. John Wade (1990) in his book 'Superstudy' talks about creating "self-reliance" among students through power of language to make them super students. He stresses on not to allow ownself to be victimized through verbal acceptance of own deficiencies and failures. Wade points out, victims say things such as "This question is too difficult". "I will try to be clearer on my next essay", "I should not have a beer before I finish studying". An easy way to slip out of the victim state, Wade finds, "is to use the power of language." "You have said the question is too difficult. Take charge by eliminating 'too'. Change the last word into 'challenging'. See what a difference it makes when you avoid giving your power away. Instead say, 'This question is challenging', Wade advices. Likewise, in the sentence, "you are going to 'try' to be clearer on your essays, going to 'try' to do anything", Wade says, "implies failure". You have to confirm it with positive power like "I will be clearer on my next essay." Similarly, in the sentence, "I should not have a beer before I finish studying", "should not" implies some invisible force outside you trying to stop you from doing something. But Wade suggests, "always acknowledge your power to chose". Say either, "I will have" or "I won't have" a beer. Language shapes particularly when it comes to self-talk (Ostrander and Schroeder, 1996). A conscious control of inner chat acts as a magic ward to shift you to more competent state of being. Actually, "smart thinking" as told by OHO Altorfer (1990), "fulfils the innate deficiency" and resolves logical emotional and ethical blocks which squeeze out the life juices (Borysenko, 1990). One should be emotionally literate to face these learning blocks.

It is said that failure is the pillar of success. From failures individual learns and corrects his/her course to attain success. One should use failure as an immediate guide to success. So Ostrander and Schroeder (1997) quote, "if you do not make a friend of failure, you will never excel." Accordingly, Libyan Cassone (1997) gives stress on the sportive bearing of negative result or failure along with positive reinforcement to produce positive result. She points out, "when somebody makes a mistake, instead of having a figurative alram go off and a hook emerge to drag the student out of the classroom, we would say, 'That is okay. You made an error—that is part of life, and you will get it better next time'. It is because we are not to be judged once, rather we are to be judged in a great by and by. So, amidst of failures and odds one should not be frustrated. Rather one should boldfully capitalize on those failures and learn the intelligent way to tacling those for success. One should have to womp up a lot of defensive energy-emotional, intellectual and creative when the mode of learning is anti to the prevailing environment or experience (Ostrander and Schroeder, 1997). Accordingly, when Mother Teresa, the peace pigeon, was asked by a group of anti-war demonstrators, "would she protest war leading a huge anti-war demonstration ?" She replied, "No", I won't march against war. If you ever hold a demonstration for peace, call me. And Thomas Edison sail through numerous unsuccessful attempts to invent the lightbulb. Accordingly, Lang (1989), from her research findings, reported that knowing how to let anger—a generally accepted negative attribute of personality-lend your power not reduce you to impotency. Therefore, it is good turn-around training for learning how to change. And superlearning should try to cultivate such affirmation among the learners. Children must learn to accept negative feedback as a source of information for future efforts rather than as a judgement about their ability (Henderson and Dweck, 1997). The "helpless responses" (of failed attempt) always lead to the mastery responses (of successful attempt) and our tryst should be on to achieve mastery on desired objective. Affirmation develops self-reliance to get mastery through failures.

Primarily, the person should always try to affirm in the positive and in the present tense. For it one has to shape and deliver affirmation correctly and to give them room to breathe by doing some housecleaning to get rid of negative or obsolete affirmations through most positive affirmations. "To develop such affirmation within self", the most surprisingly powerful technique", as told by Altorfer (1993), is to stand and deliver your affirmations in front of a mirror and let that person reflect the affirmation back to you in an authoritative and commanding way." Affirmations like 'I am intelligent', 'I am creative', 'I learn easily', 'I remember perfectly', will go a long way in removing years of negative thought patterns which might have blocked effective learning in the past (Passi and Prabhu, 1997). As depicted by Ostrander and Schroeder (1996) the following precautions should be kept in mind while we train our students for developing affirmation.

- Always phrase affirmation in the present tense, not in future. This is acknowledging the fact that everything is created on the mental-plane before it can manifest itself in actual reality.
- Always phrase affirmations in the most positive way.
- The shorter and simpler the affirmations, the more effective they are.
- Suspend doubts and hesitation. A feeling of belief that the affirmations can be true is very essential (Passi & Prabhu, 1997).

Step 4 : Breathing Exercise

Super learning technique is based on the assumption of mind body synchronization. Breath is the link between these two entities of the individual. The first expression of life would be the breath and the motion of lungs produces the breath (Abhedanda, 1999). It is the primary function which leads the function of other organs. Breathing deeply and rhythmically brings oxygen to the brain and activates the blood circulation through adequate pressure and thereby human mind-body get activated. We can not get hold of that force which moves the lung. But we know its outword manifestation in the form of inspiration and expiration. Breath or inspiration and expiration keeps the lungs active from the grosses to subtle. The first action of *Prana* is expansion and contraction—that is the first motion of life force. Therefore, breath, or expansion and contraction which is the gross manifestation and the holder of force energy, if can be guided and controlled, the individual, would have mastery over all mind-body activities. As swami Abhedananda says, "that is the aim of science of breath". It is based on Indian *"Pranayama"* which refers to control of breath or vital energy or life force (Prana means life force or vital energy ; Ayma means control). Through it one can acquire mastery over the organic activities and the life force is vital energy which keeps us alive. Whereever there is an activity in the physical, mental or spiritual world, this prana or life force or vital energy acts as the mother of other forces. Since every atom is charged with prana, then by stimulating the vibratory conditions of that prana would stimulate all atoms which make up the molecules and cells of the body and manifest more energy and powers. Such process of manifestation of power is also possible in the lower animals, in plants and vegetables as they have cells and molecules in their existence (Vishnu Devananda, 2001).

Realizing the importance of breath and its control to develop the many sided activity of individual personality, the ancient Rishis have developed Pranayama system. Before that, as told by Patanjali, the propounder of yoga, appropriate posture is to be mastered which releases tension of mind and body. In pranayama, control of inhalation and exhalation of breath is made. "Pranayama", as told by Swami Vishnu Devananda (2001), "includes specific breathing exercises for healing and raising its energy levels." Breathing directly controls the mind as the process of pranayama includes inhalation, exhalation or retention of breath; it is regulated by place, time and number and (becomes progressively) prolonged and subtle (Patanjali's Yogasutra). It also stresses on Kundalini, development of which leads to enlightement. Therefore, relating the effort of breathing exercise for benefit of students, Swami Abhedananda (2001) says, "Practise everyday a little of the breathing exercises which you have taken—start and study. Regulate your breath. By regulating your breath you will be able to get a rhythm in your system and that rhythm will produce wonderful result". By breathing, the body and mind cells get oxygen for development and meditation calms the mind state. When mind is concentrated, breath becomes slow and deep. A concentrated individual becomes a different being. By it, says Swami Abhedananda, all things, that you do not know, you will know, and all question that arise in your mind will gradually becomes awared in silence". It changes the chemistry of consciousness (Passi and Prabhu, 1997). Several research studies have shown that breathing rhythmically increases one's personal charisma, strengthens will, clears the mind, calms nervousness, increases vitality and pleasure and improves mental functions and concentration (Lang, 1980). As told by Ostrander and Schroeder (1996), "breathing, deeply and rhythmically brings oxygen to your brain and oxygen fuels learning and memory. Rhythmic breathing also synchronizes brain hemispheres and such synchronization fuels creativity. In addition, slow, rhythmic breathing helps slow mind body rhythms to the optimal state for learning".

Under Super Learning Technique (SLT) there are some principles for such breathing exercise. The general procedure of taking breathing exercise, as stated by Ostrander and Schroeder (1996) is as follows:

> "Sit comfortably in a chair or lie down on a couch or bed. Relax by your preferred method. Close your eyes and take a slow, deep breath through your nose. Inhale as much air as you can hold comfortably. Try for just a little bit more air. Now exhale very slowly. Feel a deep sense of relaxation as you exhale. Try to force out just a little bit more air."

Such activities of breath are to be practised for a few moments. One should inhale as much air as possible with a real belly breath, Slowly exhale and pull in the abdomen and take another breath as much air as possible. Thus, the breathing is based on inhale, hold, exhale and pause. Gradually, the process of inhale, hold, exhale and pause should proceed from the count of 3 to a count of 8. At first phase, one should inhale, hold exhale and pause the air upto a count of three in an even and continuous breath. Then the rhythm of such breathing should rhythmically go up to a count of four, five, six and the like as follows.

Inhale	2	3	4	5	6	7	8
Hold	2	3	4	5	6	7	8
Exhale	2	3	4	5	6	7	8
Pause	2	3	4	5	6	7	8

Such exercise should be repeated for several times. Most specifically, rhythmic breathing is a must before a super learning session, if the learner desires to achieve something extraordinary. Such breathing can be practised though nostril, which has been a long practice of yoga (Schroeder and Ostrander, 1997). Scientist of Dalhousie University found that verbal (left brain) and spatial (right brain) abilities vary markedly as breath switched and a hemisphere cycled to dominance. What the neurophysiology explains, generally the left brain controls the right side of the body and right brain controls the left side. Dr David Shannahaff-khalsa of Salt Institute (1987) states that switching the breath to stimulate the left brain, could give an edge in reasoning, and in using language or doing mathematics. Altering to the right will develop spatial, creative and synthesizing thought. In order to energize the verbal left brain, one has to press the finger against the left nostril and breath deeply through the right nostril. One way to switch the whole cycle is to lie down, stay on right side for a while to bring left brain dominance and stay on left side to bring right-brain dominance. Brian Hamilton (1996) have a series of positive experiences of the fluent use of such nostril breathing in his super learning classes. By following a time—tested yoga approach he used such nostril breathing in sectarianizing the whole brain for better mind-body coordination before the learning activity. The procedure which is related to nostril breathing is as follows:

" Do belly breathing for a couple of minutes. Then assume a hand position that lets you close either or both nostrils.

Hold up the thumb and the last two fingers of your hand, curl the middle fingers in out of the way. Close off your right nostril and take a long, slow, gentle breath through the left. Switch the pressure and exhale through the right nostril. Do this three times. Then reverse for another cycle of three. Put your hands in your lap and take three more deep, slow breathe. Then 'palm' your eyes by holding your hands over your eyes for a minute as you continue belly breathing". Here the nose becomes an instrument to fine tune the brain. Its role relating inward and outward breathing organizes the whole mind-body systems which includes sympathetic and para sympathetic nervous systems (Ostrander and Schroeder, 1996). But the rhythmic breathing or the alteration rhythm helps in solving the problems most effectively, as reported by the ground breaking researches of famous Jungian psychologist Dr. Ernest Rossi (1988). Rossi stresses on the practice of rhythmic breathing to resolve the problem automatically while he says that when you are in an inward cycle, breathing through your left nostril, go with nature, relax for a few minutes. And wander about your problem don't work at it. Just idly, lazily wander and let your inner mind do its work for five or ten minutes. Your probem will be resolved by itself and we will find yourself refreshed (Ostrander and Schroeder, 1990). The "Underwater Therapy" of Wenger (1993) created history in the field of education and learning. His research is a breakthrough which experimentally established that by holding breath under the water, carbon dioxide (CO_2) builds up in the blood stream and it expands the carotid arteries that carry oxygen to the brain. For an intensive three week exercise with one hour a day under water, holding the breath is at least two to three minute span will permanently expand one's carotid arteries. It brings more oxygen, more fuel, more toxins washed away and thereby the brain gets new life. What Wenger found, "One can own" a physically healthier, more intelligent brain gaining five to the ten IQ points and improving in all areas for life even it eradicates crebrovascular or stroke problems. (Wenger, 1993) The "waterbaby" experiments of Charkovsky (1988) the father of under water birthing "The Triune Brain concept" (Thinking Cap—the hemispheres, memory and learning) of Maclean (1990) also coroborate the findings of Wenger. The ancient Taoist's concept of "Golden Room" and ancient Egyptian psycho-physiology also stresses on this area of brain. However, for Indian yogic tradition this "under-water birthing" is not at all new. From very ancient time Rishis and yogins were practising the mediation being under water for a long time. In modern era also Swami Vivekananda, Thakur Ankulachandra, Sri Amarendra Chakrobarti (Sri Sri Borda) are the practitioners of such mediation which has brought transcendental development to their brain powers (Biswas, 1971). As reported by Yoshiro Nakamats, the famous Japanese inventor, such under water birthing brings super intelligence, superb memory, fine physical coordination—the traits of water babies.

Therefore, Super Learning Techniques (SLT) has accepted such rhythmic breathing exercise as a means to energize the brain cells through synchronizing hemispheric activities and by supplying more oxygen to the brain cells. Before the learning starts, it has become imperative to make the learner hundred percent fit—both mentally and physically, to bring superb productions in all round.

Phase II—Memory Session

The first phase of Super Learning Technique (SLT), i.e., The Mind Calming session, not only brings calmness to the distorted mind of the learner, but also develops psycho-physical readiness for learning. Through mind-body coordination and hemispheric synchronisation, the learner makes a mind-set for superb learning. Relaxation, visualization, affirmation and breathing exercise are the sequential steps for harmonization of mind and body in forming a conducive environment for fruitful super learning. The learning activities are obtained through memory session. Basically, this memory session has two steps.

Step 1 : Learning/Teaching Session

During this step, the learning goes on without music. Here

one has to read silently. If necessary, repetition should be made. If the teacher has to present a new topic before the students, the learning matters should be developed accordingly, which will facilitate memorization. Presentation needs to be most interesting, relational, comparative and motivating. Learner should be instructed to breath rhythmically. During this step breath should be held at least for four seconds at the time of learning or listening the presentation of the teacher. The teacher has to present the learning matters rhythmically. Learning matters, if will be presented diagramatically or with some significance of 'get up' and 'looking', that will create 'images' in learner's mind which is easier for quick memorization. Compare and contrast, and simultaneity of occurrences will develop critical thoughts of learner and forgetfulness of those matters get minimized.

The instructor may take the help of audiovisual aids, may write the important information on cardboards, ask the learners to make small chits or cards on different concepts, facts, etc. to paste the charts, information cardboards, different concepts, facts, etc. before the reading table to create their images in the mind, to underline materials with markers of different colours and scents to frame new abbreviation, catchy rhymes or pop songs for easy memorization. The most important and valuable activity relating development of super memory is to do five minutes review before going to sleep in night and five minutes perspective thinking on whole day's work just after getting up in morning. It is because mind is in absolute calmness and peaceful condition during these time.

Step 2 : Remembering Session/Practising Session

After learning a concept or matter, the learner has to practise those for long-term incorporation in the memory-section. At this step, super learning recommends memorization of learned things with music and in closed eyes. Things will be read alongwith background music of 60 beats baroque and after that the learner has to memorise the learned things. By it, one gets back to inner mood and listens to the rhythmic recitation of material by holding the breath to count of four. Listening to the content with rhythmic breathing acts well to carry the new learning matter to the long-term memory section of the brain.

But the selection of music should be right one. Slow stately music helps to maintain a state of relaxed concentration. According to Lozanov the music should have a tempo of about sixty beats to the minute and is generally in 4/4 or 3/4 times. The music should not over power the text being read out.

It has been proved in several research works of Jamee Cathcart that, super learning music can make one smarter, speed learning, expand memory, release stress, help concentration and visulization and open inner awareness. Such a revolutionary discovery as a long scientific pedigree was originally made by the scientists of former Soviet bloc. Taking the ancient music guilds, Baroque composers like Vivaldi, Telemann, Bach, etc. have great fame to have powerful effects on mind and memory. Slow, soothing, serene music of string instruments—the violin, mandolin, guitar and harpsichord impart energy to the brain and body. Research found a slow tempo section in Baroque concertos—the largo or ardante movement with a restful tempo of about 60 beats a minute—that brings the impute up learning effect. As the tranquil largos play, blood pressure of the listener relaxes and comes low, heartbeat slows to a healthy rhythm, stress factors in the blood drop and enhances the immune system.

The physiological and medical instruments like EEG indicate a change in brain wave—beta waves eventually decreases by 6 percent and the alone brain waves of relaxation increases by 6 percent. The right and left hemisphere get synchronized. Thus the rythmic music relaxes body and alerts mind. Physiological research shows that in calm and silence state the body functions more efficiently on less energy (Ostrander and Schroeder, 1996). Like the Z-meditation and Mantra Meditation, this slow baroque music when applied to the memory activities, makes the brain's activities coherent, laserlike and highly productive. Researches of Lozanov (1971, 1978), in Knarkar University in Ukraine relating suggestopedia, study of Cooper and report of Erikson (1960s) on the effect of 60 beat music, report of Masters and Houston's (1996) on effect of music in promoting graphic skills and studies of Lozanov and Novakov (1978) reported benefit of classical music on developing the mind-body coordination for successful activity. Besides the field of learning, this slow baroque music has proved its effectiveness in increasing intellligence of baby, who is in the mother's womb, minimizing labour pain of pregnant mother, increasing output of human resources of business and industrial organisation, curing the patients, etc. (Neill, 1996). Mahaney's (1989) super learning programme—"Change your mind " has proved to be dynamite for reaching and repatterning the powerful sub-conscious mind. Since, the sound is regarded as the linking means to super consciousness or cosmos, enchanting rhythmic music helps in bringing enlightenment in every sphere.

Such multi-dimensionality of slow rhythmic music concert, thus, has created a special place in super learning strategy. Most specifically, in the field of teaching and learning memorisation of learned things becomes more concrete and long lasting when it is accompanied by a slow rhythmic background music. What Ostrander and Schroeder (1996) state, the following steps are to be followed to facilitate super learning memory concert.

1. Follow the four step relaxation routine to get into optimal state for learning.
2. Turn on your superlearning centre. It may be prepared by self or be obtained from Superlearning cermet. The voice will read the material rhythmically—four second of data then four second pause. Varied intonations will keep the material interesting.
3. Silently read your course data following alongwith the recited material. Try to hold your breath when you hear the data. Breath out and in during passess. If you find this breathing pattern difficult omit it for the time being and just let your breathing flow alongwith the rhythm of music and it will pace itself naturally. If possible try to form images of data during the pauses.
4. Once you have gone through the whole lesson, you will hear the slow, 60 beat music begin. Lean back, relax, close your eyes and listen to the same material again. Don't stain, just let your mind float between music and data. The concert will last about twelve to fifteen minutes.

After memory expansion session one should check the

quantity of retention and recall through some puzzles, or games or questions. Super learning depends on practice. More one does, better it works. But it is clear that initially the result becomes low. So more repetition is needed during that phase. But towards the latter sessions learning becomes more with less or no repetitions.

1.4 YOGA, MEDITATION AND SUPER LEARNING—A COMPARATIVE ANALYSIS

When it is learnt that Lozanov has developed super learning on the basis of Indian Raja Yoga with some principles of Bulgarian Yogic culture, since then, a question i.e., "What is the difference between super learning and Yoga ?" always needs to be clarified. It has also become imperative to know the basic objective, principles and procedures of yoga and to understand whether some changes has crept into it through the process of its westernization in the nomenclature of "Super learning".

By literary meaning, Yoga refers "to yoke" or "to link" or "to add" : But, What are the elements or matters to be yoked or linked or added ? Since time immemorial, this has been a matter of investigation for Indian metaphysics. The epistemological analysis of the word accepts it as the means of communion of the petty self with the higher one or union of the *Jivatman* with the *Paramatman* (Prajnananda, 1999). It is a means to attain super-conscious knowledge (Freud, 1979) or God consciousness. It seems as the conscious of opinion of the great minds of the world, and it has been nearly demonstrated by researches into physical nature, that we are the outcome and manifestation of an absolute condition back of our present relative condition and are going forward to return to that absolute. In case of electricity, the modern theory is that the power leaves the dynamo and completes the circle back to the dynamo. The plant takes materials from the earth, dissolves and gives it back. Every form in this world is taken out of surrounding atoms and goes back to these atoms. The same law is applied everywhere. Law is uniform, "Whether we will it or not, we shall have to return to our origin, which is called God", says Swami Vivekananda. (Raja Yoga, 1923, 2002). The metaphysical idea believes that we all came from God, and we all bound to go back to God. Such idealistic thought believes that from whom all this universe comes out, in whom all that is born, live and to whom all returns may be called as the absolute or the almighty or the God, but the fact remains same. This is the religious approach rooted in revelatory experiences relating the human quest to know the ultimate nature of reality, the nature of life and existance and the inquisitiveness to realize the almighty and to be mingled with that supreme entity. This is the dualistic school of thought of Vedanta Philosophy. The orthodox system of Indian religion which accepts Veda, also recognises *samkhya, Naiyayika* and *Mimamsaka* as three systems of studying religion. But vedantins are the actual followers of upanisadic ideas which signify the phiposophy of veda through *mimamsaka.* In the earlier non-vedantic dualisms, all the concepts of God, soul and nature are three distinct .and independent entities. But the nondualistic theory of vedanta is different from Patanjali's Yagadarshana and Kapila's *Sankhya.* So, Sankara accepts Sankhyans and Yogins as dualists when he said: *"dvaitino hite sankhya-yogascha namaikattva-darshinah"*, i.e., as the upholders of the *sankhya* and *yogadarshana* are not believer on the non-dualistic Atman or Brahman, they are known as dualists. (Bramhasutra, II, 1.3). So the upholders of non-dualistic vedanta, including Sankara, have clearly explained that *Mukti* or knowledge of the Brahman is attained through deep meditation upon the Mahavakyas of the Upanishad: *tattva-jnanam tu vedanta-vakabhya eva bhavati,—navedavin-monutetam vrihantam, tam tvauapanisadam purusham pruchhami".* For this reason only Sankara has refuted the theory of *naiyayikas* and *mimansakas* as well as *Sankhya* and *yogadarshana* (Avedananda, 1999). In contrast, vedantic dualism holds that God alone is an independent entity, while others are absolutely dependent upon Him. (Tapasynanda, 2000). Besides that concept of Jiva or Atman, Paramatman, God, Salvation, Vaikuntha, Satya-loka, etc., vedantic dualism, also accepts that the God manifests the universe and rules over it. Nature and soul are involved in this manifestation and they undergo change, but God is unchanging. God is personal in that. He has an infinite number of blessed qualities and attributes. Soul is coming with endowments gained in past births. Our present work determines the fate for future. We are the makers of our own destiny. As we sow, so we reap. In broader sense, the present suffering of the society is due to the past wickedness of man. God has nothing to do with it. He is independent of the soul and nature.

But, the dualistic vedanta stresses on the supreme abode of the divine person which has to be attained by the individual and such attainment is the supreme goal to get rid of the birth cycle and worldly sufferings. The dualists call the attainment as salvation or 'Mokshya' or 'Nirvan' and the Divine Abode as *satya-Loka, Vaikuntha* or *Kailash,* etc. Coming out of the worldly bondage *(Samsara)* or *Maya* is the primary process of getting salvation, as accepted by the Dualistic Vedanta philosophy. Here God, soul and nature are accepted as three inseparable entities related as one organic whole. Accordingly Swami Tapasyananda says, "As the body of God, soul and nature are with him, here, no question of finite limiting the infinite arises. It is because the finite itself is a constitutive factor in the totality of infinite. The Jiva's spiritual consciousness contracts in the state of ignorance and expands in liberation. Prakriti also contracts and expands. Its expansion is the projection of the universe into the manifested or effect state. Its contraction is *pralaya* or dissolution. This process goes on eternally like night and day. The creative state gives opportunity for Jivas to enjoy the fruits of karma in repeated embodiments, gain experience and ultimately be blessed with divine love and thereby attain salvation" (The Four Yogas, 2000).

Advaitism is another strand of Upanisadic thought on religion and man-God aphorism. It exerts that every one and everything is Atman. It is the name, form, the bodies which are material; and they make all these differences. If we take away these differentiating factors, the whole universe, will be visible as one. There is but one soul in the universe, not two. It neither borns, nor dies nor reincarnates. Advaitists dethrone the existence of God and accept Atman—the self of the man as the higher embodiment than sun, heaven and even than the universe. This school of thought accepts "I am He and He is I"—i.e., none but I am God and God is I (So Aham, Aham Brahmansmi).

The cosmic mind, which is sum total of individual minds and is known as *Isvara, Avyakta,* etc. create the world appearance. Advaita vedanta accepts Isvara or Avyakta as

Hiranyagarbha-Isvara or Hiranyagarbha-Brahman as it does not create although it has will-to-create. Such cosmic mind is called *Prakriti* or *Visva-Prakrit* as Hiranyagarva-Brahman combines sagunatva and nirgunatva. The Brahma is the transcendental essence which is one without the second. Although it appears as both ground and cause of the changing world appearace, coming in contact with the inscrutable *maya* or *nescience,* it is originaly one and only one (Prajnanananda, 1999).

In short, the epistemological analysis of Indian religious thought discusses God on the basis Dualism, Non-dualism and Advaitism. It went from the external God to internal cosmic person. God emanent in the universe and ended in identifying the soul itself with God and that God with whom this soul is one, as the basis of this manifestation as the universe. But Swami Tapasyananda (2000) says that as society exists, today all these stages are necessary to suit the needs of men at different stages of evolution. The three stages are not contradictory. Each succeeding one is the fulfilment of the earlier one. Each man has to be taken where he stands and given a helping hand to go forward.

From the above discussion, it is clearly evident that irrespective of different bases of spiritual thoughts and varied contradiction among different philosophical speculations, all agreed on the point of knowing and understanding the self. Salvation, though spiritually refers to the attainment of Nirvan or Moksha (Prabhupad, 2002), most scientifically it is related to enlightenment, by acquiring true knowledge which emanates individual from ignorance, blind beliefs, superstitions, sufferings and exploitations. It is a way of making the existance of the individual superior and developed (Prusty, 2002). Therefore the religious doctrine of India stresses on knowing and understanding the own self by the individual and accordingly it has developed some methods to attain such perfection.

In this respect, Probhupad (2002) asserted, "our natural desire for ultimate meaning, happiness, enlightenment, liberation and salvation has become the most exploited commodity of the twentieth century, creating what one contemporary theologian termed a disastrous "seduction of the spirit". This seduction is indeed the most tragic kind of exploitation. And the unfortunate consequences of this exploitation is a kind of dreadening cynicism that discourages our search for self-fulfilment and the means to attain it (The Path of Yoga, 2002)"

All the orthodox systems of Indian philosophy have one goal in view—the liberation of the soul through perfection. The method to it is Yoga. It covers *sankhya* and *vedanta* schools' views in some form or other. Accordingly, Swami Vivekananda (Meditation and Its Methods, 2003), while taking of the means of realizing the self, says, "as every science has its methods, so has every religion". The methods of attaining the end of religion are called Yoga, that we teach are adapted to the different natures and temperaments of men. We classify them in the following way, under four heads:

1. *Karma Yoga* : The manner in which a man realizes his own divinity through works and duty.
2. *Bhakti Yoga*: The realization of the divinity through devotion to and love of a personal God.
3. *Raja Yoga* : The realization of divinity through the control of mind.
4. *Jnana-Yoga* : The realization of a man's own divinity through knowledge. Swami Vivekananda accepts these as different roads to leading to the same centre—the God.

According to Swami Abhedananda (2000), "Yoga is a Sanskrit word commonly used to signify the practical side of religion; and the first concern of the training for which it stands is to enforce proper obedience to the laws of our moral and physical nature upon which depends the attainment of perfect health, moral and spiritual perfection". After enunciating eleven kinds of definition in favour of the word Yoga, Swami has devided the sincere students of Yoga into three main classes; first, those who born Yogins; second, those who are born as half awakened souls; and third, all those unawakened souls who practise Yoga for first time in their life in the way of begining their serch after truth.

Swami Vivekananda, amalgamating the concept of religion and Yoga, says that each soul is potentially divine. The goal is to manifest this divinity within by controlling external and internal nature either by work or worship or psychic control or philosophy—by one, or more or all of these.

From the description of the Srimad Bhagavad Gita, it is clear that Yoga has been accepted as the most oldest and widely applauded system of spiritual development of the mankind. In a remarkable psycho-therapeutic and extraordinary dialogue between Lord Krishna, the supreme personality of Godhood and his warrier disciple Arjuna, it is revealed that Yoga is the path of perfection through which union between individual consciousness and supreme consciousness, self and superself, the soul and God become possible (Srimad Bhagavatgita, Chapters VI and VIII). The Bhagavatgita deseribes about the aim, process and methods of various Yogas in its different chapters as follows:

Chapter—I	Bisad Yoga
Chapter—II	Sankhy Yoga
Chapter—III	Karma Yoga
Chapter—IV	Jnana Yoga
Chapter—V	Karmasanyasa Yoga
Chapter—VI	Atman-Sanjam Yoga
Chapter—VII	Jnana-Bigyan Yoga
Chapter—VIII	Akhyara Brahaman Yoga
Chapter—IX	Rajaguhya Yoga
Chapter—X	Bibhuti Yoga
Chapter—XI	Viswarup Darsan Yoga
Chapter—XII	Bhakti Yoga
Chapter—XIII	Kshetra-Kshetrajna Bibhaga Yoga
Chapter—XIV	Gunatraya Bibhaga Yoga
Chapter—XV	Purusottam Yoga
Chapter—XVII	Sradhatraya Bibhaga Yoga
Chapter—XVIII	Mokshya Sanayas Yoga

Looking at these descriptions befor Arjuna by Lord Krishna from the time immemorial, some theologists are also of opinion that there are eighteen sequential stages in the Yoga through which super consciousness can be attained (Dharma—The Upholdor of Existance, Biswas, 1977). Among all these types only four types of Yoga prevail much. Four types of spiritual aspirants follow four different types of Yoga. They are discriminating reasoning type, who have a philosophiclal mind and respond quickly to this process; the psychic type, who respond more to mental stimuli than to sense stimuli; the devotional loving type, who has great capacity for feeling and the active type who prefer to be energetic and outgoing. Each type follow specific and systematic method to achieve the goal which is Yoga.

Each Yoga can lead the aspirant to the goal, independent of any of the other Yogas. But specifically, the discriminative type follows Jnana Yoga, psychic type follows Raja Yoga, Devotional type follow Bhakti Yoga and active type of people follow Karma Yoga in attaining their goal. But any type of yoga followed to its logical conclusion, would lead one to the highest goal (Gnaneswarananda, 2001)

Patanjali in his famous book "Yoga Sutra" defines Yoga as the means of controlling the agitations in the mind stuff *(Chitta-Vritti Nirodha)*. Chitta which is always like a highly agitated sea, get more disturbed by innumerable waves in the form of *Vrittis*. Yoga brings those Vrittis under control, makes *mind* or *Chitta* calm and unruffled and make the person feel the distinctiveness of spirit *(Purusha)* and matter of mind-body *(Prakriti)* (Yoga Sutra, Chapter-I, 1-4). Out of the five vrittis—right knowledge *(Pramana)*, false cognition *(Viprajaya)*, fancy *(Vikalpa)*, sleep *(Nidra)* and memory *(Smriti)*, some are painful and some pleasant. But their control is necessary for attaining the state of super conscioueness *(Samadhi)*—the supreme goal of Yoga (Yoga Sutra, Chapter-I, 17-18). Patanjali also states that success of attaining *Samadhi* or the state of super consciousness differs according to the nature of practice of Yoga—mild, moderate and intense. And the *Prakriti-linas* (Yogins who are dissolved in Prakriti but retain their ego sense based on some noble desires of gettings another suitable embodiment), naturally enjoy such, supreme bliss as they practise yoga strenuously (Yoga Sutra, Chapter-I, 19-22) and become able to supress all *vrittis* through *Nirvitarka Samadhi*, which is preceded by *Savitraka Samadhi* and succeeded by *Savichara Samadhi, Nirvichara Samadhi, Samprajnata Samadhi, Asamprajnata Samadhi* (objectless awareness) and end in *Kaivalya* or aloofness of the sprit from matters (Yoga Sutra, Chapter-I, 42-51). For it the Yogins are to overcome the obstacles like ill-health, feeling of helpnessnes, doublt or vacillation, lack of enthusiasm, stupar due to dullness of body and mind, sensuousness, false perception, not reaching the state of communion and falling away for it when attained.

All the yoga systems are capable of attaining super consciousness or God consciousness either by independently or by combined effort (Vivekananda, 2002). Among the four major kinds of yoga such as Raja Yoga, Jnana Yoga, Bhakti Yoga and Karma Yoga, Raja Yoga is said to be the best means. Swami Abhedananda (1999) called it as "the royal road to God consciouness." This is also called Astanga Yoga as it has eight sequential steps to attain super consciousness.

As described in Patanjali Yoga Sutra the "the first step, *Yama* includes non-killing, truthfulness, non-stealing, continence and non-receiving of gifts" : *ahimsa-satyasteya-brahmacharya-parigraha yamah"* (Yoga Sutra, Chaper-II, 30). Then comes *Niyama* comprising of cleanliness, contentment, mortification, study and self-surrender to God : *"soucha-santosha-tapah-svadhyayeshvarapranidhanani niyamah"* (Yoga Sutra, Chapter-II, 32). Then comes *asana* or the sitting posture and they are the means to get control over the breath (Pranayama)—the vital air or Pranavayu. In this regard Patanjali says, *"tasmin satisvasa-prasvasayorgativi chedah pranayamah* (Yoga Sutra, Chaper II, 49). The fifth step is called *pratyahara* which makes the mind introspective : *"sva-vishaya-samprayoge chitasya svarupanukara ivendriyanam pratyahararh"* (Yoga Sutra, Chapter-II, 54). Then comes *dharana* which means concentration. It is the means of concentrating different modifications of the mind on to point or on to a particular object : *"desavandhaschittassya dharana"* (Yoga Sutra, Chapter-III, 01). The seventh step is *dhyana* or meditation which refers to an unbroken flow of knowledge in that point or object on which *dharana* was made : *"tatra pratyayaikatanata dhyanam"* (Yoga Sutra, Chapter-III, 2). The last step which leads to superconsciousness or God consciousness is called *samadhi*: *"tadevartha-mantra-nibhasam svrupa-sunyamiva samadhi"* (Yoga Sutra, Chapter III, 3). Patanjali accepts *Dharana, Dhyana* and *Samadhi* combindly as *samyama* where one follows other in making one. A man can direct his mind to any particular object and fix it there and then keep it there for long time separating the object from the internal part. These three are more internal than those precede that. *Yama, Niyama, Asana, Pranayama* and *Parigraha* are external part of *Dharana, Dhyana* and *Samadhi* these three would not make the mind *Nirvikalpa*—changeless, but would leave the seeds for getting bodies again, which is the object of Yoga and Yogins.

From the above analysis it is clear that, meditation is a means of yoga. Patanjali's yoga aphorism state that meditation or dhyana is the major step of samyama, which concentrates the mind on to a point or object and lead the individual to samadhi or the highest realization of God consciousness. Taking all these things Swami Vivekananda says, "fixing mind on the lotus of the heart or on the centre of the head, is what is called Dharana (concentration). When remaining in one place, making one place as the base, when the waves of mind rise up, without being touched by other waves—when all other waves have stopped and one wave only rise in the mind, that is called Dhyana (meditation). When no basis is necessary, when the whole of the mind has become one wave, "one-formedness", it is called samadhi or superconsciousness (Paramananda, 2002). Accordingly, in Vyasa's commentary it is stated that when the flow of our mental energy is absoultely fixed on to a point—the naval base or the lotus of the heart or intelligence of the brain or on the tip of the nose or on some external divine symbol—it is called dharana or concentration. When such flow continues for sometime without interruption, the object of concentration becomes one with the mental energy, i.e. called dhyana or meditation (Abhedananda, 1999). Thus concentration is the precondition of meditation. Therefore, one who tries to realise the infinite, should pactise concentration and meditation alone, so that he would not be disturbed by the distractions or the modifications of the mind (chitta-vritti). Accordingly, different yoga systems have their respective meditation strategies like Hatha yoga meditation, Jnana yoga meditation, Bhakti yoga meditation, Raja yoga meditation etc. Though Japa mediation, has a long history, electronic meditaton is an emerging trend in the field of science of yoga and meditation (Vishnu Devananda, 2001). Speaking of the importance of Japa or Mantra yoga, Swami Sivananda says, "Mantra yoga is an exact science. *Mananat trayete iti Mantrah*—by the constant thinking of Mantra one is protected and released from the cycle of birth and death.

A mantra is so-called because it is achieved by the mental process. A mantra when constantly repeated awakens the consciousness." Advent of finer electronic technique and their use in making the system of meditation more profitable and easy is called electronic meditation.

The meditations, of course, require some preparation and those preparations may come in the form of concentration and other pre-conditions of yoga. Thus the yogic practices facilitate meditational activities and thereby achieving the state of super consciousness becomes easy (Abhedananda, 1999). There are two nerve currents in the spinal column, called *pingala* and *ida* and there are hallow canal called *sushumna* running through the spinal cord. At the lower end of the hallow canal lies the seat of *Kundalini* or *Muladhar*. Here, the *Kamakala* lies in the lower end of spinal column and yagins consider it as lotus bud. As the energy awakes such lotus bud opens and the coiled up energy goes spiraly up to brain. When the conscious reaches brain the lower parts of the body become numb. The mind gets fixed on something higher, more abstract and gradually it leads to absolute or to the state of Samadhi or God consciousness or super consciousness. The yogin wants to transmute the physical forces into mental and intellectual forces through proper regulation of the vibration of molecules of the body by breathing exercises *(Pranayam)*, as done by Raja yogins or through rare and devotional exercises done by Bhakti Yogins or so concentration by Japa Yogins or through prayer self-analysis of Jnana Yogins. Specifically, in Bhakti Yoga we have five meditative contemplations such as—*Shanta, Dashya, Sakhya, Batsalya* and *Mathurya* based on nine forms of devotions like *Sravanam, Kirtanam, Smaranam, Padasevanam, Archanam, Vandanam, Dasyam, Sakhyam* and *Atmanivedanam*. So as there are different types of meditation in other types of yogas. But, all either separately or combinedly can develop the magnetic capacity of the performers' sense organs. In making difference between yoga and meditation Kumar (2002) says, "in the contemporary psychological literature meditaion is used as a broad and generic term" which refers to a sort of "mental devices or techniques" and also found in all spiritual practices in other traditions like Buddhism, Christianity, Jewish kabalah, Taoism, etc. Carrington (1987), after a vivid investigation into the concept and practices of meditation, defined it as a "conglomerate word" under which number of different "techniques and intents such as sitting quietly, relaxing, closing the eyes, breathing deliberately, focusing attention on an object or image non-analytically, observing the thought process without judging, repeating sounds mentally, rhythmic moving of the body are included." Studying different meditative practices Naranjo and Ornstein (1971) categorised it into three types viz., the ways of forms (concentration, absorption, union, outerdirected, Apollonian), the expressive way (freedom, transparence, surrender, inner directed, Dionysian) and negetive way (elimination, detachment, emptiness, centred, the middle way). Goleman (1977) groups meditaton into two types, such as, "concentration type meditation" and "opening up type meditation". Carrington (1987) distinguished meditaton on the basis of its technique. He found that "centering technique" is somehow different from "meditation". While refering all such centring techniques as practical meditation, Carrington (1987) stated that because of limitation in vocabulary and confusion of west relating means and ends of meditation, it is widely confused and misinterpreted. The changes which was brought in western country in the original system of meditation was primarily intended to make the system easy for the novices and accordingly it simplified the concept to centring technique so that there will be easy understanding and practice. In actual sence, centring is part and parcel of meditation where the person focuses attention to a point (Dharana) to stabilize the body-mind imbalances, which pulls attention away from the centre of the self. But meditation, as described in Patanjali's Yoga Sutra, is Dhyna—the practice of fixing the mind to a point for a time period (Bhajanananda, 1980) which leads the person to the state of superconsciousness or Samadhi (Bhajanananda, 1981).

In this regard, Kumar's (2002) Three-factor Model of meditation divides meditation on the basis of nature (Category-I), influencing factors (Category-II) and effects of meditation (Category-III). The first category of meditation stresses on the attention strategy like Goleman's (1978) "concentration and opening up meditation"; the second category devides meditation on the ground of procedure adopted and experiences acquired by the practitioner (Naranjo and Ornstein, 1971) like Carrington's (1987) "spiritual and practical meditation" and Johnson's (1982) "extrinsic and intrinsic factor-based meditaion" and third category meditation is based on their effects like "self-regulation meditation" (Shapiro and Giber, 1978) and "relaxation response" oriented meditation (Benson, 1975).

The contextual base divides meditation on the ground of its purpose or aims and objective. On this base, meditaton can be divided into three types—spiritual, material and psycho-scientific. In spiritual meditation, the purpose is to attain salvation or *Moskha* or realization of almighty or Godconsciousness. It believes that meditation can lead the man (Atma) to be mingled with Parambramha or Paramatma. Followers of such idea are generally idealistic and religious persons and they practise different meditative practices of Bhakti Yoga, Kriya Yoga and some processes of Raja Yoga also. The material meditation is quite westernisation and modernizaton of spiritual meditation. In the modern industrial society when people are entangled with innumerable desires, requirements and problems of solving those, they are accepting meditation to get solace. Looking at their desires some experienced persons have brought some changes in the spriritual meditation to make it the short-cut way of achieving expected goal. Western societies are also widely acknowledged as materialistic, as opposed to spiritual, in their outlook. Their active persuit of science and technology approaching meditation from practical and concrete point of view (Kumar, 2002). Give and take principle with profit-making attitude also prevails on it. They never consider meditation as "a deep spiritual commitment, if they think of it as being spiritual at all" (Carrington, 1987). So, they learn meditation to make the life easier and more pleasant. Accordingly, the fundamental process of meditation has been changed into different forms in consideration to its need in solving various problems to attain material prosperity. This is why, now meditation is used in business, management, industry, medical science, defence and military science, agriculture, personal management, personality development and the like. Accordingly, people having some experience 'on yoga and meditation, have incorporated some feasible and local-based principles into original strategy of yoga and meditation in order to make it easy for people of variety of culture. Todays development in the field of spa, tai chi, varied massages, Rave Parties, Yogaerobics, Kripalu yoga, Surya Yoga, Artistic yoga of Bharat Thakur, Naturopathy, Aurvedic healing, Reiki,Therapy (Beam, cosmetic, Shiatsu therapy, beauty therapy, aromatherapy), store therapy hypnoses, etc. though are proving their effectiveness in solving one or more problems of the individual, in real sense, these all have incorporated one or many principles of ancient yoga or meditation. Therefore, Smita Bhatia says "de-stressing is the buzzword as every one looks to discover the perfect antidote to their busy lives. Just take your pick of any of the following : A royal thai massage, a rejuvenator package at spa, a Swedish massage or even bio-face lift-you could also join a fitness centre (or simply hire a personal trainer), pamper yourself at a day spa or at a beauty salon; relish great tasting health foods and juices, enjoy a favourite sport or take up a new one" (*The Telegraph-Weekend*, February 14, 2004). Thus, doing activity at spa, meditating at home and practising yoga or just listening to music have their internal similarity in system and approach, which is the part and percel of our material meditation. The concept of phycho-scientific meditation is emerged out of east-west integration on the concept of yoga and meditation. Though meditation, from its true meaning, refers to the means of attainment of superconsciousness, the western culture mainly consider it as the centring technique, which concentrates all distracted mental forces of the individual on to a point. Carrington (1987) calls the technique as "practical meditation", while he distinguished meditation from dharana-like pshychological centring activities. Human mind is the combination of various faculties and its harmonious development depends on development of 9/10th portion of unconscious mind (Freud, 1976). Meditation is a technique of sharpening the mind (Bhajanananda, 1980). It fixes the mind through *Dharana,* and leads to *Samadhi* or superconsciousness, as told by Patanjali's Yoga Sutra (Bhajanananda, 1980a, b, c,). Such scientificity of meditation has been found by various research studies conducted in abroad. As studies revealed, meditation has become instrumental in increasing achievement, enhancing intelligence, making the person creative, developing better problem-solving ability and igniting a dynamic personality. Most significantly, average western researcher do not consider meditation as a deep spiritual commitment, if they think of it as being spriritual at all (Corrington, 1987). In every aspect of western culture and people's actions, meditation has been considered and approached with par to science and technology (Kumar, 2000). The asana, pranayama etc. those precede meditation or dhyana and dharana are means of regulating the prana which pumps air into different lungs and nervous systems and energizes these for effective action. By getting required oxygen, the brain cells get activated and the person becomes more active and developed. Such scientific base of meditation, at many times, is shrouded by spiritual mysticism of India. But, an east-west amalgamation has given true psycho-scientific mode to the Indian meditative contemplation. Such psycho-scientific approach accepts life-force as the basis of every existance. In material bodies, this life force is present as atoms. All activity in the material world, produced by vibration and such vibration is caused by prana. As the *Prana* is controlled by breathing exercises, the physical, mental and spiritual world is regulated. Therefore, Swami Abhedananda (2001) says, "the power itself is in each one of us, even in the lower animals, in plants and vegitables. If every atom of a body or matter is charged with prana, then by stimulating the vibratory conditions of that prana, which are now going on in our system, we shall be able to stimulate all the atoms, which make up the molecules and cells of the body and make them vibrate on a higher plane and manifest more energy and more powers, as we wish to express." In practice, meditaion is psycho-scientific as it trains the psycho-physical systems in scientific way for all round achievement by the individual. A person, who has awakened his/her own *prana* and properly vibrated the atoms of the system, can also have the power to heal other creatures and develop the environment for desired perspective. Such socio-scientific base of meditation has been applauded in present world.

On the basis of technique and principles, meditation can be grouped into three types such as, rigid, flexible and *laissez faire*. The meditative systems, originally developed in Indian society, specifically during vedic period, can be considered as rigid meditations, if those will be practised without any dilution. If we take the example of the meditational practices of Raja Yoga or Hatha Yoga, it is clear that one has to follow the sequencial steps and principles lie therein to attain the goal. If some steps will be skipped or missed or some principle will be forgotten to be practised, the goal will be far away from the practitioner, causing irrepairable phycho-physical loss. So, regarding Hatha Yoga, it is said that, it requires thorough knowledge of the psychic body and its structure as well as great purification of the physical and psychic bodies. *Kundalini Shakti* is primordial cosmic power and can not be trifled with. Premature attempts to arouse it without proper preparation can cause great damage to the aspirant's mental, physical and psychic balance (Vishnu Devananda, 2001). Likewise, the principles and steps of Raja Yoga are to be followed strictly in order to reach the superconscious stage. All the preconditions are to be cautiously adhered to without which a *Yogin* can not even practise first step. But from post-vedic period some dilution crept into the rigidity of vedic meditative practices with the entry of tantric upasana of Upanishad. Vedic images of fire, sun, air etc., were replaced with images of Gods and Godesses, meditational approach became indirect and use of words with purported mystic power to produce changes in consciousness achieved central position in meditation process till today (Bhajanananda, 1981(b). During sixth century B.C., Buddhism and Jainism also brought some changes in the meditation process. The objective and subjective types of meditation of Buddhist doctrine signify such changes. *Vipasana*, practised by *Southern* Buddhist tradition and *Samartha* observed by Tibetan Buddhists have incorporated some changes into the basic nature of meditation. As time passed the Hinayan and Mahayan sects also added different practices in the original middle path meditative strategies, propounded by Lord Buddha after his years long experimentation on various meditation systems leading to his illumination. The contribution of Islamic suffism, Christian contemplation, Sikh's concentration process are, somehow or other, the modified form of vedic meditation system. Such dilutions made the meditation easy and approachable for all people and give birth to flexible type meditation. Now-a-days, the vedic meditation has also acquired many new forms by various modern foreign meditation gurus and resarchers. Some of them have changed its original Indian strategies into different forms by incorporating the foreign religious or metaphysical practices to make this system feasible for their people. The materialstic attitude of foreigners also gave birth to a new system of meditation which can help them in achieving their desired goal. Jacobson's Self Regulation Strategy, Progressive Muscular Relaxation, Bio-feedback, Autogenic Training, Mahesh Yogi's Transcendental Meditation, Meditative Process of Freud and Osho, Lozanav's Super Learning are some examples of such flexible and modified form of meditation. Though such changed forms seem more scientific and concrete in their product and effect, still those can't be treated as original meditation. But these Trans-meditations have become more popular than rigid meditational systems as their psudo-scientific nature satisfies the emerging human needs in more profitable and tangible manner.

In this juncture, there are religious practitioners who are trying to make vedic meditative system need-based by not diluting its basic nature and without any major changes in its basic principles. In this regard the works of Swami Dayananda, Sri Aurobindo, Swami Vivekananda, Swami Yogananda, Swami Sivananda are worthnoting. Basing on the crude philosophy of Yoga and meditation, they have tried to bring desired development of the human, society and of other creatures. When required they have made the scientific changes within the framework of its original dictum. Probably for such scientific and tangible interpretation of meditation their organisations have attracted the people of the globe to follow such practices to fulfil all of their requirements. As this meditative practices deny unnecessary changes which affect the basic characteristics of yoga and meditation, but welcomes desired situation-based scientific changes considering valuable cultural differences, those may be treated as *laissez faire* type of meditation.

Further, on the basis of ethnoepistemological analysis, meditation can be divided into two types such as classical and modern. Considering its origin and development, it is generally accepted that, although meditation is the original product of eastern culture, it has been changed to a massive movement only for its westernization. Cultural mentality, maturity in knowledge development, cosmopolitan outlook of the society and people, socio-economic standard and techno-scientific and eternal value-directed attitude have been recognised as determining factors of approaching to a specific meditative contemplation. Now-a-days, organisations are taking care of developing and accelerating the overall development by enhancing efficiency of reserved human resource through meditation (Shapiro, 1991). Because of these factors, researches have always viewed difference between western and eastern meditative practices and processes. Meditation as we see in the east, in connection with its objectives and processes, are quite different in west, which is based on scientific considerations (West, 1986). Meditation is accepted as a means of attaining the state of superconsiousness to bring total life development (Corrnigton, 1987). As perception of people relating development of their lives differ from one socio-cultural tradition to other, so the meditation in various social set-ups. According to Locke and Kelly (1986), such difference is due to ethnoepistemological factors. Such factors mainly accept eastern and western meditation systems as classical and modern type respectively. Thus the socio-cultural dynamics, techno-scientific attitude, and psychological considerations determine the various types of meditation. A detail typology of meditation is given in Figure 1.2. However, through meditation the magnetic forces of mental and intellectural abilities get transmuted into higher will power which can acquire different manifestations as per the will of the individual. Anybody can generate such rhythmic action in all the organic function by such yogic will power. It is clear that the matured and pointed will power, which is based on the attainment of super consciousness, is stronger than all the organic functions. And the person who attains super-conscious stage is capable of utilizing his power successfully in every field of activity.

Thus super learning technique seems as the cream of yoga and meditation, most specifically of Raja Yoga, which enables the individual to attain the state of super-consciousness within a short time span. It develops the extraordinary rationality within the practitioner to apply such scientific technique in energizing and activating the sense organs throguh practising the yoga for activating the *Chakars* or *Kundalini* or *psychic centres*

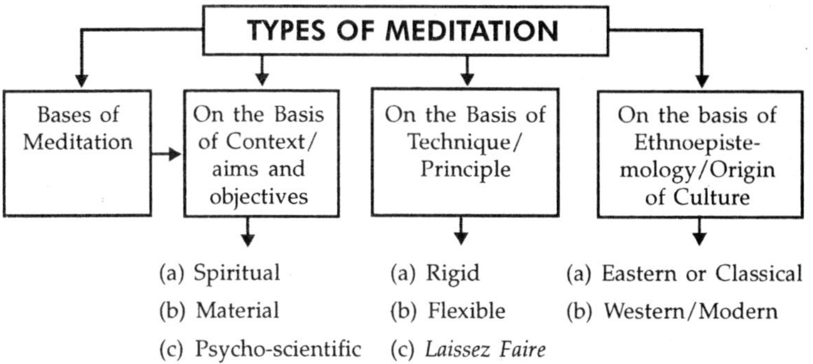

Fig. 1.2 Types of Meditation

and leading the individual to *Samadhi* or reaching the goal. Therefore, it is accepted that yoga is a system, where meditation is a sub-system or attribute. But super-learning is a system in miniature. Like meditation and yoga, super learning has become today's well known prescription for solution of varieties of problems. Taking the experiences from eastern and western religious and philosophical contemplations, the ancient meditation, has been transformed to transcedental meditation, electronic meditation, massage technique, Spa, Alexander technique, Fldenkrie's method, clinically standardized meditation and so many with addition or elimination of some aspects. At many instances, meditation and yoga has been used as a means of stress-management and self-regulation strategey (Shapiro and Giber, 1978) by adding progressive muscular relaxation, biofeedback, autogenic training and many other techniques (Jacobson, 1986).

From the above typology of meditation, it is clear that super learning is a materialistic type of meditation developed in the western socio-cultural dynamics taking its base from Indian Raja Yoga and adding something from Bulgarian Yogic culture. Research studies conducted in foreign lands shown that super learning is widely used as a psycho-scientific technique of igniting life-force in the organism and activating their atoms and molecules to super-consciousness. It has been scientifically experimented in varied cultural settings and found that superlearning technique is profitable in solving all problems and enhancing the dormated human capacities to uptimum possibiilities. Comparatively the eastern yoga and meditation which are purely based on spiritual or metaphysical speculations, are given a scientific and materialistic approach through super learning technique. It has considered the cognitive affective and psycho-moter domains with ethnographical or cultural diversities and have developed a system technology for developing human potential and social condition. It has studied the physiology of human being and has developed an exercise technique with visualization and affirmation in a *laissez faire* manner which has been proved effective in varied research studies. Thus, super learning has been accepted as a developed and modified form of yoga and meditation and has paved the way for accelerated socio-individual well-being.

1.5 SUPER LEARNING IN INDIAN SCHOOLS—A RETROSPECTION

In strict sense, super learning as it is, is not found in curricular and co-curricular practices of any Indian school. It may be due to its western nature. But a retrospection into the school system of India through ages and existence of varied nature of schools and their activities in independent India provide the signal of super learning-like practices basad on modified forms of Yoga and meditation, somehow and other. It is because the Indian education system, starting from vedic age through modern time, has been based on spiritual and metaphysical speculations (Mukherjee, 1989). The pre-Aryan *rishi yati* culture (Dandekar, 1981) and ancient Indian *ashramas* or *gurukulas* were the epitoms of spiritual practices where *sravana, manana* and *nididhyasana* were the methods (Keay, 1962) alongwith *prayer, dhyana* or *meditation, concentration* and *worship of nature*. In later or post-vedic age, the spiritual practices like prayer, worship of Gods and Goddesses, performing yajna, chanting mantras or hymns (Dasgupta, 1927) were done alongwith learning the diversified curriculum (Rawat, 1989). During that age the *gurukulas* were stressing more on *upasana* which included subjective and objective meditation in form of *service, attendance, adoration, practice of archery, religious meditation,* etc. (Dasgupta, 1927; Apte, 1970; Bhajanananda,

1981(a). Such upasana seems similiar to super learning activities as it brings psychic concentration, inspires devotional feeling, frees mind from subjective preoccupation and desires, brings relaxation, fosters psychic attitude, which allows communication with the heart of reality (Sircar, 1974). Three types of upasana- *pratimopasana* (upasana in form), *namopasana* (*upasana* in name) and *anamgrahopasana* (Upasana on self) achieve central theme in that upanisadic curriculum which were the bases of various meditation (Kumar, 2002). Mainly analogical meditation and symbolic meditation were found in upanisadic era and substitution meditation was prevailing during vedic period (Bhajanananda, 1981a, b). *Acharyas* were torch-bearers for *dwijas* (sishyas). The *dwijas* were observing *brahmacharya*—the life of complete celibacy, which was considered as the basic necessity to acquire knowledge. The muniyati tradition had brought some changes in meditative practices of this age. Begging alms was compulsory to develop competency within the learner for acquiring deep concentration to reach the supreme goal. Though salvation or *Moksha* was the main idealistic objective of that educational system, nurishing the inherent qualities of the learner for full-fledged development of personality was the central goal of Acharyas. The upanisadic tests emphasise on control of desires, high moral elevation and on meditation as necessary conditions for realization of *brahman.*

Buddhist educational system also stressed on the Arya-Astanga Marg (Nobel eight-fold path) and Arya Chatwari satya (four nobel truths) which were the pre-conditions of a Bhikhu to be a perfect learner. Through *upasampad* that system tried to make a *Bhikhu* the *monk* who practises meditations, worship and prayer to acquire true knowledge—the gate-way for *nirvañ* (Das, 1989). In later Buddhist age, when Buddhism divided into Hinayana and Mahayan sects and tantra crept into the original system, the education system also became more upasana-centred and practice of prayer, dhyana and dharana achieved central position (Maiti, 1985). Likewise, during mediaval period, Islamic *Khanquas* (Kutub) and *Maktab* and *Madarasha* were the religious shrines where education was imparted alongwith spiritual practices—*prayer, reading Quran* and *meditating Allah*—the prophet (Rawat, 1989; Srivastav, 1986). Religious curriculum of orthodox rulers made their education system more metaphysical than secular. Accordingly, their curricular practices were predominated by prayer, reading Quran, remembering the activities and sayings of the prophet and meditating on Him, those were more or less analogous to *sravan, manana* and *nididhyasana*.

All those things changed into a different set in modern India with the promulgation of English education. The entire thing took a scientific turn in independent India. The modern Indian educational system capitalized on her spiritual posterity for tangible socio-individual development. Looking at the degradation in human value system and understanding the psycho-scientific approaches of ancient yogic culture in moulding the individual and social life, the modern education system has incorporated such spiritual practices in some acceptable and modified forms, considering the secular and democratic characteristics of Indian republic. The education commissions and committees like Secondary Education Commission (1952-54), Sri Prakasha Committee (1959), Education Commission (1964-66), National Policy on Education (1968, 1979, 1986 and 1992), those have stressed on varied activities in one way or other, seems similar or as part and parcel of the activities concerned to meditation and yoga.

Considering the multi-cultural, multi-religious and diversed ethnological characteristic of numerous communities (Shapiro, 1990) those were living in India, the republic has devised an educational system giving freedom to religious communities, minorities and various sects to open their learning centres. Therefore, India has government, aided, private and minority educational institutions. Though, at school level, it has CBSE, ICSE and state-sponsored courses of studies, in all these courses there are some moral practices added with a view to develop humantarian values (West, 1987) and increase concentration among students. In courses of studies also, life and teachings of various religious leaders, prophets, great men are incorporated to inculcate such values among learners, Prayer classes, reading the sayings of great men, seminars and talks on spiritual topics and prophets are recommended activities, those, to some extent, create the environment for meditative practices. In residential schools morning and evening prayers and study hours are maintained believing of creation of concentration within the learners. But there are schools in India where meditation, pranayama, yoga, prayer, religious observances like Saraswati Puja, Ganesh Puja (Goddess and God of knowledge and learning), Viswakarma Puja (God of Engineering and Technology), etc. are practised as part and parcel of their curricular programme, Saraswati Shishu/Vidya Mandir, Vivekananda Shiksha Kendra, Maharshi Vidya Mandir, Shivananda School, Tapoban School, Integral Education centre are some of those schools where such practices of yoga and meditation are common activities. Arya Vidya Mandir, Arya Yogashram, Bihar School of Yoga, Munger, Ambica Yoga Kutir, International centre for Yoga Education and Research. Pondichery, Ramamani Iyenger Memorial Yoga Research Institute of Mysore, Krishnamachari Yoga Mandiram of Chennai, The Yoga Institute of Mumbai are some of leading Yoga institutes of India those have contributed a lot in institutionalising Yoga and meditation.

Gandhiji's Wardha scheme of Basic Education, Tagore's Shantiniketan, Gopabandhu's Statyabadi System and Sri Aurobindo's Integral Education had made education a part of their curriculum alongwith conggregational prayer (assembly) and other moral teachings. In this connection Gurudev Tagore wrote, "I insist on this period of meditation, not however expecting the boys to be hypocrites and to make believe, they are meditating. But I do insist that they remain quiet; that they exert the power of self-control, even though instead of contemplating on God they may be watching the squirrels, running up the tree." This is why, while teaching in Shantiniketan and some birds were making sound or wind was flowing, Tagore used to stop teaching and instruct students to listen to them in quiet and in closed eyes. Now, inspite of many demotivating tendencies and apathy, a few positive efforts of innovative schooling are seen in India. Bal Bhawan, Jena Prabodhini Mirambika, Rishi Vally School, Netarhat Residential School, a few public schools and some emerging schools by private organisations also stress on such spiritual activities in their schools to develop creative thinking and intelligence (Passi and Prabhu, 1997). Now, with the recommendation of central government and CABE (Central Advisory Board of Education)

Yoga has been included in ICSE and CBSE courses as an elective subject. In many Universities, Department of Yoga has been opened. Bombay University is offering diploma course in yoga. At present, private persons, having expertise in yoga and meditation and in their materialistic approach for solving various problems, are opening a large number of yoga centres all over the country. Research studies shown that, in these centres people of all age level and almost all categories of the society are attending the courses (Bhatia, 2004). Personality development centres, guidance counsellors, therapists, physiotherapist, healing centres touch techniques, coaching centres, and Arya Yogashram are using material meditation and analogical meditation in solving diverse problems and thereby inviting people of every walks of life to upgrade their lifestyle.

An analytical speculation on the metaphysical tradition of spiritual India and the "interority" (Bhajanananda, 1980, a, b, c, d, and e) of Indians show that there is a cultural mentality and human motivation within every Indian towards such spiritual activity. Such permanent internal inclination is seen in the flesh and blood of every Indian which is exemplified in their "*Gotra*"—the title showing their inheritance from a specific vedic Rishi. It is believed that there is an inceasant flow of blood of those vedic *Rishis* and *Munis* within the persons bearing the respective Gotra. Through these blood cells the characteristics and temperaments of those Rishis are obviously present in the persons, who have obtained their gotras. As the Vedic Rishis were the embodiments of high level spiritual and meditative resources, their ancestors in these age are expected to have those tremendous tendencies as inherent qualities. The concept of *Dharma, Artha, Kama* and *Moksha* seem to be their requirements and all internally try to achieve the state of *gunateeta* (Srimad Bhagbad Geeta) by surpassing the three constituent principles of human mind (Guna)—*Sattva, Rajas* and *Tamas* (Kuppuswamy, 1985). The ancient Rishis and Munis have been responsible for integrating meditative practices in all their diversities into daily life. This find expression in personal, social, religious and universal attitudes and values. Tresspassing all cultural and geographical boundries, meditational practices seem very popular for all (Kumar, 2002). But it is irony that not everyone pursues a spiritual path actively. However such ideas are interwoven there in the societal system in various practices and forms. For common individual, those austere practices have been simplified for making its practice easy in daily life. Kumar (2002) stated morning prayers, evening prayers, ritual workship, chanting mantra, devotional singing (bhajan), listening to spiritual discourses, viewing dramatic performances having religious themes, reading books about great saints, going on pilgrimage, and visiting ashrams are some examples of the ways by which the religio-mystical outlook of the culture is integrated into the "ethos" or life ways and *'eidos'* or thought ways of Indian masses. The Indian schools, now-a-days, are also following one or some of these aesthetic practices to bring out the inner potentialities of the learners. Though meditation is not taught in all schools, these altered activities are serving the purpose to some extent. Such altered meditational practices, though are not similar to super learning techniques, are fulfilling some of its components and preparing learners for developing concentration and consciousness. If attaining superconscious state is a far away dream of this process, it can not be accepted as unreachable.

1.6 SUPER LEARNING AND ISSUES RELATING CREATIVE THINKING

Although super learning is mainly regarded as a technique of achieving extraordinary out put in any field of activity, it is based on the sound theoretical foundation. Since Lozanov developed this technique taking the yogic principles of India and Bulgeria, it is crystal clear that the technique is embodied with the psychophysical, philosophical and metaphysical theories relating Yoga and meditation of both the cultures. As super learning acts as Vitamin E supplements in energizng the fundamental organismic constituents, it creates and supplies amino-acid which fuels whole-brain synchronization, that is related to creative thinking (Garreet, 1967). When US government realized the effect of super learning in making the people 25% smarter and in increasing creative thinking, intelligence, memory, concentration, mastering skills and relieving stress from psychophysical systems, it is evidenced, that super learning is a multi-dimensional approach. Strategies of super learning are very much scientific and systematic which energizes the left and right hemispheric function of human mind. It combines the activities of intelligence and creative thinking into a whole which were respectively called cognitive creativity and affective creativity (Vargiu, 1973). So far as the psychoanalysis and sociological aspect of psychoanalysis are concerned, super learning also acts as a means of digging out the inherent potentials from unconscious level (Frend; 1971). Such levels though seem synonymous to Kubie's (1958) pre-conscious or Cannon's extraconscious (Wason and Laird, 1968) or Eharenzweig's principles of dedifferentiation (Rothenbeog and Housman, 1976) levels however, their contribution for the development of creative thoughts are very much important. It acts as a means of developing the intelligence, creative power and so many other attributes. The concept of creativity is interpreted as the ground of 5-P's, namely, person, process, product, press and potentialy. Likewise, super learning can be interpreted on these five gounds. The persons those show extraordinary dispositions in any field of activity may be called as superman—the concept analagous to the philosophical metaphysics of Sri Aurobindo. In the spiritual lader Sri Aurobindo stated that the man who bears the ordinary mind called "Manas" can go up to "Superman" or 'Ati-manab with an upgraded mind-state called "Ati-manas"'. At this state, the five beings—physical, psychic, mental, spiritual and vital, are found their full-fledged development within the superman. It is believed that a superman has the potency of showing extraordinary achievement in any field of activity. Any kind of person—political, economic, social, artistic, cultural, according to Lozanov, can develop the super memory and engage that ability in being extraordinary.

Creative thinking comes to exist through a systematic process. That may depend on Wallas's is preparation, incubation, illumination and verification or seven passages which include framing, probing, explaining, revaluating, affirming, reaffirming and realizing (Motamedi, 1982). Meanwhile, the traditional processes of bringing development of creative thinking have been modernised with the impact of science and technology. Osborn's brainstorming has been developed to electronic brainstorming (Siau, 1995). Likewise super learning has developed a scientific process to upgrade the mind and its function to Alpha level. Through mind calming session it stresses on simple exercises for relaxing the mind-body condition. The affirmation stage develops confirmation in the individual and through breathing exercise it tries to develop concentration and supply of more oxygen to the brain cells which helps in activating the mental organs and their activities—intelligence, thinking, reasoning, analysis, synthesis, creative thinking and many others. While employing the technique in teaching and learning, it stresses on teaching session and memorizing session which is conducted in closed eye with and without music. Thus, super learning technique has very scientific process. The principles of Raja Yoga and Meditation are clearly evident in this technique. Now-a-days, the use the technology like audio-visual aids, computer, internet, e-mail etc. has made super learning more advanced. Development of electronic meditation bio-feedback (Vishnu Devanada, 2002) has also exerted significant influence on the process and practices of yoga and meditaiton in modern era. Super learning, in turn, is getting new dimension in its approach to solve various problems.

Super learning, to its core of action, is product-centred. As reported by several research studies, super learning makes the normal individual the learning superstar. It brings extraordinary discoveries, memory expansion and transforms ordinary life time into quality time and anxiety into soaring self-confidence. It is always recognised by top performance in art, sports, creative thinking, problem solving and in different fields of life, such as, economics, social, cultural, science and technology, sport, politics, infotainment, etc. But, in every field, whether super learning is applied there, will be known only from the spectacular achievement achieved by the concerned person. Relating the output of super learning Siegel (2003) says "super learning is full of new breakthroughs in use of sound, brain patterns, music, nature, nutrients, imagery and much more to open potential—yours for the taking plus how to super learn almost anything and excel at work, school, sports and the arts." Its achievement or success is measured by multi-dimensional mind/memory power, multi-level stress relief techniques, cope with change with easy, dream realization and goal attainment with 2 to 10 times faster and so on. Likewise, the field of expanded realm of memory can be measured in the form of turbocharge intelligence and memory, created physical, mental and spiritual wellness, rebalanced life conditions, release of exhilarating potentials and speed learning. If an individual actively acquires such qualities, it will be presumed from those productions that he/she has super learning ability. It is clear that if the person achieve super learning he would excel in every field of activity and such excellence is the prove that super learning has taken place there.

Press, in the theory of creative thinking, refers to the environment. Arieti's (1976) concept of creativogenic society is quite similar to it. A congenial environment helps in generating creative talents. In exception also, some, exceptional creative persons have came from general societal situation. There, their hereditary qualities play a strong role. Overall, a creative environment begets creative persons (Prusty, 1996). Super learning stresses on the psycho-physical environment of the indivisual. It also accepts quiet and tranquil environment as the source of psycho-physical well-being. That is why people of ancient India were practising yoga and meditation in deep dense forest and during early morning called *"Bramhamuhurrta"* and in evening called *"Sayankala"* (Bhajanananda, 1981). Some of the experiments those are conducted in west have capitalised on the yogic and meditative practices. The mind-body relaxation which brings excellence to individual in any field, is attained by mind calming activities like simple exercise. Under such exercise simple yogic asanas are practised which paves the way for fixing the mind on to a point, as is done in practical meditation of Carrington (Kumar, 2001). As the process of yoga and meditation has acquired a change on the basis of east-west cultural influence, so the change has also been crept into the super learning system. This ethnoepistemological nature which affects ceative thinking is also seem influential in super learning. Such ethnoepistemology refers to complex of beliefs, values and recipes—social, psychological, cultural, technical and the like. Therefore, Lozanov brought some changes in Indian Raja Yoga with Bulgarian Yogic principles while he was applying that in Bulgaria. Materialistic interpretation of yoga and meditation by the westerners put a different strategic plan to the eastern spiritualistic approach of yoga and meditation (West, 1986). Such attitudinal influence has been well tackled by super learning system. It has brought a middle path-like compromise for the development of a sound technique for bringing unprecedented development in any field of endeavour (Locke and Kely, 1986).

On the feature of potential, theory of super learning expresses very much optimism. It accepts every individual as full up with maximum possibilities. Favouring Freudian and neo-Freudian theory of consciousness, super learning believes that 9/10th portion of human mind is remained uncultivated. If that portion of hidden qualities will be developed to their maximum potentiality, then the individual would be super individual. The modern psychologists have redefined meditation on the ground of different theoretical orientations, such as, behaviorism, constructivism, cognitive, humanistic and psychoanalytic. Taking this analysis into view, it is realised that super learning accomplished the essence of all those theoretical descriptions and tries to bring transcendental development through proper processes and practices. As told by White (2001), Super learning connects with expanded realms of memory to turbocharg intelligence and memory, find fulfil work and relationship and to release exhilarating potentials. Through visualization super learning sharpens the mind to self- visualize the inherent potentials and capabilities. Affirmation consolidates such visions by putting positive and optimistic confidence on the self. It is a method of understanding the self through knowing thyself. So, Ostrander and Schroeder says, "super learning (r) your own and find out how to uncover unconscious learning blocks". Thus super learning is a technique which capitalizes on the process of revealing long suppressed, explosive secrets and discovering the fascinating roots lies in individual by undertaking stunning voyages into the far galaxies of human potential and the psychic realms. Having much resemblance with meditation sphorology, suggestology, telepathy, healing, chi energy, and transcendental meditation, super learning has made a strand over in bringing all hidden potentialities out and investing those in super creations. The psychokinetic power get accelerated by it. For such, vibrative activity superlearning is called as "psychotronic generator"—a device that harness psychic force and put it to work. Eli Bay of Toronto says, by super learning "you will learn to relax and relax to learn. With mind-body relaxation, mind calming and the joy of learning experience, you will dissolve IQ-hampering anxiety and fast forward to new creativity."

Creative thinking which has become a mysterious phenomenon because of definitional differences and conceptual variations, has been accepted by super learning as a natural human phenomenon. This technique can enhance the fluency, flexibility, originality, elaboration, inquisitiveness and persistence of the individual those constitute creative thinking. The imagery thoughts, concept of serendipity, effect of training, development of correlates of creative thinking like intelligence, attitude, aptitude, right and left brain synchronization, use of technology in the development of creative thinking to metacreativity all can get well-treatment from this super learning. Super learning, thus, has become a major training model which has proved its applicability in developing originality in thought and exceptionality in application in the field of business, medicine, science and technology, art, politics, social relation, military science and in varied personality attributes (Kirkus, 2002). Robinson (2001) says use of super learning improved learning by 24% and enhanced memory by 26% with the use of Baroque music. Like the development of electronic meditation, electronic brain storming and bio-feedback process of developing human potentials, super learning has taken the help of rhythmic music, baroque music, relaxation music, meditative chanting, mantras or hymas and devotional song composed and recorded with required beats or vibrations in energizing body cells and atoms those constitute the human body. The brain cells and memory section—short-term memory and long-term memory get sharpened by it. Over all, super learning as a technique tries to touch all aspects of creative thinking and bring appropriate development to its multi-dimensionality.

2 STUDIES ON SUPER LEARNING

2.1 Studies on Super Learning—A Cross-cultural Analysis

2.2 Super Learning with Academic Achievement, Intelligence and Sex

2.3 Super Learning and Creative Thinking

2.4 Yoga and Meditation with Super Learning

STUDIES ON SUPER LEARNING

2.1 STUDIES ON SUPER LEARNING—A CROSS-CULTURAL ANALYSIS

Super learning is the brain child of Georgy Lozanov, who developed it in Bulgaria. But the features of the technique were taken from the principles of Indian Raja Yoga and Bulgarian Yogic culture. Therefore, it can be told that Super Learning Technique (SLT) is the output of east-west cultural convergence. Such ethnoepistemological admixture has been practically experimented in many countries of the globe. Psychologists, educationists, administrators, businessmen, military scientists and researchers of almost all fields have utilized it and reported its significant impact. Raja yoga of Indian spiritual tradition is known as Astanga Yoga in Patanjali's Yogasutra. The eight steps are sequencial and very much systematic. But Lozanov, the Bulgarian doctor had added some principles and strategies of Bulgarian yogic system to make it more practical and usable in every field of activity. He made the *asanas*—the postural technique of meditation, more flexible with a view to bring mind-body relaxation. Not including the strict yogasanas like Utthita Lolasana, Hasta Utthan Asana, Vagu Nishkasana, Bhujangasana, Uttharapadasana, Shavasana (Kapil Murti, 2004), Lozanov made it very easy so as one can practise at any place and being in any condition. Then visualization is a step where a mixed activity of dharana, dhyana and some activities of *Niyama,* like *soucha, Santosh* and *swadhyaya* is done. Here individual sees either by objects or in abstract; either in closed eyes or in open eyes, depending on visualizing capacity. The natural scenes or things of love and affection are to be concentrated and visualized to make the mind calm and peaceful. Affirmation technique is an adoption of Bulgarian yogic principle where individual has to realize the self. Breathing exercise progresses through rhythmic inhaling, holding, exhaling and pause of breath. It is analogous to yogic pranayam. The second phase which deals with memory session is the scientific thought of Lozanov. Here, the learner will be taught something in first phase which will be remembered in closed eyes with music in latter phase.

However, bearing a western origin, the influence of super learning techique is not confined to Bulgaria only. Researchers of all over world are using it to study its effect on different walks of life. Most specifically the research studies conducted by Lozanov himself in the then Russia, Canada, USA and in several other western countries have exerted significant impact of super learning technique on varied fields.

The works of Lozanov was accelerated by Ostrander and Schroeder (1994) who wrote three major books such as, "Super learning", "Superlearning 2000" and "Supermemory—The Revolution". These creations have become the milestones in the history of super learning technique. They have also prepared six cassettes and 40 pages interactive handbook depicting the process of making learning enjoyable, exhilarating and knowing how to learn successfully in the 21st century. Through many experimental works they have proved this technique as profitable means of learning facts, figures, languages two to five times faster without stress.

Heidenhain, the business trainer of an US-based company, asserted, "It changed my life. It provides the fuel for awakening and suynchronizing yourself with success consciousness." Dr. Lee, CEO of Canada-based lifelong communications, expressed, "it added to my creative thinking by lessening self-doubt and fear of failure". Superlearning (r) workshop of USA developed a package on it containing six tapes where subjects like secrets of superlearning, disolving blocks, the right state—the right stuff, super learning music, experience fast learning with Spanish, subliminal connections, etc. are found.

The researches conducted in the former Soviet Block by Sheila Ostrander, Lynn Schroeder and Nancy Ostrander (2002) were breakthroughs. They have reported that super learning transformed the ordinary people into learning superstars. First breakthrough tests that let people learn 2 to 5 times even 50 times faster than before. Learning progressed without stress and learners benefitted from the scientifically charted powers of certain kind of music to influence, body, mind and spirit.

Mind-body mental training programmes for ultimate fitness mind training secrets was successfully used by Russian cosmonauts and European Olympic stars that open new dimensions of mind power, health and physical skill. It is also used by them for mental and physical wellness, sports, public performance from acting to guitar playing. Bancroft of University of Toronto, Australia and Kryzanowski, Special Education Branch of Alberta (2002) have appreciated and excelled such extraordinary output. Super Memory which is a correlate of super learning is accepted as a knockout, jammed with astonishing facts and ideas (White, 2002). The use of super learning extends from Pargue to Moscow to Siberia where the scientists, physicists and biologists tested and used psychokinetic-mind over matter, the telepathic knockout, psychic machines effectively, speaks *Publisher Weekly* (2000). Such activities also created sensation up to Pentagon (Kirkus, 2002). To explore new dimensions of super learning United State's *Foreign Service Journal* formed Washington Research and Development Farm. NASA scientists were also using this technique for enhancing their capacity (Beal, 2002). The Russian scientists and psychic superstars were using SLT in developing psychokinetic power to move objects at a distance. Czech scientists used to turn on lights or machines with the psychic power of eyes (Ostrander, 2002). Kirlian (1981) reported that during cold war the Soviet scientists were succeeded in using super learning technique in harnessing psychic weapons which were used in Espionage, politics, military and sports. They were effective in developing telepathy, combating UFO's that were swarming and landing all over Russia. (Lozanov, 1979).

The researchers of Norway are also using SLT in wide range. The Saga reports (nancy@superlearning.ca). People of California also shown effective result in improving learning to 20% and developing memory to 26% by using super learning music (Robinson, 2002). Taking the guidelines of SLT, Dr Alfred Tomatis, a French scientist proved the effectiveness of high frequency sounds in turbo charging brain, revitalizing the body and overcoming learning problems. The Mozart-violin concertos were also used in Turkish culture and proved their effectiveness in super learning (Super learning.com). Pat Joudry (2000), the Canadian novelist reported the effectiveness of electronically altered high frequency music created by Tomatis in exploration of seeming wonders—the retarded to bright. Likewise, the research activities of Eli Bay (1984) in Toronto, Al Boothby of California, Allyn Prichard and Jean Taylar of USA, Janalea Hoffman, Liz Belson of Florida, USA, Hal Beeker and Lloyd Silverman of USA achieved central position in the super learning research. Bay (1984) conducted research on use of super learning music in Japan alongwith Japanese researchers and found that it takes the person's mind to alpha level. John Wade of Woden TAFE college, Australia (2002) reported that superlearning is found more popular and widely effective in the Australia, Mexico and Spain. In this regard, the work of George Jacobson Corporation on NYC founded by George Jacobson is worthnoting. Ostrander's super learning language programmes which were published in French, Spanish, German, Italian and in Indonesian languages also proved astonishing results (Hunter Galt; 2002). Duffy (2000) says that it has also become popular in England. Super learning technique is also used in the field of health and medical science in Swizerland (Abrezol, 1990). He has also switched over from medicine to learning or education relating application of super learning music. He had recorded the super learning music in a Swiss cathedral and then electronically altered those as per the cultural characteristics of

Swizerland and also found its effectiveness in enhancing hemispheric function of the individual.

The research activities of Lisa Curtis through her International Sophrology Institute is also very commendable (Tape # 593). Likewise, the activities of Doe Lang relating development of self confidence through super learning are being realised and appreciated by the publics and executives from companies like Honeywell, IBM & EXXON, Fulbright scholars, artists and teachers. Dyvekes's superlearning music (1990) has its tone of success in Asia, America and Africa. Dyveke's Scandinavian floklore music has also become effective in relaxation and developing concentration. Accordingly his compositions on Russian, Indian, Spanish and American spirits and musical culture have proved their effectiveness in solving manifold problems (morning Dance Tape # 325, High Sierra Suite Tape #327). Dr. Teri Mahaney, professor of Business and Education, had developed "Change your Mind Tapes" on 60 beats of super learning (r) music to fill up the mind with positive healthy and motivating impulses (Soer, 2002). In this regard, the works of Fryling of USA and Johannes of Germany are very much Popular. Fryling's autogenic technique helps in developing vitality and energy, relaxing body-mind and enhances self-esteem and success by imaging techniques. (Tape # 731, 732 & 733). In this regard, the studies of Christian Drapeau of Montreal, Heidenhain of Germany and Dr Lee Pulos of University of British Columbia of Canada are very important. Accordingly, the works of Centre for Accelerated Learning founded by David Meier is worthnoting.

Being inspired by communist experiment of super learning, the psychologists and educationists of North America started utilizing it. Pentagon's Institute of Defence Analysis also exploited the benefits of suggestology. In Das Moines, Toronto, Antlanta, super learning achieved the popularity. Society for Accelerative Learning and Teaching (SALT) founded by Dr. Doland Schuster of University of Iowa at Ames and International Society for Effective and Affective Learning (SEAL) in England, Japanese Society for Accelerative and Integrative Learning (SAIL) founded by Moyumi Mori and Wagner's (1984) Skill Training Institute in Heidelberg, Germany were leading Super Learning Corporations those have contributed a lot in popularising and developing this new approach. Taylor's (1988) Accelerative Introductory Method (AIM) also created a new history in learning in Australia and California. Guthridge's (1992) Reverse Instruction has also made landmark stride in Japan, Russia, Alaska, etc.

Abrezol (1990) popularised his "autogenics" and "progressive relaxation" in and out of Swizerland. Bay (1984) became a famous stress control trainer in canada and Frying (1982) made autogenic super learning famous in America. Jafri Zanial, a Malaysian trainer who worked with engineers, state police and disables, states that super learning can create better people for better world. Expressing the importance of super learning Dr Hartmut Wagner (1984) states, "super learning has special appeal for the citizens of the old Germany Democratic Republic, because of its humanistic effect, its holistic and personal atmosphere and the respect for the learning personality, which they experience as new and fascinating". Wagner's (1984) *skill* team at IBM training centre in Herrenberg and Heidenhain's (1982) DGSL in the Dolphin Training Company tried to bring strategic change in the teacher training practices of Germany for identification of barriers and their solution process for students' all round development.

During the hot-pot of Cold War, Bulgarian government with the help of Mankind Research Unlimited of Washington, D.C., worked to set-up franchaised Lozanov learning. Thereafter Lozanov travelled internationally to make his technique and suggestopedic centres popular. Activities of these centres in making language learning ease spreaded in many European cities. By and by, Baltics and Finland started faimilarizing super learning for language learning and learning other courses of school curriculum (SEAL Journal, 1992). The Danish government recently funded the accelerated language learning projects in schools and Swedes used it to make the immigrants learn Latin quickly. The exchange of Suggestopedic ideas between Russia and England alongwith the exchange of suggestopedic teachers of both the states show how superlearning blends naturally with western mind techniques like kinesiology, psychosynthesis and the Alexandar Technique (Ostrander, Schroeder and Ostrander, 1997).

Ostrander and Schroeder (1994), so said, "if you join learning revolution you will be part of a phenomenon that does not recognise national boundaries any more than seeds riding the inter-continental winds. The seeds seem to thrive in any place in the crowded avenues of Mexico city or in Vanuatu, a dot of an Island, so tiny on the map that a pin obliterates it." Such inter-cultural traverse gave rise to many synonyms to Super-learning, such as, Optiomal Learning, Power Learning, Sound Learning, Inner Track Learning, Reverse Instruction, Super Study, Project Renaissance and many others. As told by Ostrander and Schroeder (1971), "they are all branches of the same tree". Sleep Learning-using music during sleeping; relaxopedia-using autogenics; hypnopedia using hypnosis are some of the innovations in the field of super learning developed and experimented by Lozanov (1970s) in Ukraine, Russia and Bulgaria.

Alongwith the above research support, there are hundreds of tapes, CDs and packages developed on Super Learning Technique (SLT) considering the changing cultural ethos. During such culture-specific changes some alterations have been crept into the original Super Learning Techniques, developed by Lozanov during 1970s. But it is the matter of great regret that super learning being a product of Indian yogic culture, has not yet been experimented in Indian soil either in its original form or in any altered from. However, it can be asserted that this new technique has world-wide application, In spite of ethnological diversities, the effectiveness of SLT, though is visualized at many places in varied fields of activities, its benefit specifically in Indian educational ecology is to be ascertained.

2.2 SUPER LEARNING WITH ACADEMIC ACHIEVEMENT, INTELLIGENCE AND SEX

Academic achievement or scholastic performance is related to the performance of the student in the field of study. Intelligence and sex are personality variables which also become cariterion for other variables. Here, super learning has become independent variable and its impact on the development of academic achievement and intelligence was studied. The effectiveness of super learning was again analysed on the groud of gender.

Today's education world is full of with innumerable problems. Even the US has a third world labour force. Thirty percent US kids drop out of school. Canada has 30% failure rate. Comparatively India has millions of educated unemployeds and illiterates. Our education system has become directive and stereotyped. In the sphere of achieving academic excellence, Lozanov (1971) discovered a new malady namely "didactogenic syndrome"—sickness caused by poor teaching methods—and advocated to heal it with suggestopedia. Like the philosophical speculations of Socrates, Aristotle, Plato, Froebel, Montessori, etc., Super Learning considers each individual as the storehouse of all possibilities and the role of education as the means of drawing the genius out. Lozanov stresses on suggestology and supermemory for emergence of all those hidden powers.

Seki (1983) conducted a study in Tokai University on effectiveness of super learning. He reported that the number of students who scored high grades increased dramatically, while the number of low grades decreased. The group was very large. The study also shows the success of SLT for large groups. Suggestology approves the development of super memory (hypermnesia) which is a variable of learning and achievement (Lozanov, 1983). Expressing the effect of SLT on own life, Brian Hamilton says, "in just two weeks of super learning, I went from 'B-minus' to A's. Sometimes, when I go to Carnegie Hall and hear vivaldi, trigonometry, Identities start reeting off in my head." Subliminal learning, which trains supermemory for accelerated learning, was also found very much effective in the learning of emotionally troubled and generally delinquent children (Silverman and Bryant Tucker, 1988) and learning language (Mahaney, 1989). Likewise, autogenics or self-birthing found by German M.D. Johannes Schultz as an alternative of super learning was experimented by various researchers and reported successful in accelerating language vocabulary learning (Stefanishin, 1983), relaxing the mind, draining out physical and muscular tension (Bay, 1984). Wagner (1984), through the Skill Training Institute of Heidelberg found super learning, weak students averaged to 92 percent and got 100 percent score in multiple choice type examination.

Hoffman (1990) reported that during 1970s American defence department had successfully used super learning to speed up the learning of weapon systems, languages even for basic learning skills. Wenger's (1984) 'Image Streaming' is found very fruitful in bringing development of intellectual abilities, creative thinking and scholastic achievement with logical thinking and imagination (Reinert, 1989). Cook, as reported by Ostrander and Schroeder (1997), found imagery practices beneficial for science students of Toronto's Upper Cânada College in developing their scholastic performance to a super level. Like electroacupunture of Dr H.L. Wen and electrostimulator of Dr Margaret Patterson those help neurotransmission in brain cells, David Graham's couch is also used to sharpen the mind, increase learning abilities of disables, accelerate the learning of mathematics, reading and spelling. Basing on Graham's "Couch potato", Schulz developed integrated motion system (IMS) and IQ Synmetron and Marvin Sams designed sensory and mind stimulation (SAMS) those were found effective in developing neuroefficiency. Similarly, Bio-Battery of Edgar Cayce, Alpha-Stim—the cranial—Electro-Stimulation, Mind-Man are also developed on the basis of super learning principles to develop achievement, memory, learning, IQ and creative potentials of people.

Croucher (1981), through a self-experiment, found himself learned 94% of what he studied. His wife, as controlled one, learned 95% of the material. They say that they used to absorb 20 to 25 Japanese phrases per day. It showed that by studying half an hour in a weekday one can learn Japanese and retain those perfectly within one month. Thus, super learning technique trains our memory section for long-term absorption of learning tasks and for quick learning. It is also equally influensive for old people (if will be followed with principles) in developing their language learning, solving vocabulary puzzles and learning and memorizing history tasks (Ostrander, Schroeder and Ostrander, 1997).

In this regard, it has been seen that super learning is used divergently all over the world on development of different personality attributes. Lynn had made super learning a major factor of alternative education (Ostrander, 2002) in putting superlearning (r) workshop in a Box which explains the way to learn how to learn facts, figures, languages 2 to 5 times faster without stress. As experimented and reported by Ostrander and Schroeder (2002) super learning uses music and sound in making learning ease and bringing super achievement with 'mind-body relaxation'. They reported that executives, school children, medical students and language learners have excelled in their respective fields by using super learning technique. Ostrander, Schroeder and Ostrander (1997) reported a breakthrough in learning and achievement, acquired by using super learning to increase their speed of learning up to 50 times faster than before. By developing focused concentration it acts as a boon to learners and teachers in speed learning, overcoming blocks and awakening achievement potential (Quality Trade Edition # 100-A). It taps dynamic inner memory states of the individual and heals mind body to release new abilities, beats intelligence robbing diseases and disabilities and acts as genius-level mind machines (Atkins, 1992). Fre (1992) advocates that the memory, which acts as a major means of developing intelligence and achievement of the learner is developed to supermemory powers and memory weapons and protects the learners from memory pollutions. It is reported that super learning music enhances learning faster to 24% (Robinson, 1998). It is vividly experimented the neuroacoustical musical format and string instruments rich in natural harmonics are designed for maximum mind-body benefits, development of hemispheric function and accelerates factual learning by easing stress (Ostrander, 1979; Superlearning (r) (r) music, Vol. one). By it learning facts, figures, languages goes on ultrarapidly. (Super Learning. (r) all music, Vol. Two). Janalea Hoffman's super learning music (mind-body Tempo) was experimented by Hoffman himself on the school graduates of Kansas Medical School University. From the analysis, she found her 60 beat super learning music very much effective in significantly boosting the student's examination scores. Her related research experiments to know the effectiveness of musical bio-feedback, musical acupuncture in synchronizing internal rhythm, relaxing mind-body by releasing tension and stress are also helpful in increasing academic performance of students. The heavy curricular load and impact of socio-economic condition, over-crowded classroom, impatience of teachers and group competitiveness among students increasing their tension and hampering their academic performance. At this stage, super learning music acts as a panacea (Ostrander and Schroeder, 1979). The Mozart sound sharpens the mind and enhances intelligence by recharging the brain, checks learning disabilities and creates access to intelligence (Tomatis, 2000). The sound therapy prepared in the light of super learning by Jourdy (2002) experimented by him on monks and school going students and found very significant in producing unbelievable results and changing the retarded students to bright. Soar into the first lane with super learning acts as accelerater of learning in producing A+ learning outcome (Ostrander, 2002).

Bay's (1998) "Relaxation response", "Progressive Relaxation" and "Autogenics" proved effective in dissolving IQ hampering anxiety and relaxing the individual for better learning outcomes (Fryling, 2000). Al Boothby (2002), a teacher in Sacramento of California used super learning and reported that it is impossible for children not to learn with super learning programme. Allyn Prichard's (2000) super learning (r) Arithmetic programme was used by many teachers and found effective in developing elementary level students' understanding and achievement in multiplication table, basic formula for square, rectangle, triangle, circle, etc. Prichard's (2000) super learning (r) Mathematics was also found effective in increasing achievement of secondary level students in SAT Math. Examination relating geometry and trigonometry. On the other hand, this super learning technique helped students in overcoming mathophobia and anxiety with the built in stress control programme. By using super learning (r) Vocabulary, Prichard found the high achievement of high school and college students in learning new vocabulary through musical memory format, Prichard and Taylor (2002) get eye-catching result of use of super learning in speeding up remedial reading. Using it on his students in Alaska, Rosella Wallace (2000) said "my class has scored 91% in SRA tests over the past 2 years. Their scores have been highest in the school." As memory acts as a prominent factor of increasing achievement of students, so Ostrander and Ostrander (1979) found super learning (r) guided imagery for children very much fruitful in producing superior academic performance by enhancing memory and increasing remembering or recalling capacity—the two major factors of increasing scholastic achievement. The second nature subliminal tapes of Sheila Ostrander and Lynn Schroeder (1979) increase motivation, enhance ability and help in learning quickly and well. Tape # 003, 003 and Tape-005 developed by Lynn help in developing performance and efficiency at school level.

Deo Lang (1984) stresses on the effectiveness of super learning in increasing rediance, magnetism and attractiveness (Tape # 928). The editorial of *Wall Street Journal* reported that superlearn a language at laser speed proved effective for American Managers in enhancing their language skills at multiplied speed. Ostrander (1979) reported the effectiveness of accelerated superleap (r) languages through music in developing super memory to six-fold. Abrezol, the Swiss sophrologist, who claims reputation all over Europe for his effective sophrology sports training has developed a system on super learning technique namely, adventuring with the brain, which shows the way of getting acquainted with left and right hemispheres of individual's brain. It also paves the way of getting super-success in any type of competition (Spino, 2000; Mahaney, 2000). Realizing the multidimensional approach of super learning William James says, "we bungle our way through life as if only half awake. Super learning (r) provided the fuel for awakening and synchronizing yourself with success consciousness". By using SLT, the passing rate of electrical cable splicing course soared 70% (Pulos, 2000). Mahaney (1989) studied the effect of super learning process in achieving success through women and found the effect most satisfactory.

2.3 SUPER LEARNING AND CREATIVE THINKING

After reviewing 22 definitions of creative thinking Welsch, P.K. (1980) found significant levels of agreement on the key attributes of these definitions. She defines creative thinking as "the process of generating unique products by transformation of existing products. These products, tangible and intangible, must be unique only to the creator and must meet the criteria of purpose and value established by the creator". On the other hand, Passi (1972) defined creative thinking as "a multi-dimensional (verbal and non-verbal)" attribute differentially distributed among people and includes chiefly the factors of seeing problems, fluency, flexibility, originality, inquisitiveness and persistency. Likewise, after critical analysis of 34 different definitions on creative thinking Prusty (1996) stated that creative thinking which has varied connotation like creative thinking, reflective thinking, divergent thinking, lateral thinking, etc. with a little difference in its meaning, is multidimensional in its approach and product. Though some accept it as serendipity, the modern psychologists and creativity rescarchers like Osborn, Gordon, Edward De Bono, Guilford, etc. have a common belief that such synchronized hemispheric function can be enhanced to optimum. Each and every individual is full up with innumerable creative possibilities and what they want is a systematic, planned and psychological approach of developing such dormated qualities of the individual. The primitive belief of God's bless has now been replaced by electronic treatment to the human potentialities for its hyperproduction.

In this regard, Super Learning Technique (SLT) is accepted as an innovation. Considering various approaches of creative thinking—process, product, person, press and potentiality, and different theories related to it—cognitive, psychoanalysis, behaviourism, structuralism, functionalism, constructivist, humanistic and ethgnoepistemslogy, it can be asserted that super learning is an ultra-modern super-technique of unveiling the untapped energy cells of the individual. Like the theory of creativogenic society (Arieti, 1976), super learning regards each individual as the storehouse of all potentialities. Such limitless capacities are culture-bound. Mind-body harmonization and right brain-left brain synchronization (Garrett, 1971; Abrezol, 1986) pave the way for optimum illumination of such qualities. Today's human society is greatly suffering from deadlocks for creative production either for lack of creativogenic societal condition or for hyper-tension or stressful situation surrounding the individual and not allowing any imagery thoughts to come up. Super learning technique hits there to bring mind-body relaxation for making the individual stressfree and for paving the way for creative expression (Passi, 1970). It takes the human mind from Beta Level (H_z 14-22) to Alpha level (H_z 8-14), where the whole brain get involved in effective learning and retention

(Ostrander and Schroeder, 1979). They again stated that use of super learning music sparks problem-solving and creative thinking. Salter, R., who used super learning in the field of literary production says, "it added to my creative thinking by lessening self-doubt and fear of failure". Application of super learning technique is accepted as a unique creativity training programme which develops intuition and creative talents (Ostrander, Schroeder and Ostrander, 1979). White (1982), who used super learning in different fields reported that super learning plug into memory's creative power to build new behaviours and draw wealth, success and serenity into your life. Hugh Lynn Cayce, Director of Edgar Cayce Association, who used super learning in varied fields says, "super learning is woven in an vivid style that will stimulate and intrigue every imagination, fascinating a potential bomb shell". Eminent music composer Janalea Hoffman (1980) composed and used super learning music and found stress released and creative thinking produced. The deep daydream Tape of Hoffman which incorporates slow melodies of 50 beats found ideal for imagery, imaginative rehearsal for increasing creativity. Tomatis (2000) reported positive impact of 'sound of smartness' in bringing landmark discoveries. Joudry used sound therapy of Tomatis and proved successful in providing access for exploring seeming wonders. Lang (1984) reported the effectiveness of Prichard's super learning (r) for children in developing positive imagination. Likewise, the "relaxation tape" of Hoffman, as reported by Lang (1984), also develops creativity and imagination. The subliminal Tape No. 005 of Ostrander and Schroeder (1979) also proved beneficial in developing sparks of creative power within the learner. Lisa Curtis (1989) used seven minute stress breakers to turn stress into energy for creative advantage. Bernard's Dream Incubation and problem-solving method, which was developed on the principle of super learning has been proved effective at several times in bringing out great scientific discoveries, sparks of dream incubation renaissance—the basic of imagery production and in preparing the individual for creative problem-solving. Dyveke Spino's (2002), super learning based Mental Rehearsal develops imagination capacity of people and thereby helps in creating new and original productions. It sparks of the mental stuff by empowering the self through enjoying a liberated life. Such super learning activity accelerates learning by developing self-reliance (Ostrander and Schroeder, 1979) and makes the individual bestowed with new potentials. At many times, super learning music and its rhythmic activities also exert positive impact on individuals brain cells and develops the creative activities originated from the combined effort of left brain and right brain. It provides oxygen into brain cells through proper exercises which facilitates the innovative thinking (Ostrander and Schroeder, 1979).

Robina Salter (1980s) who used super learning for herself and for others, shares her experience relating effectiveness of super learning as follows.

"I observed the students lying on their gym mats learning and recalling science and mathematics tables. They were also learning how to overcome pre-exam. and pre-sports competition jitters. . . . I saw how Super Learning class clears the mind before sleep, possibly enhancing the two-way traffic between the conscious and unconscious, making dreams more memorable and vivid. . . . I have been using super learning to prepare my material for workshops in keeping with super leaning teaching, I record my material, carefully spacing each unit of information. I also visualize an audience, a lectern words going forth clearly, steadily to receptive ears. The method frees a speaker from the need of notes, the recall being in a reliable sequence. . . . The material for the whole work (writing a new novel) come to me in three nights of dreaming." Relating her practice of superleaning process, Salter says, "Every morning I would lie down, follow the steps of the super learning tape (relaxation, mind calming, positive suggestion), and then begin to write. Ideas flowed freely, unhampered by resistance from the analytical left brain. The method began to add to my creative thinking by lessening self-doubt, fear of failing and by quieting the inner critic".

The students of USA and Canada were found to be more creative by using Jourdy's (1984) Sound Therapy. Marian Bainsworth, a Vancouver artist, says that after six months of practice of sound therapy he overcame the depression he had succumbed and felt an inner strength by which his buried artistic talents pushed up. Likewise, Delehanty (1994), the famous journalist checked the performance of clients of super learning researchers Ivan Barzakov and Pamela Rand and stated, "almost every optimal learning graduate I interviewed, talked at length about experiencing a quantum leap of creativity. One woman who had not written more than a paragraph in years suddenly started creating magazine articles in her head and jotting them down feverishly during lunch break. A man who had been an occasional painter found himself coming home from work and painting abstract canvases until the wee hours of the morning (Ostrander and Schroeder, 1997)". Super learning technique can flash out creative thinking everywhere—in legal brief, teaching mathetics, cooking class, a new gadget, a fully realised life in a globalised, perspective.

But researchers have given a little attention to such area and have conducted a small number of studies in the field. Out of those studies not a single one has undertaken in India. Though Chopra (1997) and other spiritual leaders like Bhajanananda (1980, 1981), Abhedananda (2001), Vishnu Devananda (2002) and several other Indian authors have investigated into the theoretical and spiritual speculations of yoga and meditation and their strategic plans for creative expression of inherent human potentials, they have given no concrete scientific expressions which can be shown to others besides self-realization. Such conditions warrant a scientific and experimental enquiry into the benefits of Super Learning Technique on creative thinking.

2.4 YOGA AND MEDITATION WITH SUPER LEARNING

While we discuss the East-West amalgamation in super learning technique, it is clear that Indian Yoga and Meditational culture have exerted significant impact on it. The eight-fold path of Raja Yoga includes *dhyana* or meditation as a major step of attaining the state of super consciousness (Patanjali's Yoga sutra). Introduction of Yoga and other meditative practices in western cultures has significant cultural, religious, contemplative and intellectual effect in the western world (Kumar, 2002). Now-a-days, yoga and meditation has not been remained as the resource of India. Culturally they have made world-wide travel with a globalization spirit. Inter-cultural transformation has given some other form to it in changed socio-cultural and metaphysical surroundings. Still, Indian metaphysics and epistemology, those lie in meditation and yoga, have fostered a resurgence of western meditative disciplines such as Christen contemplation, Jewish Kabalah and Islamic suffism. Intellectually, they have led to new interest in Asian psyhologies and philosophies laying the foundation of new disciplines such as transpersonal psychology, transcendental meditation, sociology, sophrology, Autogenics, etc. (Walsh, 1999). Todays yoga and meditation has become the effective technique of stress management or self-regulation strategies (Shapiro and Giber, 1978). Now-a-days, when the stress-ridden individual searches for a spa-centre, healing guru, taichi, bio-feedback, relaxation exercises, reiki some other take the excuse of antidepressants, sleeping pills, synthetic drugs (ecstacy, LSD, speed, smack, crank, chalk, etc.) and organic drugs, rave parties (an abbreviation of raw and virtual energy) to have a psudo-feeling of potential energy through raw energy and to have a false state of relaxation (Bhowmik, 2003). Being the master of wide range of mental power the stress ridden people, now, are taking Vitamin E supplements, Vitamine-12 and antioxidants to enhance memory power (Zandi, 2003). Most surprisingly, we forget the most effective and 100% positive effect bearing panacea i.e., Yoga and meditation.

'Yoga', say Bhatia (2004), "is the spiritual and physical practice that originates in India some 5000 years ago, is the flavor of the movement worldwide and is sweeping through the globe in a variety of names such as, Raja Yoga, Bhakti Yoga, Hatha Yoga, Gyana Yoga, Karma Yoga, Yoga erobics, Artistic Yoga, Kundalini Yoga, Smriti Yoga, Mantra Yoga, Laya Yoga, Tantra Yoga, etc. Though Raja Yoga, Bhakti Yoga, are of vedic period, Yoga aerobics, Artistic Yoga, Surya Yoga, and Smriti Yoga are product of modern time by the practitioners of materialistic meditation. However, it is clear that even the people of Mahenjodaro were practising such yogas during 2300 to 2000 B.C." (Varughese, 2003). There is much scientificity of Yoga in relaxing mind-body, recovering from illness, losing weight-getting slim, calming woriness, getting contact of God by sage (Varughese, 2004), making spine flexible, reducing stress level, and stimulating nervous system, getting enlightenment and salvation (Bhatia, 2004). Yoga and meditation are interlinked in Indian spiritual civilization and both have been spreaded all over world. "People are looking for greater direction and purpose in life. They are realizing that solutions cannot be piecemeal. The answer is Yoga, which does not neglect any aspect of our live and integrates it". (Vyas, 2003) However, the ancient spiritualism of yoga and meditation has changed to some what for fulfilling the increasing materialistic demand of the modern society and of practical life. Unlike the side effects of modern medicine yoga takes care of the body and mind (Aggarwal, 2003). Accordingly, the modern yoga teachers have developed various yogas taking changing demands into account. Kripalu Yoga is known as meditation in motion, Artistic Yoga, the brain child of Bharat Thakur is a synthesis of chanting, postures and breathing techniques. It has cosmopolitan applause all over world. Yogoerobics, which is an admixture of yoga and modern aerobics, has been used by young students, to develop their concentration, achievement, etc. (Bhatia, 2004). Iyengar yoga produced by B.K.S. Iyengar who accepts Yoga as synonymous to asanas has international demand. Dehypnotic meditation, biofeedback and electronic meditation are also proved beneficial in problem-solving, enhancing memory, creative thinking and also in developing intelligence. and in excavating one's unlimited hidden potentiality (Nanak, 2003).

Meditation rids the mind of unnecessary clutter by reducing irrelevant thinking. Meditation on sixth Chakra or third eye where pituiary gland is located, activates the brain and makes mind concentrated. Different asanas—shavasana, yoganidra and Hamsa Yoga of Gurunath were experimented and are found effective in enhancing scholastic performance, memory, intelligence and creative potentials. Japa meditation where some mantra or words like 'Aum' are chanted by the performer enhances the activities of brain cells and develops memory and concentration (Sukla, 2003). Likewise, Lozanov's super learning accepts individual as a psycho-physical being produced in an environmental condition, Body-mind and left-right brain coordination brings his development. It accepts each individual as the epitome of innumerable possibility and takes the technique of body-mind relaxation alongwith visualization, affirmation and breathing exercise to energize the brain cells for enhancing memory, intelligence, creativity, etc. All these behavioural qualities are not merely the functions of physical cerebrum, but are there in individual's blood cells in the form of *samskara*. Each human mind is capable of producing enormous possibilities. But only irony is that those are in dormat state in the individual. So, Super Learning Teachnique (SLT), like the Yoga and meditation always tries to activate and energize the brain cells by super learning music and allied exercises. All these activate the nervous system and thereby sharpens the memory, retention, problem-solving abilities and rational thinking or intelligence. (Passi and Prabhu, 1997). Like Brainstorming of Osborn, Syntectics of Gordon, Lateral Thinking of Edward de Bono, the transpersonal theory of yoga and meditation sticks to the original and inherent nature of the individual and tries to enlighten the areas or capabilities those are shrouded in obscurity of ignorance and uncultivation. Yoga and meditation, in modern era, try to shift their spiritual bent of analysis and action to practical one. Likewise, Super Learning Technique (SLT) considered meditation and Yogic exercises as the means to make individual super-individual or super man embodied with enlightened memory, intelligence, creative thinking, problem-solving attitude and adjustment ability.

The attempt of materialization of yoga and meditation on ethnoepistemological considerations has given rise to psychotherapy-like pseudo-meditative contemplations. The steps of super learning technique also combined the steps of Raja Yoga, Kundalini Yoga, Hatha Yoga and some aspects of Bulgarian Yoga. The ethico-religious, psycho-physical and spiritual aspects those are revealed in the eight-fold path of Raja yoga are very much systematic in attaining psycho-physical and psycho-moter development of the learner. Visualization and breathing exercise of SLT tries to concentrate all the powers of the individual on to a point, i.e., goal. Such concentration activates mind and digs out the creative thoughts from the subconscious and unconscious levels of the individual. It approves mnemonic exercises, psycho-pedagogical teaching principles to improve memory and creative thinking of the children. There are schools in India those have made yoga and meditation their routine activity and have shown significant result in students' performance and personality. Therefore, Yoga, is accepted as a means of yoking one thing to the other.

Twenty minutes of chanting Mantra or Meditation brings mind-body relaxation (Bay, 1984; Curtis, 1989). Curtis's Seven Minute Stress Buster is an important innovation in the field of breathing. She (1990) advocated "Sabasana", which, "not only relaxes the muscle tension but also stimulates the thyroid and carotoid arteries that carry blood-oxygen to the brain. As told by Ostrander and Schroeder (1994) such Baroque Music match with many of the physical benefits of Mantra and Meditation, except that unlike chanting mantra or doing meditation routines". Studies at the Menninger Foundation in Kansas found that synchronizing the hemispheres of the brain (which super learning music can do in minutes) is at the physical heart of the zen-meditation. This synchronization makes the activities of the brain coherent, laserlike and highly productive (Ostrander, Schroeder and Ostrander, 1997). Classical musics of Shamans of Central Asia, the Jajouka Musicians of Northern Morocco and Indian Oriental Musics help in mind expansion, pain control, getting enlightenment and performing miracle-like activities. The compositions of famous Indian Sitarist Pandit Ravishankar on the fundamental tone of 'OM' (AUM) is a classic which brings primodial vibration and thereby activates all the organs of mind-body state. Such music is also related to concentration on to a point or object which brings Bliss (Chopra, 1992) and prepares the individual for creative exploration. It heals mental and physical wounds and acts a booster to IQ and memory (Tomatis, 1988)

In a critical analysis of the status and nature of researches conducted on yoga, meditation, super learning and super learning music, Ostrander, Schroeder and Ostrander (1997) say, "scientific research on music and yoga for mind sharpening was still scarce in the west. The system was so inter-disciplinary, that a few were expert in all aspects. People followed false instructions ritualistically not having a clue about neuro-acoustics. They substituted wrong music which deflected memory. Some tried party animal antics as language practice. Alleged suggestopedia vanished thunderous music and dashing waves. Even the Canadian government, after complex negotiations with the Bulgarians, brought a definitely decelerated disastrous failure of French programme for their civil service employees."[3] Under such circumstances, the research activities conducted so far in India is under serious setback because of its methods, techniques and adulteration in the original framework of yoga and meditation. Although theoretical analysis express optimism on accelerated performance the practical experiments are scarce in quantity either for lack of adequate research interest or for inefficiency of education researchers to undertake related experimental studies thereof to prove the scientificity of theoretical abstractness and metaphysical speculations.

Thus, there are maximum resemblance among yoga, meditation and super learning. Accordingly, super learning has proved its effectiveness in enhancing memory, intelligence, problem-solving ability, creative thinking, etc. by relaxing the mind-body state, as done by meditative practices. The spiritual meditation when was transformed to material meditation in the nomenclature of Super Learning Technique (SLT) has been proved beneficial to maximum extent. Still, Super Learning is not the substitution or synonymous to Yoga and meditation. It has been regarded as a modified form of Yoga and meditation. Its result is realized substantially and in tangible forms, whereas the impact of Yoga and meditation are personal, abstract and depends on auto-realization.

3 THE STUDY OF SUPER LEARNING TECHNIQUE

3.1 Rationale

3.2 Statement of the Problem

3.3 Scope and Delimitations

3.4 Objectives

3.5 Hypotheses

3.6 Operational Definition of the Terms Used

3.7 Design

3.8 The Sample

3.9 Tools Used

3

THE STUDY OF SUPER LEARNING TECHNIQUE

3.1 RATIONALE

Yoga and meditation are oldest concepts to super learning. Their prevalence traced from 3000 B.C. or before. During Rig vedic period literature of yoga and meditation were consolidated (Kumar, 2002). The archeological excavations of Mahenjodaro (2300 to 2000 B.C.) provide prove that people of Indus valley were practizing Yoga and meditation then and there. The meditative state of Lord Shiva corroborates such statement (Varughese, 2003). Patanjali's yogasutra, which was composed during 200 A.D. proves the wide use of yoga and meditation in ancient India. The eight-fold path of Raja Yoga resembles with the Arya Astanga Marg of Buddhism, raised during sixth century B.C. toward the end of post-vedic age. Contrastically, super learning is a new method which came to exist during twentieth century by Bulgarian doctor Lozanov. Such newness of the technique demands a wide range research on super learning.

Second, Yoga and meditation are spiritual whereas super learning is materialistic. Yoga and meditation are the products of age-long spiritual search of Rishis of ancient India. Such practices revolve round spiritual and metaphysial speculations of Indian culture. *Purusartha* (attaining Dharma, Artha, Kama and Moksha) is the main objective of human life. Ancient Rishis were practising these for getting over the *Rajasic* and *Tamasic* for attainment of *sattvic guna* or even to attain the state of *gunateeta* (Kuppuswamy, 1985). The eight-limbs of Raja Yoga, system, Upasanna, different meditations—analogical, symbolic, substitution, objective, subjective, intend to control desires with high moral elevation and to attend *brahman* (Dasgupta, 1927) or to connect *Purusha*—the transcendent consciousness with *prakriti* (Ajaya, 1983). It may be acquired through yogic process of *Nididhyasana*, the upper level of *sravana* and *manana* (Bhajanananda, 1981). Irrespective of different philosophical bases of spiritualism—*Dualism* and *Monoism*, yoga and meditation aspire either for samadhi or nirvikalpa samadhi or realization of brahman or paramatma. All these are relative terms and needs self-realization. Such vedic practices demand unfailing obedience and submission. But super learning teachnique analysed meditation and yoga in contextual considerations. Besides cultural mentality as a primary contextual variable, there are many other factors those determine the way through which materialistic meditation is approached, understood, practised and experienced. Like the meditative practices of Transcendental meditation, Buddhist meditation (which intends for compassion, love, equality and change in society) and the rapuic meditation, super learning has blend the spiritual meditation into material form to solve day-to-day problems. Therefore, meditation, in now-a-days, is practised in consideration of cultural mentality (Sorokin, 1937), Paradigm (Kuhn, 1962; Lifton, 1976), sociology of knowledge (Berger and Luckmana, 1966; Schutz, 1967), Metascience (Habermas, 1968; Radnitzki, 1968) and of psycho-physical and philosophical considerations (Metzner, 1971, Wilson, 1977). Likewise, super learning is used for stress relief, increasing body-mind relaxation and developing intelligence, solving adjustment problems in workplace and bringing personality development (Ostrander and Schroeder, 1979). But, in the field of education, meditation and Yoga has a little or no use except some schools established on religious thoughts by some spiritual organisations. Therefore, the applicaiton of super learning needs more experimental proof in developing scientific approach in materialistic persuit.

Third, Yoga and meditation are contributions of eastern world, whereas super learning is the outcome of east-west cultural integration. Lozanov developed it by taking Indian Raja Yoga and Bulgarian yogic principles together. But matter of research concern is its experimentation in Indian context. Inspite of westernization of Indian yogic principles, super learning technique has been proved effective throughout the world. Cross-cultural approach proves a strong ethnoepistemological base of super learning whereas India has failed till now to have a research experience on its usability and effectiveness. The learners, businessmen, reformers, technocrats, astronauts, scientists, poets, novelists and hundred others of varied faculties of Australia, America, Russia, Canada, UK, etc. have expressed their accelerated success in respective fields by using the super learning technique. But the motherland of the technique is still languishing on its subjective approach. Therefore, it is barely felt to have an Indian experiment of super learning technique.

Fourth, the researchers of super learning demand that the technique has a strong psycho-physical and scientific approach. Yoga and meditation are more spiritual than psycho-physical. Though their espistemological and metaphysical speculations greatly stress on the scientificity of the techniques in bringing psycho-physical changes in the person, their societal approach is mostly predominated by religiosity and orthodox interpretations and unnecessary austerities. In this respect, super learning is very much popular in ventilating its scientific and psycho-physical considerations thereby attracting people to use it for development of cognitive, psycho-moter and affective domains of personality. Therefore, researching such applicability in Indian context is the intention of present study.

Fifth, Yoga and meditation have rigid principles whereas super learning is flexible. The principles of an activity when do not suit the practitioners, more people do not want to follow it. Moreover, in the modern democratic set-ups each person needs some freedom and flexibility in activities. But the vedic-age yoga and meditation, as depicted in Patanjalis Yoga Sutra, is very much strict and needs austere practices. Although some changes in those system was made by Lord Buddha in the name of Buddhist meditation or middle path, in latter time, that was also changed to its ancient form by different sects of Buddhism (Kumar, 2002; Varughese, 2003). On the ground of anthropological and sociocultural considerations, when Indian Yoga and meditation shows reluctance for any sort of humanitarian result-oriented flexibility, people turn down to apply it with suspicion of its desirable result. Therefore, at present, Yoga and meditation are seen in many forms—biofeedback, electronic meditation, objective meditation, etc. Under such circumstance, it has become necessary to know the effectiveness of super learning—the flexible form of Indian Yoga and meditation, in the Indian soil.

Sixth, super learning seems as an amalgamated form of yoga and meditation. The essence of Raja Yoga, Kundalini yoga, Hatha yoga are found in super learning technique in flexible form. The principles and practices of objective or malerialistic meditation, electronic meditation and simple dhyana and dharana are found to be incorporated in super learning. Alongwith, some foreign techniques of learning and memorising are also found in it. All together act for making the individual super-man bearing a super-mind and super-memory within himself. Therefore, it is matter of interest to see whether the said technique is becoming effective in making our students super-learner ?

Seventh, research experience of Lazanov himself, Ostrander, Schroedeer and Ostrander (1979), Lang (1984) and Huffman (2000) showed that supercharging music and super learning technique has multipronged effect. It has been fruitful on developing intelligence, memory and generating discoveries (Tomatis, 2000) and profitable for releasing stress, increasing health standard and sports achievement (Abrezol, 1990s). Likewise, yoga and meditation have that power of creation. It, as reported by Bhatia (2004), heads injuries, relaxes body-mind tension, develops memory and creates self-concept. It also cures diseases and enhances performance of sports persons, students and people of different fields (Kumar, 2002). Likewise, the ethno-religious, psycho-physical and spiritual classification of effects of Raja Yoga, basing on its eight-fold path, also gives hints of solving manifold problems (Chaudhury, 1975). Still, the circumference of super learning is wider than the yoga and meditation. It's locus of application encompasses almost all fields- science, technology, education, medicine, military, literary, art, architecture, philosophy, sports, space science and the like. Its periphery extends all over world besides India and some other Asian countries like Pakistan, Bangladesh, Nepal, Indonesia, Bhutan and China. The practitioners of super learning have reported to have achieved extraordinary success in their related fields. Novelist Robina Salter, Business Trainer Gail Heidenhain, CEO of Life-long Communication Dr Pulos are some of the excellent achievers who praise the effectiveness of super learning in high tones (Ostrander and Schroeder, 2002). Such wider spread of super learning technique than yoga and meditation may be due to its westernization, flexibility and interest of researchers to see its effectiveness. The inter-cultural adaptability of the super learning system also increases its usability. Taking such wide use of SLT in foreign lands and in various fields, it is natural to have a research-interest to know its effectiveness in the field of education and its related variables in India from where it has been imported by Lozanov.

Eighth, super learning has a less number of studies relating development of creative thinking. Robin Salter accepts that super learning has developed his creative thinking. Hoffman (2000) found super learning music effective in enhancing intelligence imagination, whole brain synchronization, problem-solving ability, right-left hemispheric function which are related to creative thinking (Curtis, 1994; Abrezol, 2000; Tomatis, 2000; Ostrander and Schroeder, 2002). But quite a few number of study have been reported on the effect of SLT on development of creative thinking. Besides the above idiosyncratic experiences relating influence of SLT, till now no such experimental study has been conducted to know its significance on creative thinking of school students. Therefore, it has become a matter of interest to see what SLT does for making our normal students creative?

Ninth, effect of SLT on developing the scholastic performance of students is yet to be fully exploited. In countries like USSR, UK and USA, adults have learnts a language in 24 days, retardeds have become super learners and students learnt

Spanish in a month (Ostrander and Schroeder, 1979; Passi and Prabhu, 1997). But when no such study has yet been undertaken in Asian states and it has been widely acclaimed that students of formal schools of India are suffering from "didactogency" (Lozanov, 1974), at that time, how can we say that the SLT, which has been proved fruitful in developing academic achievement of students of European and American Nations will also act profitably in Indian sub-continent ? To have a correct answer to this research question, undertaking an experimental study is felt more intelligent than believing on any hunch. On The other hand, in growing curriculum load, if we can have a super learning technique, which will actually help in accelerating the learning speed of students and making the difficult tasks easy for them, there would be no other good news for our teachers, students parents and educationists but to universalize SLT.

Tenth, effectiveness of SLT on the basis of sex has not yet been widely studied. Comparatively, during vedic era the females had right of reading Veda, doing meditation and yoga. Though this trend was stopped during post-vedic era, still, at present, ladies have come up as Yoga-teachers. They have established yoga schools and providing training on yoga to learners. Many foreigners are coming to India to practise Yoga and meditation and some of them have established Yoga ashramas in India. All these explain that yoga and meditation has also become fruitful for both male and females. Lady yoga and meditation teachers are healing the patients, curing diseases, helping people in releasing tension as their male counterparts. But a small number of study show that SLT is used by researchers on the females. It has also been reported that girls are faring well in SLT intervention. Whether boys or girls are doing better in developing their intelligence or creativity or memory is not clear as researches conducted on these aspects are silent. Therefore, it is also a challenging aspect of SLT and its effect thereof.

Eleventh, the method of teaching prevailing in present India is suffering from didactogenic syndromes. Our schools have become knowledge markets. Over-loaded curriculum developing throat-cut copmpetitions among students. Both teacher and students are stressing on completion of courses.

High ambitious parents becoming result-oriented. Examination system encourages rote learning and creating stress, tension and insecurity in a vast majority of students. Failure in examination and intellectual poverty developing learning detaste among them and mars joy of learning. Various methods of teaching proved their failure in perpetuating the aim of education and becoming time-consuming, costly and tasteless. But we can not entirely change the prevailing system of education. Therefore, we have to experiment SLT on our prevailing system of school education to remedy the defects (Passi, 1997). It helps learners to learn more within less time. It makes learning joyful and accelerated by developing quick memory among learners. If all these findings of Ostrander, Schroeder and Ostrander (1979) will be found positive in our educational ecology, no doubt, our educationist, students, teachers and parent would get solace from the prevailing educational mess of India. Therefore, it is felt inevitable to take up an experiment of SLT on secondary level students of India.

Twelfth, unfortunately, there is no research on SLT in India til yet. Fortunately, in the interest of research, there is no more interesting and challenging news for a researcher besides it. Actually, maximum studies related to SLT have been conducted in foreign lands. Out of these some are descriptive and biographical whereas others are experimental. But there are less number of studies which were conducted taking pre-test post-test experimental and control group design. Maximum number of study were based on one group pre-test post-art design. Many of them have small sample goups. Another matter is variable of the study. Although it has been viewed in the previous studies that SLT is quite effective in releasing tension, bringing mind-body relaxation, developing hemispheric function and enhancing creativity, all these were done separately. Those studies are also silent regarding sample size, statistical analysis, experimental control and statistical control of variables and data analysis. Although studies have been reported in website and related source books and there is no ambiguity on their authenticity, still research demands a scientific answer. Therefore, a thorough and scientific study is needed which will findout the independent and interacting effects of some variables related to education and educand. In consideration of all these characteristics undertaking an experiment on the effect of SLT on the secondary school students seems very much logical.

3.2 STATEMENT OF THE PROBLEM

Taking the above reviews and rationale into consideration, it is felt that Super Learning Technique (SLT), which has been variedly experimented and studied all over Europe and America need to be studied in India. It is further intended that the learner's intelligence, gender, academic achievement and creative thinking will be included in the study to see the impact of SLT on them, so that the education system of India will get a new light. Therefore, the research problem is stated as follows.

"EFFECT OF SUPER LEARNING TECHNIQUE (SLT) ON DEVELOPMENT OF CREATIVE THINKING"

3.3 SCOPE AND DELIMITATIONS

The circumference of the study bears the characteristics of a behavioural research with a view of generalisation of its finding for the benefit of the students, teachers and of the system.

(a) This was an experimental study. The study was intending to experimentally prove whether super learning technique is effective in developing creative potentiality.
(b) The study was conducted in Indian cultural milieu, specifically in Orissa. Therefore, the implications of the study is more applicable to India than to any foreign cultural tradition.
(c) The experiment was conducted on secondary level students. Since the school was a co-educational institution, the study included both boys and girls.
(d) The experiment was undertaken on students of class-IX, those belong to the age group of 14 to 15 years.
(e) "History" was chosen as the subject to be taught and learned through super learning technique.

(f) Super Learning Technique (SLT) developed by Lozanov, the Bulgarian doctor was regarded as independent variable of the study. Effectiveness of SLT was verified through teaching history.

(g) Creative thinking and achievement in History were considered as dependent variables of the study. Effect of SLT on these dependent variables was statistically analysed.

(h) Intelligence and sex were considered as extraneous variables. Their relative impact during experiment process were also studied.

(i) Effect of Super Learning Technique (SLT) was compared with the conventional method of teaching history to know which method fares well.

(j) There were some changes in the teaching or learning session of super learning technique to generate creative thinking among students. Gordon's syntectic approach combined with electronic brains storming the modified form of Osborn's brainstorming were incorporated in SLT's learning session activity relating to the teaching of history.

3.4 OBJECTIVES

The study was conducted on the following objectives:

(i) To find out the effect of Super Learning Technique (SLT) on development of creative thinking.

(ii) To find out effect of Super Learning Technique (SLT) on students' achievement in History.

(iii) To find out the relationship that existed between intelligence and development of creative thinking as an effect of Super Learning Technique (SLT).

(iv) To study the rate of development of achievement scores in History in relation to levels of intelligence as an impact of Super Learning Technique (SLT).

(v) To find out the relationship between change in creative thinking scores and change in achievement test scores as an effect of Super Learning Technique (SLT).

(vi) To find out the difference in creative thinking scores of boys and girls as an effect of Super Learning Technique (SLT).

(vii) To find out the difference in academic achievement scores of boys and girls as an effect of Super Learning Technique (SLT).

3.5 HYPOTHESES

Taking the above stated objectives into consideration and to study the objectives in scientific process, following null hypotheses (H_{0s}) were formulated for the study. The hypotheses were objective-based.

H_{01} (a) There was no significant difference between the experimental group and control group in their pre-test creative thinking scores.

(b) There was no significant difference between the experimental group and control group in their post-test creative thinking scores.

(c) There was no significant difference between the experimental group and control group in their mean gain scores in creative thinking.

H_{02} (a) There was no significant difference between the experimental group and control group in their pre-test mean achievement scores in history.

(b) There was no significant difference between the experimental group and control group in their post-test mean achievement scores in history.

(c) There was no significant difference between the experimental group and control group in their mean gain scores in achievement test in History.

H_{03} (a) There was no significant difference in pre-test creative thinking mean scores of high-intelligence group and low-intelligence group of:

(i) Control Group, and

(ii) Experimental Group

(b) There was no significant difference in the post-test creative thinking mean scores of high-intelligence group and low-intelligence group of:

(i) Control Group, and
(ii) Experimental Group.

(c) There was no significant difference in the gain scores in creative thinking of high-intelligence group and low-intelligence group of—
(i) Control Group, and
(ii) Experimental Group.

H_{04} (a) There was no significant difference in the pre-test achievement mean scores in history of high-intelligence and low-intelligence groups of—
(i) Experimental Group, and
(ii) Control Group.

(b) There was no significant difference in post-test achievement mean scores in history of high-intelligence and low-intelligence groups of—
(i) Experimental Group, and
(ii) Control Group.

(c) There was no significant difference in mean achievement gain scores of high-intelligence and low-intelligence groups of experimental group.

H_{05} (a) There was no significant difference in mean creative thinking gain scores of high-achievers and low-achievers in history achievement test scores of the experimental group.

(b) There was no significant difference in mean achievement gain scores in history of high-creative group and low-creative group of Experimental Group.

(c) There was no significant correlation between creative thinking gain scores and achievement gain scores.

H_{06} (a) There was no significant difference between boys and girls in their mean creative thinking scores at pre-test stage.

(b) There was no significant difference between boys and girls in their mean creative thinking scores at post-test stage.

(c) There was no significant difference between the boys and girls of the experimental group in their gain scores in creative thinking tests.

H_{07} (a) There was no significant difference in mean achievement scores in History of boys and girls at pre-test stage.

(b) There was no significant difference in mean achievement scores in History of boys and girls at post-test stage.

(c) There was no significant difference between boys and girls in their gain scores in academic achievement in History.

3.6 OPERATIONAL DEFINITION OF THE TERMS USED

If one will go into the study, he will come across a number of new words and terms. Although many of those terms are not at all new, still their use in this study bears some different meaning. Therefore, the new terms are defined in following ways:

(A) Super Learning Technique (SLT)

Super learning is a technique of learning or teaching which brings out the hidden possibilities from the unconscious level to make the individual super-conscious. This technique was developed by George Lozanov, a Bulgarian Doctor and Psychiatrist. Thus, SLT has now been accepted as a means of accelerated learning, mind-body relaxation, enhancing memory, developing intelligence and creative thinking.

This technique has two phases of activities—

Phase I : The Mind calming session.

Phase II : The Memory session.

Phase I : Mind Calming Session

It has four steps, such as, relaxation, visualization, affirmation and breathing exercise. Simple physical exercise is recommended for mind-body relaxation and for releasing body tension. Visualization stresses on simple meditation or memorisation of peaceful and calm situation with a view to develop concentration by erasing worries and distractions. Affirmation is a step of creating self-confidence or self-concept within the individual. It is an attempt of creating the mental set of "I can win" within the individual. Breathing exercise is recommended to be practised through rhythmic inhaling, holding, exhaling and pause.

Phase II : The Memory Session

Here, the learners learn different topics of History. This phase has two steps. In the first step the topic is to be produced in condensed form so as to make it fit to be easily grasped and memorized by the learners. Divergent questions in the form of electronic brainstorming are to be asked on the topic to generate creative thinking among students. In the second step the learners are to remember the things taught to them in first step with a background flute sound of 60 beats. This memorisation is to be conducted in closed eyes.

(B) Creative Thinking

Creative thinking is the mental power of creating new and novel things. Researchers interpret it as power, process, product, person and press. Psychologists define it as divergent thinking (Guilford, 1957). Many opine that creative thinking in the activity of whole brain synchronization being characterised by fluency, flexibility, originality and elaboration. But, here, creative thinking referred to the scores obtained by Mehdi's Group Test on Creative Thinking (verbal).

(C) Intelligence

Psychologists accept intelligence as convergent thinking (Guilford, 1957), abstract thinking (Terman, 1960), ability of analysis and synthesis (Spearman, 1904) and capacity relating reasoning, thinking and effective environmental adjustment (Wechsler, 1958). Here, intelligence was defined as scores obtained from Tondon's Verbal Group Test of Intelligence (2/70).

(D) Achievement

Successfulness of individuals in different fields of life is generally accepted as achievement. The sportsman, scientist, artist, technocrat show their achievement in their respective fields. In the field of education, students' scholastic performance or academic brilliance is regarded as their academic achievement. Here, academic achievement referred to the scores obtained by the students in the achievements test on History developed by Orissa Secondary School Teachers' Association (OSSTA) and administered by the school.

(E) Secondary School

In connection to implementation of National Policy on Education-1986, there is the prevalence of 10+2+3 pattern of education all over the state. On the same ground, in Orissa, the secondary level of education consists of Lower Secondary Level (Class IX and X) and Higher Secondary Level (Class XI and XII /+2 Level). Here, the Secondary Level referred to the class IX and X, i.e., lower secondary level and the experiment was conducted on the students of Class-IX.

(F) History

In Orissa, History has been taught as a school subject from lower primary level under social studies. From upper primary level, it is taught as a separate subject. Sequentially, it includes the local history, regional history, history of the state, national history and world history keeping pace with the development of students and progress of classes. Such history content also varies from class to class basing on the nature of course—ICSSC, CBSE, ICSE and State Boards, prevailing in concerned school. In this study, ninth class students were taught the topics included in the history book of Class-IX prepared and published by Board of Secondary Education, Orissa.

(G) Sex

Since the study was conducted in a co-educational institution, both boys and girls were found in the classes. Though generally sex refers to male and female, here such dichotomy referred to Boys and girls those were included in the study as participants or sample.

(H) Control Group and Experimental Group

It was an experimental study which followed Pre-test Post-test Parallel Group Design. Accordingly, the study had a control group, where students were taught the subject in conventional method and an experimental group, where history was taught to students through Super Learning Technique (SLT).

3.7 DESIGN

There was a need to know the effectiveness of Super Learning Technique (SLT) on the development of creative thinking. So, it is experimental research which was found absolutely fit to the purpose. There are various designs of an experimental study those answer about the future perspective of a matter. Amidst pre-experimental, quasi-experimental and true-experimental designs, the last type proved to be most appropriate design to produce scientifically generalizable results (Koul, 1993). Taking all these things into consideration the study had followed two research designs—one was Pilot Study Design and other was Experimental Design.

3.7.1 Pilot Study Design

Super Learning Technique, which was originally formulated by Lozanov, has been experimented world-wide with some culture-specific and field-related alterations. Accordingly, when it was thought to see the effectiveness of SLT in India and specifically in the Indian educational system, it was felt inevitable to have some Indian adaptability in super learning techniques. But such culture and field-oriented changes raise question of sanctity and solidarity of SLT in serving the prime purpose. Therefore, the researcher felt justified to test the solidarity of SLT with the altered elements through a pilot study. Another intention of the pilot study was to observe and diagnose the defect of SLT, if any, during the transaction and to bring necessary changes thereof to avoid any sort of experimental error. Such pilot study will also increase experimental effectiveness of SLT.

Therefore, the first draft of SLT was tried out through One Group Pre-test Post-test Design which is presented in Table 3.1

TABLE 3.1
Paradigm of One Group Pre-test Post-test Design for Pilot Study

Test	*Variable*	*Test*
Pre-test (T_1)	Independent Variable SLT(x)	Post-test (T_2)

To undertake the pilot study through the above design, the researcher randomly selected a section of Class-IX students from Dabaraj Vidyapitha, Bhubaneswar. As creative thinking was chosen as dependent variable, it was measured at pre test stage and also at post-test stage. Super Learning Technique (SLT), developed by the investigator on the basis of Lozanov's directives, was regarded as independent variable. Mehdi's Verbal Test on Creative Thinking was used to measure students' creative thinking.

The randomly selected group was administered Mehdi's VTCT (T_1) first before the intervention. Then teaching of history started according to Super Learning Technique (x). It lasted for two weeks. After two months of intervention post-test on creative thinking (T_2) was given.

The collected data was analysed by the application of SE_D (significance of difference between means) and 't' test. Table 3.2 shows the significance of difference between the mean creative thinking scores of pre-test and post-test stages. Calculated result shown a significant difference ($t = 5.8976$, $P < 0.01$). Thus, the null hypothesis which stated, "There is no significant difference between pre-test and post-test mean creative thinking scores as an impact of SLT" was refuted at 0.01 level of significance. The post-test creative thinking mean score is found at higher level (M= 153.6578, SD = 36.0240) than the pre-test creative thinking mean scores (M=107. 0263, SD = 27.8201).

TABLE 4.2

Significance of Difference between Pre-test and Post-test Creative Thinking Mean Scores in Pilot Study

Tests	*N*	*M*	*SD*	*t*
Pre-test	38	107.0263	27.8201	5-8976*
Post-test	38	153.6578	36.0240	

* Significant at 0.01 level (P < 0.01).

3.7.2 Observations and Remedials on Pilot Study

It is ovious that the One Group Pre-test Post-test Design which was employed for pilot study to test the effectiveness of SLT is a weak experimental design. Since there was no control group, the obtained data from one group lacks scientific generalisation. On the other hand, although there were sufficient number of extraneous variables those have maximum possibilities and capacities to influence the result, no effort was taken to subside their impact so that the actual effect of SLT would have been known. There may be carry over impact in the result of post-test. As the investigator wanted just to know the loopholes of SLT, and it was a pilot study, he undertook this weak design. But it would be wise to follow a strong true experimental design at the stage of experiment and try to equalize control group and experimental group on various grounds. Accordingly, the researcher took the safeguards during experiment.

During pilot study intervention, it was seen that students were not interested towards the SLT during first phase. It created problem in attaining objectives. It may be because of the new technique. Therefore, it would be intelligent to give sometime for environment building and making the experimental group, teachers and students conversant to the SLT and motivated to work with the technique. All these should be made much before the actual intervention.

The students were not found duly acquainted to the super learning music, so some irregularities were noticed in practising memorisation while listening to music. Primarily they felt disturbed. So, such situation should be tackled carefully. First, they are to be made familiar with the music and its rhythm. They are to be trained on the process of memorisation and visualization with the music. Since everything has to be performed within the class, special care be taken in this regard.

During the transaction of topic through SLT, it was observed that time was short and remaining tasks were more. Such situations created problematic condition with regard to the attainment of instructional objectives. Therefore, the entire class-time should be intelligently distributed among the activities of SLT. More time should be given to the memory session and less time be devoted for the mind calming activities, as because students have practised likewise exercises before and will carry on those during each SLT session.

It was found that students have much leisure time in their out of school life. On the other hand, such meditation-like activities are easy to be practised in lisure time, even at home. Therefore, simple and as less as possible home tasks are advisable to be given to students at the end of each class.

The pilot study was conducted during January and February 2002 after which the annual examination of the school was held. It was reported by the Headmaster, teachers and even by some students that the result of some students were found excellent. Students, those were practising super learning principle effectively during pilot study and were continuing their practice after the pilot study, have fared well in their achievement in history subject. Some had also done better in other subjects. As the news came to the researcher very late, i.e. during experiment time, it was decided to stick to learning history through super learning process and to measure those during analysis.

Taking the above observations on the Pilot Study, the investigator incorporated the suggested remedial measures in improving the effect of Super Learning Technique (SLT) at experimental stage. It is hoped that the experimental process will be very much effective in knowing the multi-sided impact of super learning.

3.7.3 The Experimental Design

Since the study was experimental and there was a weak design in pilot study, the researcher selected a strong experimental design, i.e., Randomized Matched Groups Pre-test Post-test Design as shown in Table 3.3. The design will study the impact of SLT on creative thinking of the learners.

TABLE 3.3
Paradigm of Randomized Matched Groups Pre-test Post-test Design

Randomly Assigned Matched Groups	*Pre-test*	*Independent Variables*	*Post-test*
Control Groups (C)	T_1C	Teaching through Traditional Method	T_2C
Experimental Group (E)	T_1E	Learning Through SLT	T_2E

3.7.4. Description of the Design

Two sections of Class-IX of University High School, Vani Vihar, Bhubaneswar were chosen for the study at random. Assignment of control group and experimental group to both the sections were also made at random. The control group and experimental group were named as 'C' and 'E' respectively. Pre-tests on creative thinking, achievement and intelligence were administered on both the groups. Pre-test on control group was symbolized as T_1C. and on Experimental group was symbolized as T_1E. Then, the control group was taught by traditional method and experimental group was taught by Super Learning Technique (SLT). History was taught to both the groups by the investigator himself. The experimental treatment continued for two months. After the intervention period post-test on creative thinking was administered and scores in History of Annual Examination was considered as the post-test scores in history, whereas students' marks in History obtained in half-yearly examination was considered as pre-test scores in History. Post-test scores of control and experimental groups were symbolized as 'T_2C' and 'T_2E' respectively.

3.7.5 Variables

The study had different variables of varied nature. The study had included creative thinking, intelligence, achievement, sex, Super Learning Teachnique (SLT) and the traditional method of teaching as it variables. Among these, creative thinking and achievement were considered as dependent variables, Super Learning Technique was accepted as independent variable whereas sex, intelligence and the traditional method of teaching History were treated as intervening variables. The intervening variables were taken only to facilitate the analysis by finding out their influence on the dependent and independent variables. But the sole objective of the study was to determine the influences of Super Learning Technique on the development of creative thinking and achievement in History.

3.8 THE SAMPLE

3.8.1 Area of Sample

The sample for the study was drawn from the capital city

(Grade A) of Orissa, i.e., Bhubaneswar. The School was University High School situated in the Utkal University Campus and is under the administration of Utkal University, Vani Vihar, Bhubaneswar (Orissa). It was a co-educational institution. The sample was the students of Class-IX, who were within the average age of 14 years. Though the mother tongue of maximum students was Oriya, students of other mother tongues like Bengali, Punjabi and Hindi were also in the class. But all the students were able to read, write and speak Oriya, English and Hindi fluently and correctly. Some were also very much conversant to other regional Indian languages like Bengali, Urdu, Telugu, etc. The city had the status of municipal corporation. Though there are Government Schools, Central School, Sainik School, Special School and so many Public Schools, overall three types of courses—CBSE, ICSE and state Board of Secondary Education, are taught in different types of schools. But the University High School, where the experiment was conducted was following the courses designed by Board of Secondary Education, Orissa. However, the sample was a heterogenous group consisting of boys and girls.

3.8.2 Selection of Sections

There were five sections in the school. Two sections were chosen at random and from among the two sections, experimental and control group was assigned at random. In final, one group was assigned as control group and one group was assigned as experimental group. Both the groups include boys and girls.

3.8.3 Recruitment of Sample

The experimental group and control group had varied number of students on roll. As per the nature of experimental study, though record of each student was maintained throughout the study, the actual sampling was done after the post-test data was collected and before analysis. Out of total 122 students, which included 60 boys and 62 girls, 109 students (Boys—53; Girls—50) appeared in different tests. Out of 109 students 96 students were recruited as sample of the study with inclusion of equal number of boys and girls (B—48; G—48). Such selection was done at random. But the exclusion of many students from the study was due to the absence of students in different testing programmes, lack of necessary data required to be furnished by them and by their school authority relating their scholastic achievement and because of experimental mortality. Application of random method to fulfil the necessity of equalizing the control and experimental group also brought some loss to sampling strength. Some students those had changed their sections during the intervention period and those were present in either of the pre-test or post-test, were not included in the study as sample. A group-wise sampling data is presented in Table 3.4 followed by a sampling Framework of the study given in Figuie 3.1.

TABLE 3.4
Data on the Sample of the Study

Group	*Total No. of students (Boys, Girls)*	*Students appeared in the Tests (Boys, Girls)*	*Students Recruited as Sample (Boys, Girls)*
Control Group	62 (B-32, G-30)	56 (B-27, G-29)	48 (B-24, G-24)
Experimental Group	60 (B-28, 4-32)	53 (B-25, G-28)	48 (B-24, G-24)
Grand Total	122 (B-60, G-62)	109 (B-52, G-56)	96 (B-48, G-48)

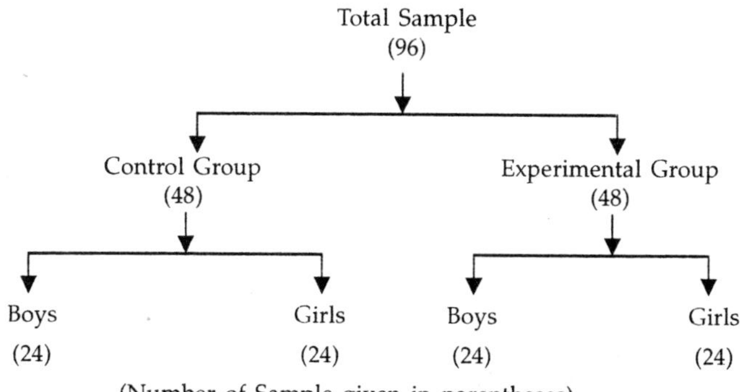

(Number of Sample given in parentheses)

Fig. 3.1 : The Sampling Framework

3.8.4 Matching of the Sample on Intelligence and Creative Thinking

Control of variables and matching the experimental and control groups are some of the important principles of controlling the impact of extraneous variables and increasing the effect of independent variable over the dependent variable. Therefore, in this study, the samples of control and experimental groups were matched on the ground of intelligence and creative thinking.

(a) Matching on Intelligence

Intelligence of students of both control group and experimental group was measured by Tondon's Verbal Group test of Intelligence. The obtained scores were analysed and the significance was studied by employing SE_D (Significance of Difference Between Meas) and by using 't' test.

There were 96 subjects in total having 48 students each in control group and experimental group. Both the groups, in total, had equal number of boys and girls. Their scores in intelligence were obtained through administration of Tondon's Verbal Group Test on Intelligence and analysed by SE_D and 't' test. Table 3.5 shows the significance of difference between control group and experimental group in their intelligence scores. It showed a non-significant difference (t=0.6054, P>0.05) between control group and experimental group in their intelligence scores. The result confirmed that both the groups were same in their intelligence. Hence, the impact of intelligence was controlled here and both the groups were matched on intelligence.

TABLE 3.5
Significance of Difference Between Means of Control Group and Experimental Group on Intelligence Mean Scores

Group	*N*	*M*	*SD*	*t*
Control Group	48	66.1251	11.8420	0.6054
Experimental Group	48	64.7708	9.9995	

n.s.—not significant at 0.05 level (P>0.05).

(b) Matching on Creative Thinking

Creative Thinking ability of students was measured by Mehdi's Verbal Test on Creative Thinking. The collected data was analysed by SE_D and 't' test to findout the significance of difference, if any. The singnificance was studied separately on different aspects of creative thinking and on total creative thinking score. Table 3.6, Table 3.7 and Table 3.8 present the data relating significance of difference between means in fluency, flexibility and originality respectively and Table 3.9 shows the singnificance of difference between means in total creative thinking scores of control group and experimental group. The analysis was made at pre-test stage. The result found non-significant difference in fluency, flexibility, originality and in total creative thinking scores of control group and experimental group with respective 't values' of 0.5733 (fluency), 1.9288 (flexibility), 1.6327 (originality) and 0.1823 (total creative thinking). All the calculated values were not significant at 0.05 level.

The above result showed that, at pre-test stage, all the groups were equal in their creative thinking mean scores. Hence, the students were matched in their creative thinking scores at pre-test stage.

TABLE 3.6

Significance of Difference between Means of Control Group and Experimental Group on Fluency

Group	*N*	*M*	*SD*	*t*
Control Group	48	52.0625	12.6925	0.5733n.s
Experimental Group	48	50.6458	11.4895	

n.s.—not significant at 0.05 level (P>0.05).

TABLE 3.7

Significance of Difference Between Means of Control Group and Experimental Group on Flexibility

Group	*N*	*M*	*SD*	*t*
Control Group	48	29.354	7.3415	1.9288 n.s
Experimental Group	48	32.4792	8.4925	

n.s.—not significant at 0.05 level (P>0.05).

TABLE 4.8

Significance of Difference Between Means of Control Group and Experimental Group on Originality

Group	*N*	*M*	*SD*	*t*
Control Group	48	12.7499	5.1537	1.6327 n.s.
Experimental Group	48	11.1875	4.1715	

n.s.—not significant at 0.05 level (P>0.05).

TABEL 3.9

Significance of Difference Between Means of Control Group and Experimental Group in Total Ceative Thinking

Group	*N*	*M*	*SD*	*t*
Control Group	48	93.00	21.937	0.8123 n.s.
Experimental Group	48	93.8333	22.852	

n.s.—not significant at 0.05 level (P>0.05).

All the above analyses showed that the samples of control group and experimental group were matched on intelligence and creative thinking.

3.9 TOOLS USED

In this study, the investigator had used the Oriya version of Verbal Group Test of Intelligence (2/70) of R.K. Tondon, Verbal Test of Creative Thinking developed by Baquer Mehdi and the Achievement Tests developed by Orissa Secondary School Teachers' Association (OSSTA) to measure intelligence, creative thinking and achievement of the sample respectively. The brief description of these tools is presented below.

3.9.1. Verbal Group Test of Intelligence (2/70) By R.K. Tondon

The Verbal Group Test of Intelligence (2/70) was developed by R.K. Tondon and published by the National Psychological Corporation, Agra. The test is meant for secondary school students. The original Hindi test was first translated into Oriya language by Basanti Pradhan (1990) and here, the investigator had used that Oriya version of the test.

The test consists of 91 omnibus type of items like number series, correlating relationship, hypothetical arguments, synonyms, antonyms, difference analysis and the like. The test is proceeded by some examples for practice and instructions. The students are to answer all the questions within twenty minutes and they are instructed to write the number of correct answer in the attached answer sheet. Each correct answer carries one mark and each wrong answer carries zero. The sample of this test and its scoring key are attached in Appendices A and B respectively.

3.9.2 Verbal Test of Creative Thinking By Baquer Mehdi

Dr. Baquer Mehdi, Ex-Professor of Education, NCERT, New Delhi had developed this test battery for measurement of creative thinking ability. He had realized the importance of developing separate creativity tests specifically relevant to a given culture and attempted to solve this problem by preparing his creative test battery. Before it, Torrance, Guilford and Wallach and Kogan had brought out their creativity tests which are being extensively used not only in United States, but also in other countries including India either as such or with some Indian adaptations. But with consideration of Indian cultural ethos, Mehdi's test has a distinction. His test was first published in 1973 by Mrs. Qamar Fatima under the sole distributorship of National psychological corporation, Agra. This test is meant for a wide range of sample starting from students of middle school and going upto the graduation level.

This test has been used by different researchers at different times in various studies. Prasad (1979) and Singh (1984) had used this test to ascertain the effect of teaching methods like problem-solving and specially designed teaching strategy on creative thinking. Both the methods were found effective in developing creative thinking abilities of the children. Singh (1984) studied the relationship between creative thinking and other variables like adjustment, frustration and level of aspiration. Significant relationship was found between creativity and level of aspiration and between creativity and adjustment. Insignificant relationship was found between creativity and frustration. Mehra and Singh (1982) found low correlation between creativity and intelligence. Agarwal (1882) found solid relationship between creative thinking and risk taking by using this creative thinking test. Oriya version of this test was first used by Pradhan (1990) to measure the effect of teaching science by creative method of teaching on the development of creative thinking. Later on, Prusty (2004) measured creative thinking of students and its development through it in an experimental study to know the effect of self-developed CMTE model.

The theoretical framework for the preparation of this test is based on Guilford's divergent thinking process of mental operation. It measures fluency, flexibility and originality aspects of ceative thinking. It includes four sub-tests namely, consequences test, unusual uses tests, similarity test, and product improvement test.

(i) Consequences Test

The basis of this activity is Guilford's "Consequences Test" or "Torrance's Just Suppose Activity". The tests included in this activity are based on familiar things but are presented in the form of "hypothetical situations". (Mehdi, 1985). The consequences test consists of three hypothetical situations : (a) what would happen if man could fly like birds?; (b) what would happen if our school has wheels?, and (c) what would happen if man does not have any need for food? These tesks confront the subject with a situation for which he can think of with a large number of possible consequences. This implies cause and effect thinking or stimulus-response activity of the individual's thinking process. The happenings may be usual or unusual, logical or illogical, but the subject is required to think as many consequences of these situations as he can and write them under each situation in the space provided. The test encourages free play of imagination and originality. The time allowed is four minuets for each of the three problems. The number of relevant responses produced by the subject yields the measure of his ideational fluency, the number of shifts in the thinking trends of consequences gives the measures of verbal flexibility and statistical infrequency of response or the departure of thinking from the common place gives the measure of originality.

(ii) Unusual Uses Test

The basic idea of these tasks comes from Guilford's "Brick Uses Test" or Torrance's "Tin Can Uses Test" or "Cardboard Boxes Uses Test." Common things like water, a stick and a piece of stone are used as stimuli to let the subjects thinking go in different directions. The activity appears playful to the child, but quickly puts him on a train of thought which will yield many novel responses. This test presents the subjects with the names of three common objects—a piece of stone, a stick and water—and requires him to write as many novel, interesting and unusual uses of these objects as he may think of. The test measures the subject's ability to retrieve items of information from his personal information in storage. Total 15 minutes duration is allowed for the test with five minutes time for each of the three objects. The number of relevant responses gives the measure of one's ideational fluency; the number of thought categories gives the measure of verbal flexibility and uncommonness of response gives the measure of originality.

(iii) New Relationships/Similarity Test

Taking Mednick's word association definition of creativity and its remoteness into consideration, in this activity, articles of daily use with which the child is quite familiar are taken so as to enable him to think more naturally about relationships between two apparently dissimilar objects. This test presents the subject with three pairs of words apparently different—tree and house, chair and ladder, air and water—and requires him to think and write as many novel relationships as possible between the two objects of each pair in the space provided. Here free play of imagination and originality of the subject is given utmost importance. For each pair of words five minutes time is allowed. The items of this activity provide possibilities for scoring responses for fluency, flexibility and originality in the same manner as for Unusual Uses Test.

(iv) Product Improvement Test

This test of verbal imagination has similarity with

Torrance's Product Improvement Activity. But the difference is that Torrance used a picture of a toy monkey, whereas, here, Mehdi asked to imagine the figure of a toy horse and to give unusual responses regarding addition of new things and accessories by which he can make it more interesting and useful for the child to play with. The task puts the child in the state of imagination and spurs him to think in different directions. For this activity six minutes time is allowed. This test measures fluency, flexibility and originality.

Hence, the total time required for the test is 48 minutes besides the time for supplying instructions, passing booklets to children and collecting them back. The test constructor gives the instruction to students to write the answer in mother tongue also. But the investigator used here the English version of the test and translated that into Oriya during administration time, when students required so. The respondents were given freedom to answer in their mother tongue, when they required to write. Mehdi's Verbal Test of Creative Thinking (English Version) is given in Appendix-C and the related scoring key in Appendix-D.

3.9.3 Achievement Test in History

History is a subject, which has been taught in Orissa from lower primary stage as social studies. From upper primary to the lower secondary level it is taught alongwith civics. In CBSE course this subject is taught as social studies. Here, the students' achievement in History, which were obtained by the school authorities through half yearly examination and annual examination were taken into analysis. As the intervention was conducted just after half yearly examination of the school, it was decided not to take another test to know the achievement of students in History, but to record their half-yearly examination marks as the pretest achievement score. Accordingly, marks in history which was obtained by the students in their annual examination that was conducted just after one month of intervention programme, were considered as their post-test achievement scores in History. However, for ready reference, the sample of History questions of half-yearly and annual examinations were given in Appendix-E and Appendix-F respectively. Since, these questions were prepared by the board of expert subject teachers under the guidance of OSSTA (Orissa Secondary School Teachers' Association) and these questions were used by all the aided and state government secondary schools of Orissa, the questions should have to be accepted as reliable and valid to serve the purpose of research.

4 SUPER LEARNING TECHNIQUE OF LEARNING HISTORY
The Intervention Strategy

SUPER LEARNING TECHNIQUE OF LEARNING HISTORY

The Intervention Strategy

4.1 HISTORY—IT'S MEANING AND MATHETICS

With the explosion of knowledge and evolution of the society, the concept of history has undergone a transitional change from Herodotus's narration of events to Thucydide's scientific and systematic analysis of facts through cause and effect relationship. History, which was primarily accepted as the record of what one age finds worthy of note in another (Burckhardt, 1954) changed to a scientific subject during 19th century (Vrajeswari, 1973). The modern concept of history has advanced to a most correct manner linking the past, present and future to this natural science (Chaudhury, 1975). Now, the historians interpret the subject as "the systematic and scientific study of past events in present context to forecast an error-free future". As a natural science, history may not be satisfied with the development of laws which would explain the happenings in the life of a nation; it may try to predict future happenings in its life with the help of these laws and within the minimum margin of errors. Whatever scientificity have been bestowed upon the nature of history, it is not yet free from its subjectivity. Objective, real and concrete description is scarce in it, as it is affected by social and human variables thereby leading in making facts to "controversial issues" (Kochhar, 2000). Religiosity, personal and group prejudices, racial and national differences have made many of the historical analyses illusive and mere propaganda. When histriography lacks histroicity and objectivity, the aims and objectives of teaching history get shrouded in obscurity, our student folk, being pray to our mathetic—disabilities, are getting outtracked.

4.2 AIMS AND OBJECTIVES OF LEARNING HISTORY

Specifically, through learning history, the secondary level students of India are expected to achieve the following aims of history, as described by NCERT, New Delhi.

(a) To know in their proper sequence the important events in national history.
(b) To comprehend historical reasoning, cause-effect relationship of the events.
(c) To appreciate the contributions of great personalities to the development of the nation.
(d) To know and understand the chronological sequence of historical events.
(e) To develop sense of national integrations and international understanding.
(f) To develop a sense of patriotism by taking pride of culture of the country.

In terms of pupil behaviour, History intends to achieve following aims and objectives (NCERT, 1975):

(a) The pupil should know the most significant happenings of past which are causally related to the present happenings in the national and state life.

(b) They should also be able to determine cause and effect relationship between them.
(c) They should be able to make critical estimates of the contributions of great personalities in the past and the present in terms of their influence over subsequent happenings in national and state history.
(d) They should be able to locate the dates of historical happenings in the time line.
(e) The pupils should be able to locate places of historical happenings in map.
(f) They should scrap books, pictures and information relevant to history; their leisure time reading should also display their interest in the study of history.
(g) The pupils should develop a strong belief in the unity of India inspite of all its diversities
(h) They should also develop a positive attitude towards the members of other religions and linguistic groups.
(i) They should take pride in the achievement of India in the past and the present.
(j) The pupil should also develop positive feeling towards people of all nationals.

When History is learned topic-wise, some objectives are expected to be acquired by the students. Those objectives encompassed by cognitive domain (Bloom, 1956), affective and psycho-moter domains of the child. (Krathwohl, Bloom and Masia, 1964). The instructional objectives of teaching History which are expected to be acquired by the students of secondary level are given below in a synchronized form.

I. Knowledge

The students will acquire knowledge of terms, concepts, facts, event, symbols, ideas, conventions, problems trends personalities, chronology and generalizations, etc. related to study of history. Acquisition of knowledge of above matters will be judged in following behavioural terms.

- Recall facts, terms, concepts, events, etc.
- Recognize facts, terms, concepts, events, etc.
- Show information on maps, charts, diagrams, etc.
- Read information presented in various forms.

II. Understanding

The pupil will develop understanding of terms, facts, principal events, trends, cause and effects, etc., related to the study of history. In this regard the students are to dispose their success in following behavioural terms:

- Classify facts, events, terms and concepts, etc.
- Illustrate events, trends, etc., by citing examples.
- Compare and contrast the events, trends and concepts.
- Explain events, terms and concepts, causes and effects, trends, etc.
- Discriminate between the significant and insignificant, important and less important cases, effect and events.
- Identify relationship between cause and effect, means and ends.
- Arrange facts, trends, etc., in a particular known order.
- Detect errors in the statement and rectify them.
- Interpret the maps, charts, etc.
- Extract from different courses of history.

III. Critical Thinking

History learning enables the pupils to develop critical thinking. By it the pupil should be judged in following behavioural dispositions:

- Identity the problem.
- Analyse the problem.
- Collect evidence.
- Shift evidence, facts and opinion.
- Select relevant evidence and facts and weigh them.
- Establish relationship and Marshal facts.
- Draw conclusions.
- Advance arguments in support of his contention.
- Verify the inference.

IV. Practical Skills

The subject will enable the pupils to develop practical skills helpful in the study and understanding the historical facts.

Acquisition of such abilities will be judged in the following behavioral terms:

- Draw maps, charts, diagrams, etc.
- Prepare models, tools, etc.

V. Interest

The subject will cultivate interest within the learners to read history and related writings. Such interest should be seen in following behavioural dispositions:

- Collect coins and other historical materials.
- Prepare illustrative material aids.
- Participate in historical dramas and mock sessions of historical events.
- Visit places of historical interest, archaeological sites, museums and archives.
- Read historical documents, maps and charts.
- Write articles on historical and other related topics.

VI. Attitude, Appreciation and Application

It enables the students to develop healthy attitude among themselves. If proper attitude is formed they will appreciate appropriate things and will try to apply those in their day-to-day life. Such acquisitions can be measured through following behavioural expressions:

- Posses a sense of patriotism
- Show respect towards other people's opinions, ideas and ways of life.
- Read about other faiths and religions.
- Establish friendship with pupils of other communities and faiths.
- Practice the spirit of noble ideals.
- Cooperate others in social and civic activities.
- Appreciate culture of others, contribution of others for democracy and independence, works of international organisations and humanitarian activities.
- Believe in the equality of man irrespective of caste, religion and colour.

4.3 LEARNING HISTORY : PROBLEMS AND PROSPECTS

A well-designed curriculum and setting of comprehensive instructional objectives would of no use if the methods used will not expose students in persuiting them. Method forms the most important link in the total teaching-learning chain (Kochhar, 1984). "Even the best curriculum and the most perfect syllabus remain dead unless quickened into life by the right methods of teaching and the right kind of teachers" (Secondary Education Commission, 1956). In this connection, recognising the best method of teaching History from among several methods needs profound experience, sharp intelligence and strong attitude of a good history teacher. She should identify the best method through recognising its various characteristics such as capacity to arouse large range of interest in the mind of students; to inculcate proper values, attitudes and interests among students; to make learning of history interesting, purposeful, real and concrete; to stimulate desire of further learning among students and overall to fulfil all the aims and objectives of history subject. It needs saturated psycho-pedagogical skills to select a most profitable method out of more than a dozon methods of teaching history—textbook, story telling, dramatisation, biographical, lecture, note dictation, conversational, narration-*cum*-discussion, unit, assignment, project, socialized recitation, supervised study and source method (Kochhar, 1984). Therefore, it is imperative that an effective history teachers needs to be well conversant with all methods so that he will use the best suitable one considering the ability, age, class and attitude of students and the nature of the topic.

But, the review of the research studies of independent India revealed that history teaching in our state is in an embarassing situation. At present, many of our schools lack a history room, adequate audio-visual aids and qualified history teacher. Besides this insufficient ecological support, our teachers those are transacting history syllabus are less-qualified, ill-equipped and lack the required attitude and aptitude of a history teacher. Incorporation of foreign history in our school curriculum, dull and uninteresting mode of presentation of curricular tasks, use of wrong methods of teaching and learning and defective text books have reduced history to a subject of cramming (NCERT, 1975). Such alarming condition, now-a-days, is becoming the causal factor of lowering student strength in history departments of colleges and universities of India and Orissa. Pupils are fearing at the subjectivity of history and teachers stress on cramming of the entire matter. Amidst all, problems, relating method of teaching and learning history sounds much, as a good method can present the defective syllabus in right form. But it needs the expertise of the subject teacher.

Under such circumstances, Super Learning Technique (SLT) has emerged as a panacea to such didactogenic syndrome (Lozanov, 1971). It tries to make learning of history amusing, stress-free and pleasurable. It shows the tricks of accumulating the learning tasks with less labour and without tension. Super learning, through its various techniques changes the chemistry of learner's consciousness, increases personal charisma, strengthens will, clears mind, claims nervousness, increases mental function and concentration and makes learning pleasurable. The details of the SLT for learning history is given below.

4.4 SUPER LEARNING TECHNIQUE OF LEARNING HISTORY—THE INTERVENTION STRATEGY

Use of the word 'learning' instead of 'teaching' itself signifies the importance and strategies of Super Learning Technique. SLT never believes in teaching which is the process of loading pupils mind with some information without considering the ability, attitude, interest and capacity of the learner. As a result, education is becoming drudgery, not interesting and redundant for the Child. Further history as a subject stands dead for the students and demotivates them towards learning. That is why, SLT does not believe on such passive teaching, rather it creates the physical, mental and non-physical atmosphere to facilitate learning. It energizes the learner with abudant self-concept and creates a strong mental set of learning with joy. It tries to put history before the learners as an interesting and pleasurable subject so that learness will be free from the prevailing phobia of learning history. SLT also accepts every pupil as the storehouse of all possibilities and tries to draw out those capacities to fullest extent.

Super learning Technique (SLT) has two phases of activities. But before starting those activities some preliminary preparations are necessary. Those preparations include the following steps:

(a) Building the Condusive Environment

Environment building includes creation of awareness among the school personnel including teachers, students, principal, administrators and parents. Such measure should intend to make the experimental situation or learning condition favourable and pleasurable.

(b) Selection of Subject and Topic

The researcher here has to select the subject/subjects that is to be transacted through super learning technique. Each topic that is to be taught should be scrutined thoroughly, because the method of super learning is quite different from the conventional methods of teaching.

(c) Setting up Instructional Objectives

Topic-wise instructional objectives should be formulated before the starting of super learning session while stating the objectives, the teacher should look at their importance and achievability within the topic. It is not that all the objectives will be found in each topic or all the objectives those are there in the topic seem equally important. Therefore, setting of objective needs rational scrutiny.

(d) Development of Super Learning Frames

Each topic should be divided into sub-themes. Each sub-theme should be transformed into super learning frame, so that the objective of the specific theme will be achieved strategically. Acquisition of one theme leads to learning of subsequent theme. Development of such Super Learning Frame should include the following items:

1. Statement of Instructional objective.
2. Stating the major themes.

3. Selecting the Minor themes.
4. Synchronized presentation of learning themes without and with music (with help of maximum possible audio-visual aids).
5. Memorisation of learned material with music.
6. Feedback Presentation.
7. Evaluation and Feedback Review.

(e) Time Allotment for Different Items of Super Learning Frame

Within the super learning frame, activities of the first three steps need no time of the class or learning session, as those need to be preplanned much more before the commencement of the learning session. But the subsequent four steps are very much important as the learning matter is acquired during such practices. So, for intelligent and successful attainment of learning objective through learning of major and minor theams, within a period needs, scientific distribution of time of the period for different activities of the super learning frame. A detail time-distribution is given in Table 4.10 in the description of the super learning class.

(f) The Super Learning Class

Many researches have used Lozanov's super learning process in original form when they tried to practise the guided super learning activities in very informal way (Tomatis, 1988; Prichard, 1983 and 1990). Some other have used the techniques in some altered from looking at the suitability of the situation (Seki, 1988; Curtis, 1989; Pillai, 1990; Ostrander and Schroeder, 1994). But using super learning technique outside the time frame of a period (class time) put question mark on its utilisation in conventional classrooms and also in teaching a subject in conventional class time (period).

In the conventional Indian schools, all subjects are learned by the students through specific classes, duration of which extends from 45 minutes to 60 minutes. Therefore, here, the researcher has tried to carry out all the techniques and activities within a class-time duration of which is confined to the average limit of 50 minutes. There is no need of changing the subject period as per the researcher's feasibility. To avoid all sorts of personal biasness, the researcher needs to stick to the pre-planned routine or time table of an institution, if he wants to check the effectiveness of super learning technique on students' academic performance and other allied variables through teaching/learning a specific subject through SLT.

With due consideration of the above facts, here the researcher has alloted the entire 50 minutes of a class-time among the super learning activities as per Table 4.1

TABLE 4.1
Time Distribution for Super Learning Class/Lesson

Sl. No.	*Activities to be Conducted*	*Time Alloted*
1.	Simple Relaxation	5 minutes
2.	Visualization with Music and Creating Affirmation	7 minutes
3.	Breathing Exercise	8 minutes
4.	Presentation of Super Learning Frame	30 minutes
	Total	50 Minutes

Further, thirty minutes alloted to various activities of Super Learning Frame is distributed according to Table 4.2.

TABLE 4.2
Time Allotment for Presentation of Super Learning Frame

Sl. No.	*Activities to be Conducted*	*Time Alloted*
1.	Synchronized Presentation of learning Theme	13 minutes
2.	Memorization of learned Matters (with music)	7 minutes
3.	Feedback Presentation	5 minutes
4.	Evaluation and Feedback Review	5 minutes
	Total	30 minutes

When the Super Leaning class follows recreation or games and sport period or gardening activities, at that time, relaxation activity need not be practised. It is because students must have engaged themselves in some physical activities or exercises through those activities. Here, the students may be directly allowed to breathing exercises and visualization activities. After getting calmness, affirmation is to be practised. However, the activities of a super learning class such as relaxation, visualization, affirmation and breathing exercise are the activities known as *Mind Calming Activities* coming under *First Phase* of Lozanov's Super Learning Teachnique and all the activities of super learning frame (which includes synchronised or condenced presentation of learning theme, memorisation of learned matters with music, feedback presentation, evaluation and feedback review) are coming under the activities of *Memory Session* of *second phase* of Lozanov's Super Learning Technique. Figure 4.1 and Figure 4.3 represent the System Approach and Cycle of Super Learning lesson for more clear understanding of this technique.

Input	*Process*	*Output*
• Learner	**Phase I : Relaxation**	• Releases stress
	• Visualicaiton	• Brings Mind-body relaxation
	• Affirmation	
• Facilitator of Learning	• Breathing Exerise	• Develops
		❖ Hemispheric Function
		❖ Intelligence
• Innovative Learning Aids	**Phase II : Learning the Condenced matter or Super Learning Frame**	❖ Creative Thinking ❖ Problem Sloving
• Condenced Topic/ Subject Matter	• Memorising with Music	❖ Achievement ❖ Imagination
		❖ Memory
• Supportive Learning Environment	• Feedback Presentation	❖ Critical Thinking
	• Evaluation and Feedback Reviewer	❖ Intelligence and many other
• Interest, Attitude and Motivaiton of teacher, learner and others	• Home Task	

Fig. 4.1 : System Approach of Super Learning

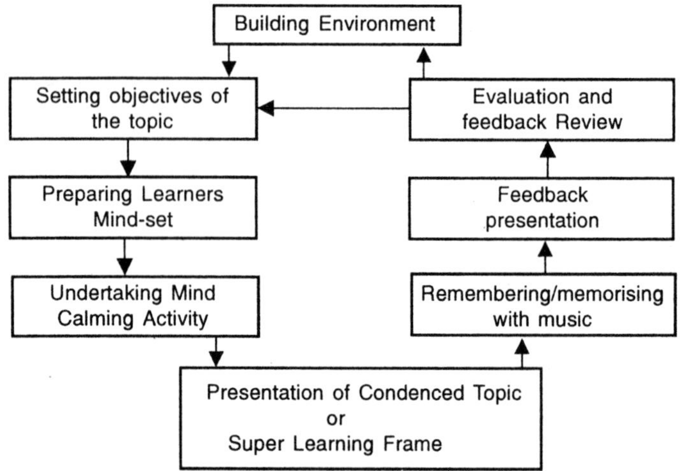

Fig. 4.2 : Cycle of Super Learning Lesson

4.5 BRIEF DESCRIPTION OF ACTIVITIES OF A SUPER LEARNING LESSON/CLASS

In the Introduction Chapter, under the sub-heading 1.3, a vivid presentation is made relating instructional strategies of super learning technique. But, while one has to incorporate all the activities within a period of 50 minutes time duration, it is ovious that an intelligent and creative consideration has to be made for the selection of nature and extent of super learning activities. All these are to be done in consideration to the time, resource, level of students and instructional objectives expected to be achieved.

Simple Relaxation is to be practised inside the class and for five minutes time duration. The objective of this exercise is to relax the body. If the super learning class follows sports period or recreation, it is clear that students have done some activities and their body is in relaxed state. So, there is no need of undertaking relaxation activity again. That time may be adjusted in visualization and breathing exercises. Simple physical exercises should be selected which are to be performed by students by sitting and standing inside the class. In each bench, maximum two students should sit keeping hand reach distance from each other. Neck rolling, stretching hands and legs, squeezing and opening fingers of hands and legs, tilting the upper part of he body from waist to right and left keeping palms in the waist, learning forward and backward should be included in relaxation activities. If all these activities will be practised in closed eyes with a feeling of each organ and nervous system that is involved in each exercise, that will exert maximum impact in making body tense-free within less time span. Then, the students should be trained to sensitize each organ of the body such as toes, legs, upper legs, lower back, abdomen, upper torso, shoulders, chest, arms, face and head through feeling the flow of a warm wave. Such feeling should be practised from bottom-up and up-bottom principle for at least twice. In continuation to this activity learner should be informed to switch over visualization-affirmation exercises. But, from the starting to few days these physical relaxation should be guided one. Teacher has to perform all the activities with, clear utterance and students are to follow in open eyes. When the relaxation wave progresses from one part to another, that should also be uttered, so that, students at primary stage, would feel the wave in their respective body-organs. When students will be found mastered over the process, they can be allowed to practise in closed eyes only by listening to teacher's guided utterance. With comfortable breathing catch the tension of particulars body point by the relaxation wave and let that tension flow out of the point with relaxation wave.

Visualizaiton and affirmation should be practised together for seven minutes for making the mind calm and for developing self-concept. Sitting in comfortable position, the students are to take easy and deep breathing. Alongwith, they are to imagine in closed eyes. The matter of imagination should be joyous, positive, exhilarating, imagery, pleasurable and power giving. Such creative imagination should be accompanied by a background music. With such music the teacher should describe a pleasant situation which will energize them and when the students will be found to have acquired full mental tranquility and pointed concentration, at that time alongwith that background music the teacher has to give some short, positive, optimistic and invigorating affirmations rhythmically. The affiramations should include sentences like "I can do it", learning is easy for me", "I am successful", "remembering is easy for me", etc.

Breathing exercise, which was there from starting of relaxation, is to be practised here very carefully and with rhythm. Sitting comfortably in relaxed position, here, the student has to centre his mind on to a point. The point should be designed before the students on a cardboard in the line of "Prosperity Tree". Here, the researcher had used the point shown in Figure 4.1. Two cardboards bearing this point were hanged before the students of two rows and they were asked to take breathing exercise with concentrating on this point. The rhythmic breathing at this point should proceed sequentially in four phases—inhale, hold, exhale and pause. Time of inhale, hold, exhale and pause should gradually increase as per the capacity of the learner. It can go from the count of two up to the count of 8 or even more. This activity will sharpen the mind and put the learner in ready situation for learning with a relaxed mind-body state.

Fig. 4.3 : Point for Breathing Concentration

Synchronised presentation of learning theme is the first step of memory session of super lerning technique, where learning takes place. Here, taking the help of possible audio visual aids, themes and sub-themes are to be presented in interesting and eye-catching manner which would have an impression on memory frame of the learners. So, presentation of history themes should be through diagrams, maps, pictures, time-line, comparative bullet points, underlined matters, cloured subjects, which can have long-term impact on memory and retention. Inspiring scope should be provided for inculcating creative thinking through presentation of thought provoking questions. A sample of Super Learning Frame is given in Table 4.2, which clearly explains the synchronised presentation of learning theme. As new learning task is to be presented at this step, 15 minutes time duration is alloted just for presentation.

After presentation, *memorisation* of learned matters is to be practised with a background slow music. It will extend for seven minutes. If learners fail to remember some learning themes and sub-themes, they are to point out those at the end of memorisation activity. The forgotten points will be presented, again with proper procedure. At last, evaluation of achievement of instructional objectives will be carried out and proper feedback will be provided for achieving complete learning objectives.

As stated by Ostrander and Schroeder (1997), it is not that a learning theme presented once through Super Learning Technique will be hundred percent effective in memorising all the matters. For initial time, it needs some repetition. When students will be conversant to the techniques, the effectiveness of the process will be increased in manifold. Therefore, it is the responsibility of the researcher, learners, teachers and others concerned to SLT to have patience and inceasant endeavour to get the success.

A model of a Super Learning Lesson is given in Appendix-E.

5 PROCEDURAL DESCRIPTION

5.1 The Mental Set

5.2 Pre-Experimental Readiness

5.3 Conduct of Experiment

5.4 Data Collection

5.5 Post-Experimental Activity and Data Compilation

PROCEDURAL DESCRIPTION

5.1 THE MENTAL SET

From the student career, the researcher has been practising yoga and meditation. After completion of Ph.D. in Education, when he was in search of another suitable topic to conduct research on creative thinking, fortunately there was a research paper of Passi and Prabhu (1997) in Progress of Education (Vol. IXXI, No. 7, Feb. 1997) on "Stress-free Super Learning". There, Passi and Prabhu gave a strong advocacy on the success of super learning method in developing intelligence, creative thinking, memory and in making learning pleasurable. One thing which made the researcher anxious to make up a mind set for research on Super Learning Technique (SLT) was the Indian origin of SLT. Lozanov developed this technique taking the essence of Indian Raja Yoga and some principles of Bulgarian yogic culture. Another challenging thing was inspite of its Indian origin, till yet not a single study was reported to have undertaken in India, whereas in Europe, Russia, Canada and USA quite a good number of studies have been conducted and reported on effectiveness of SLT. Mostly the direction given by

Passi and Prabhu on various areas of super learning research instigated the researcher to take up a study on it.

Thereafter, the researcher went on searching the source books on it through writing letters to various publishers. At last, the postal guidance of Prof. B.K. Passi, who was in Bangkok at that time, helped the researcher in getting the books on Super Learning from Strand Book Depot, Mumbai. After going through those books thoroughly, the researcher developed a mental set of undertaking an experimental study on the effect of Super Learning Technique (SLT) on development of creative thinking of school students.

5.2 PRE-EXPERIMENTAL READINESS

The researcher considers himself very fortunate to have availed the guidance of eminent Educationists like Prof. B.K. Passi, Prof R.C. Das, Prof. S.L. Jena, Dr. M.M. Mohanty and Emeritus Professor Dr. J. Mohanty in preparation of the research proposal. Taking their suggestions and guidance it was decided to see the effectiveness of SLT on creative thinking and achievement and to find out the impact of extraneous variables such as intelligence and sex on the performance of SLT. After submitting the research proposal to the University under the guidance of Prof. J. Mohanty, the researcher started his preparation for experiment. For it, the preliminary works like collection of Text books on History, selection of school, collection and printing of tools and Development of SLT learning packages for each topic were completed. The major activity at that time was collection Baroque music cassette and development of that in our context. SLT learning packages were also tried out to know their effectiveness. As it was decided to conduct the experiment at secondary level, heads of schools were contacted and approached to spare their classes for the experiment. At last, University High School of Utkal University Campus, Vani Vihar was selected for the intervention.

5.3 CONDUCT OF EXPERIMENT

Experience during experiment was very interesting. Before conducting experiment the researcher had already finished the pre-test data collection from both the groups. Then one group was made control group and other was made experimental group at random.

Being highly optimistic, when the researcher went to the experimental group to teach history as per SLT, things were not found congenial. Researcher's thought that students will appreciate and follow the super learning techniques fall flat. Students laughed at the relaxation exercises, meditative visualizations, breathing exercises even at the Baroque music which was the background music for memorization of learning materials. At that time, researcher remembered the experiment conducted by Gijubhai Botheka in Gujurat, where students, teachers and even educational administration treated Mr. Bodheka as mad. Still, the researcher had the strong morale that we can not deny our cultural characteristics those we possess in our blood and gene. Since meditation and yoga are there in our blood from ancient period, researcher hoped that students will gradually appreciate the method. Therefore, without using SLT, the researcher started infusing the importance of breathing exercises, meditation and memorisation in solving their day-to-day academic problem. He started the classes from affirmation and tried to create self-confidence among them that they are capable of doing everything for it. To the stories of successful persons, physiological analysis of memory, remembering activities were presented before them. It took two weeks to bring the experimental group on to the point. When it was seen that students asked anxiously for the teaching through the SLT method, which was shown to them on the first day of experiment, the researcher started the intervention programme. Therefore, it is said that three elements : (i) there must be desire to learn through SLT, (ii) strong belief on self and on SLT, (iii) readiness to accept the result of SLT—are necessary to make super learning popular (Passi and Prabhu, 1997). In this regard, it is necessary to create awareness among school personnel—teachers, administrators, students and parents—for effective use of SLT. Supportive environment, administrative support and adjustment of school time table and courses of study are desired for effectivity of super learning.

Thus after realizing that students have desired motivation, the researcher decided to start the intervention. The process or strategy of SLT were strategically used in the classroom. Simple relaxation exercises were practised sitting on the bench where they usually sit. Visualization was also practised in closed eyes and in meditational posture since they had created self-concept within themselves, it was needless to invest more time on that. So maximum time was laid on breathing exercises. In the second phase the topic prepared in condensed form was presented before them. Diagramatical and graphical presentation were made to facilitate the memorization of the content matters. Questions which can provoke divergent answers were put to them and they were trained to attend those accordingly. At remembering step the recorded matters were presented before the students. They were informed to listen those silently and in closed eyes.

Under this procedure the intervention lasted for two months. During those intervention classes tasks were given to students and those were collected from them in following classes. Gradually, learners started progressing and expressed their satisfaction over the method of teaching.

5.4 DATA COLLECTION

The data collection of the study was generally done in two phases. In first phase, it was collected before the experiment as pre-test data. The pre-test data were collected on creative thinking, intelligence and achievement in History. The intelligence and creative thinking tests were verbal group tests. So, those were administered on group basis. But the pre-test achievement scores were collected from the half-yearly examination result. Likewise after intervention programme, post-test data were collected on creative thinking and achievement on history. Verbal Group Test on Creative Thinking of Mehdi was administered for collection of data on creative thinking. Annual Examination marks in History was accepted as their achievement scores in history. All these data were collected both from control group and experimental group. During data collection and test administration, proper attention was given to time factor. No malpractice or proxy attendance was allowed. After distribution of tests teachers were requested to move around to check all types of malpractices. But matter of great satisfaction was that no such incident was noticed during administration of the test.

5.5 POST-EXPERIMENTAL ACTIVITY AND DATA COMPILATION

After the intervention programme, the results collected from pre-test and post-test stages were evaluated. Accordingly scores were awarded to the learners in their respective tests. At last, according to the sample a factror-wise scoring chart was framed. From the final data sheet it was revealed that from pre-test to post-test there was a great number of sampling mortality. Some were present in pre-test and were absent in post-test and *vice versa*. Some were present in all tests and absent in any one test, some learners were found in the extreme scores putting suspicion of result fluctuation. During compilation such samples were kept out of analysis. Thus, the final compilation of data gave the final sampling framework of the study and paved the way for scientific analysis of data through proper statistical procedure.

6 ANALYSIS AND INTERPRETATION

6.1 Analysis and Interpretation

6.1.1 Effect of Super Learning Technique (SLT) on Creative Thinking

6.1.2 Effect of SLT on Academic Achievement

6.1.3 Development of Creative Thinking and Level of Intelligence—An Impact Analysis of SLT

6.1.4 Development of Academic Achievement and Levels of Intelligence-Impact Analysis of SLT

6.1.5 Development of Creative Thinking and Academic Achievement—A Comparative Analysis

6.1.6 Development of Creative Thinking of Boys and Girls

6.1.7 Development of Academic Achievement of Boys and Girls

6.2 Findings of the Study

ANALYSIS AND INTERPRETATION

6.1. ANALYSIS AND INTERPRETATION

After collection of post-test data, the sampling frame of the study was finalized with due consideration of the samples affected by experimental mortality and deficiency in fulfilling allied characteristics. Thenafter, attention was given to analysis of data and interpretation of result thereof. The study had a number of hypotheses to verify the achievement of research objectives. All the hypotheses were stated in null form so that their testing would be feasible and the stated objectives will be analysed scientifically. The stated hypotheses intended to verify variety of relationships that exist between and among various variables. Accordingly, divergent statistical procedures—Scattergram correlation, Significance of Difference Between Means, 't' Test, One-way and two-way Analysis of Variance (ANOVA), etc., were followed to analyse the data and to verify the hypotheses of the study. The hypotheses were tested and the results were interpreted as follows:

6.1.1 Effect of Super Learning Technique (SLT) on Creative Thinking

The sole motive of the study was to know the effectiveness of Super Learning Technique (SLT). As per the study, the first objective was stated as "to find out the effect of Super Learning Technique (SLT) on development of creative thinking". To measure the objective, three null hypotheses were formed. These hypotheses entirely attempted to measure the differences in the creative thinking mean scores of experimental and control groups at various stages, such as, pre-test and post-test stages and also in their creative thinking gain scores. All the three sub-hypotheses were tested by the application of SE_D (Standard Error of Difference Between Means) and their significance were verified by finding out respective 't' values through the following formulae:

$$SE_D = \sqrt{\frac{\sigma_1^2}{N_1} + \frac{\sigma_2^2}{N_2}} \qquad \text{..................(Garrett, 1966)}$$

$$t = \frac{M_1 - M_2}{SE_D} \qquad \text{..................(Garrett, 1966)}$$

6.1.1 (a) Testing of First Sub-Hypothesis [$H_{01\ (a)}$]

The first sub-hypothesis of first hypothesis [$H_{01(a)}$] stated, "There was no significant difference between the experimental group and control group in their pre-test creative thinking scores."

Mehdi's verbal test on creative thinking was administered as pre-test measure of creative thinking of the sample. There were 96 students in total having 48 students each in control group and experimental group as sample of the study. The raw scores in creative thinking obtained from the sample at pre-test stage were analysed through calculation of SE_D and 't' value to verify the above stated hypothesis. Table 6.1 gives the data relating significance of difference between control group and experimental group in their mean creative thinking scores.

Table 6.1 showed no significant difference between the experimental and control groups in their pre-test creative thinking mean scores. A detailed analysis presented in the table showed that the difference was not significant in fluency

TABLE 6.1
Significance of Difference in Creative Thinking Mean Scores of Control Group and Experimental Group at Pre-test stage

Factors of Creative Thinking	*Group*	*N*	*M*	*SD*	*t*
	Control Group	48	52.0625	12.6925	
Fluency					0.5733 n.s.
	Experimental Group	48	50.6458	11. 4895	
	Control Group	48	29.3540	7.3415	
Flexibility					1.9288 n.s.
	Experimental Group	48	32.4792	8.4925	
	Control Group	48	12.7499	5.1537	
Originality					1.6327 n.s.
	Experimental Group	48	11.1875	4.1715	
	Control Group	48	93.00	21.937	
Total Creative Thinking					0.1823 n.s.
	Experimental Group	48	93.8333	22.852	

n.s. = not significant at 0.05 level (P>0.05).

(t=0.5733, P>0.05), flexibility (t=1.9288, P>0.05), originality (t=1.6327, P>0.05) and in total creative thinking mean scores (t=0.1823, P>0.05). Therefore, the sub-hypotheses which stated "no significant difference in creative thinking mean scores of control group and experimental group at pre-test stage" was rejected at 0.05 level of confidence. The result clarified that both the groups had equal creative thinking abilities at pre-test stage.

6.1.1 (b) Testing of Second Sub-Hypothesis [$H_{01(b)}$]

The second sub-hypothesis of the first hypothesis stated "There was no significant difference between the experimental group and control group in their post test creative thinking scores."

After the intervention programme, the creative thinking scores of the sample were obtained through administration of

Mehdi's verbal test on creative thinking. The obtained data were analysed by employing SE_D and 't' test. The creative thinking ability of the sample was analysed on different aspects of creative thinking such as fluency, flexibility and originality and also on total creative thinking ability. Table 6.2 showed the data relating significance of difference in post-test creative thinking scores of samples of control group and experimental group.

Table 6.2
Significance of Difference in Creative Thinking Mean Scores of Control Group and Experimental Group at Post-test stage

Factors of Creative Thinking	*Group*	*N*	*M*	*SD*	*t*
Fluency	Control Group	48	52.167	12.9435	7.2627**
	Experimental Group	48	79.583	22.726	
Flexibility	Control Group	48	28.9375	6.7435	12.7327**
	Experimental Group	48	59.1458	15.0430	
Originality	Control Group	48	20.375	5.2722	2.6100*
	Experimental Group	48	23.8125	7.4473	
Total Creative Thinking	Control Group	48	94.041	20.664	10.3910**
	Experimental Group	48	167.8749	44.6821	

* = Significant at 0.05 level (P<0.05), ** = significant at 0.01 level (P<0.01).

The analysed data presented in Table 6.2 showed that the calculated 't' values in fluency, flexibility and originality were found significant. The t value of fluency was 7.2627 (P<0.01) where as the 't' value of flexibility was 12.7327 (P<0.01) and of originality was 2.6100 (P<0.05). The 't' value of total creative thinking was 10.3910 (P<0.01). A detail analysis showed that in all the factors of creative thinking and in total creative thinking scores, the experimental group was at higher degree in post test mean creative thinking scores than the control group mean scores in creative thinking. In fluency, flexibility, originality and in total creative thinking, the control groups had 52.167, 28.9375, 20.375 and 94.041 as their respective mean scores whereas, the experimental group had 79.583, 59.1458, 23.8125 and 167.8749 as the repective mean scores. In SD scores also the experimental groups were at higher degree. All these showed that the experimental group which was at par with the control group at pre-test stage in the creative thinking, went up at post-test stage, was only because of the intervention programme. On this ground it can be asserted that the second sub-hypothesis of the first hypothesis of the study which stated that "there was no significant difference between the control group and experimental group in their post-test creative thinking mean scores" was rejected at 0.01 level of confidence. But for more scientific analysis the investigator had conducted the gain score analysis which is presented below

6.1.1 (c) Testing of Third Sub-Hypothesis [$H_{01(c)}$]

The third sub-hypothesis of the first hypothesis [$H_{01(c)}$] stated, "There was no significant difference between the experimental and control groups in their mean gain scores in creative thinking." Table 6.3 represented the data relating significance of difference in mean gain scores in creative thinking of control group and experimental group.

TABLE 6.3

Significance of Difference in Mean Gain Scores in Creative Thinking of Experimental and Control Groups

Group	*N*	*M*	*SD*	*t*
Control Group	48	0.8334	7.2725	
				16.3698**
Experimental Group	48	68.0416	27.4993	

** Significant at 0.01 level ($P < 0.01$).

Table 6.3 showed that there were 96 students in total having 48 each in control group and experimental group. Gain scores were obtained by subtracting post-test creative thinking scores from respective pre-test creative thinking scores. Significance of difference between means and 't' test were used to find out the difference in such gain scores in creative thinking of control group and experimental group. Analysis of data showed a significant difference between control group and experimental group in their creative thinking gain scores (t=16.3698, P<0.01). The experimental group showed a higher mean value (M=68.0416, SD=27.4993) than the control goup mean value in creative thinking gain scores (M=0.8334, SD = 27.25). It showed that the experimental group gained more in creative thinking scores than the control group. Hence, the sub-hypothesis which stated "no significant difference in mean gain scores in creative thinking of experimental and control groups" was refuted.

An overall analysis of the above three sub-hypotheses leads to the interpretation of first objective of the study which intended to know the effect of Super Learning Technique (SLT) on development of creative thinking. Data obtained from control group and experimental group at pre-test and post-test stages on various aspects of creative thinking was analyzed statistically. The experimental group and control group had almost equal total creative thinking scores at pre-test stage which was statistically stated as insignificant difference having 't' value 0.1823 (P>0.05). A vivid analysis into different aspects of creative thinking also gave a non-significant difference in fluency (t=0.5733, P>0.05), flexibility (t=1'9288, P>0.05) and originality (t=1.6327, P>0.05). But after the intervention programme, the post-test analysis of the creative thinking score showed a significant difference between the control group and experimental group. The difference was statistically significant in fluency (t=7.2627, P < 0.01), flexibility (12.7327, P<0.01) and in originality (t = 2.6100, P<0.05). In total creative thinking ability also the difference was significant (t=10.3910, P<0.01). In all these factors and in total creative thinking the experimental group was found at higher level in the post-test mean score in creative thinking. In fluency, flexibility and originally the respective mean scores of control group were 52.167, 28.9375 and 20.375 and the respective SD scores were 12.9435, 6.7435 and 5.2722. But in all those factors of creative thinking the mean scores of experimental group were 79.583, 59.1458 and 23.8125 and the respective SD scores were 22.726, 15.0430 and 7.4473. In respect of total creative thinking scores the experimental group was also at higher level (M=167.8749, SD=44.6821) than the control group (M=94.041, SD=20.664). All these data exemplified that the experimental goup has acquired a spectacular increment in the creative thinking score at post-test stage. To substantiate such post-test finding the mean gain scores in creative thinking of both the groups were also analysed by SE_D and 't' test. The result also gave a significant result (t = 16.3698, P<0.01) where the mean gain scores in creative thinking of experimental group was at higher level (M=68.0416, SD=27.4993) than the mean gain scores of control group (M=0.8334, SD=7.2725). Such result confirmed that the experimental group gained significantly more in creative thinking than the control group.

The above result showed that the experimental group which was almost equal to the control group in creative thinking scores at pre-test stage went upto a significant level at post-test stage. During the gap that existed between pre-test and post-test the students of control group were under as-usual teaching environment, whereas the students of experimental group were exposed to the new intervention programme, i.e., Super Learning Technique (SLT). Therefore, it was presumed that SLT was one and only factor which seemed to have created such difference in post-test creative thinking scores and also in creative thinking gain scores of the students of experimental group. Osborn's brainstorming (Osborn, 1957) when used by Fairness (1959 and 1961), Meadow (1962). Taylor and his associates (1958) and Torrance (1961) in different experimental situations was found to have exterted such significant effect on the experimental group. Similarly, Taylor's (1961) PAKSA (Pack Corp. Scientific Approach), Gordon's (1961) Synectics and Torrance's (1965) six stimulating principles were effective in developing creative thinking. Likewise, it was seen that Super Learning Technique (SLT) was very much effective in increasing the creative thinking of the students of experimental group. Studies of White (1982), Hoffman (1980), Lang (1984), Tomatis (2000) and Spino (2002) were in favour of such finding. Salter's (1980) self-observation on the positive impact of super learning also support the finding. Like the study of Kaha (1983) and

Venkatraman (1993) who studied the effect of "Synectics" on improving hemispheric functions of secondary school students and of Abrezol (1986) who found super learning much effective in developing human potential, here the SLT must have brought development to the synchronized function of whole brain and had become effective in increasing creative thinking.

The SLT programme was found effective not only in developing the total creative thinking scores but also in enhancing the scores in fluency, flexibility and originality. Such finding was also substantiated by the research findings of Curtis (1989), Jourdy (1984) and Ostrander and Schroeder (1997). Like this success of SLT, the research findings of Prasad (1979), who used discovery method; Golub and Hahn (1983) who used open class room situation; Hooda and Jarial (1983) who used role playing; Vora (1984) who experimented divergent thinking programme; Katiyar and Jarial (1985), who used verbal and non-verbal creativity development programme, were found effective in developing fluency, flexibility and originality of students. Prusty's (2004) CMTE (Creative Method of Teaching English) and Sahn's (1992) Brainstroming programme were also effective in developing total creative thinking alongwith significant incresement in fluency, flexibility and originality. Studies of Singh (1985), Nandanpower (1986), Patel (1987) and Amin (1988) were also of same finding. Like the electronic brainstorming (Siau, 1995) and use of media (Pnnusamy, 1980; Sharma, 1986), use of audio-aids, i.e., presentation of learning themes with superlearning music and visualisation and breathing alongwith music seemed effective in developing creative thinking of students (Adaman and Blaney, 1995). On the other hand, bio-feedback training, deep relaxation, sounds and images, meditation, etc. have been tried out as the effective approach of developing creative thinking (Passi, 1998). Likewise, relaxation, visualizaiton, breathing exercises and memorisaiton with music used by SLT programme have found effective in developing creative thinking of students (Jourdy, 1984; Curtis, 1989; Ostrander and Schroeder, 1997; Gulati, 2000). These findings support the result of the present study. Motamedi's (1982) seven passages of creative journey also includes affirmation, which is a step of SLT, for bringing mind to calm. Super Learning visualizaion which is, somehow and other, similar to imagination or imagery thoughts (Mc Ghee and Davis, 1994 ; Mehr and Shaver, 1996), was presumed to have influenced the post-test creative thinking scores of experimental subjects. When both control and experimental groups were matched on intelligence with no significant difference in their mean intelligence scores at pre-test stage, there was no chance of any extraordinary contribution of cognition on such meta-cognitive skill (Feldhusen, 1995). Rather, it was SLT which had effected such significant increase in creative thinking of experimental subjects. It was not that the ecology of the school, family and community became creativogenic with an immediate effect and that too for the experimental subjects only (Isaksen, Puccio and Treffinger, 1993; Davis, Kogan and Soliman, 1999) which had brought such significant increase in their post-test creative thinking scores.

From the above interpretation it is clear that there was no significant influence of ecological, behavioural and morphological factors on the development of creative thinking of the experimental subject. The only factor was Super Learning Technique (SLT) which was added to the educational environment as independent variable and produced such significant difference in favour of experimental group. Overall, it is confirmed that SLT as a method has the maximum potentiality of developing creative thinking.

6.1.2 Effect of SLT on Academic Achievement

Academic achievement or scholastic performance was another dependent variable of this research study. As per nature, academic achievement is related to memory, intelligence, sex, age, motivation and several other socio-individual characteristics. Like all other variables, relation of academic achievement with that of creative thinking has been studied by many researchers of the world. Researchers who established positive and significant relationship between these two variables also support the impact of higher creative potentials to produce higher academic success and *vice versa*. (Bentle, 1966; Gilchrist, 1970; Richardson, 1989; Carroll and Howicson, 1992; Srilatha and Srivastav, 1992). Contrastically, low and negetive relation between academic achievement and creative thinking is reported by Holland (1961), Flescher (1964),

Dewing (1970), Richardson (1989), and Toth and Baker (1990). Surprisingly, studies also showed no relation between these two variables (Torrance, 1970; Whitemore, 1980; Khatena, 1978; Dunn, 1983).

Under such controversial research findings when some researchers are trying replications, others are trying to verify such relationship in subject-specific conditions. Paramesh (1973) found that there was positive and significant relationship between creativity and student's achievement in English, Science and elective subjects respectively, whereas, no significant relationship was observed in other subjects. Joshi (1974) and Prusty (2003) found positive and significant relationship between creative thinking and achievement in English, but in case of other school subjects, a low and positive correlation was reported. Dhaliwal and Saini (1976) reported no relationship between creative thinking and achievement in mathematics but the dimensions of creativity, namely, fluency and flexibility were positively and significantly related with achievement in History and Geography separately.

Looking at such diverse relationship, researchers have also experimentally tried out various training strategies meant for developing creative thinking to see their impact on development of scholastic performance of students. Pillay (1978), Nair (1978), Shah (1981), Vora (1984), Telegaonkar (1984), Dey (1984), Rechardson (1989), Pradhan (1990), Snyman and Dekock (1991), Coleman (1992), Shan (1992), Carson and Carson (1993), Grossman and Wiseman (1993), Jampole (1993), Murdock, Isaksen and Lauer (1993), Wesenberg (1994), Mann (1994), Moon and Feldhusen (1994), Russel (1994), Adaman and Blaney (1995), Camp (1995), Klaner (1996), and Prusty (2004) through their various experimental studies, found a large number of creative methods such as—brainstorming, brain calming, mind control, Synectics, morphological analysis, bionics, value engineering, CPS, free association, scenario writing, imagery training, biofeedback training, deep relaxation, creative dreaming, sociodrama, psychodrama, etc.—significantly effective in developing student's academic performance alongwith development of creative thinking.

Under such circumstances, when the effect of Super Learning Technique (SLT) was experimentally studied in the

Indian context and history subject was taught through SLT, it was decided to test whether SLT is effective in developing academic performance of students in History subject. Accordingly, the objective was set "to find out the effect of SLT on students' achievement in History."

To verify the objective, three null hypotheses were formed relating pre-test scores, post-test scores and gain scores. Marks in History, obtained by the students of control group and experimental group in half yearly examination and annual examination were considered as pre-test and post-test achievement scores in History respectively. The questions prepared by OSSTA were administered in both,the tests. Verification of all the three sub-hypotheses were made as follows.

6.1.2 (a) Testing of First Sub-Hypothesis [$H_{02(a)}$]

The first sub-sypothesis of second hypothesis stated, "There was no significant difference between experimental group and control group in their pre-test mean achievement scores in History".

There were 96 students in total, having 48 each in control group and experimental group. Marks in history obtained by students in their half-yearly examination was considered as the pre-test achievement scores in history. The obtained data was analysed by application of SE_D and 't' test. The calculated data is presented below in Table 6.4.

TABLE 6.4
Significance of Difference in Mean Achievement Scores in History of Control Group and Experimental Group at Pre-test Stage

Group	*N*	*M*	*SD*	*t*
Control Group	48	32.7917	14.287	
				0.6398 n.s.
Experimental Group	48	34.875	17.4590	

n.s = not significant at 0.05 level (P>0.05).

Table 6.4 represented the data relating the significance of

difference in mean achievement scores in History of control group and experimental group at pre-test stage. The calculated data showed no significant difference between these two groups in their pre-test achievement scores in History (t=0.6398, P>0.05). It exemplified that on the ground of achievement scores in History both the groups were more or less same. Therefore, the sub-hypothesis [H_{02}(a)] which stated "no significant difference in mean achievement scores in History of control group and experimental group at pre-test stage" was retained at 0.05 level of confidence.

6.1.2 (b) Testing of Second Sub-Hypothesis [$H_{02(b)}$]

The second sub-hypothesis of the second hypothesis of the study stated, "There was no significant difference between the experimental and control groups in their post-test mean achievement scores in History".

To test the above hypothesis the marks in history acquired by the students in annual examination was accepted as post-test achievement scores in History. Those scores were obtained through administration of achievement question on history developed by OSSTA, Orissa. The collected data was analysed by application of SE_D and 't' test. Table 6.5 shows the significance of difference in post-test achievement scores of control group and experimental group.

TABLE 6.5
Significance of Difference in Mean Achievement Scores in History of Control Group and Experimental Group at Post-test Stage

Group	*N*	*M*	*SD*	*t*
Control Group	48	37.375	15.056	
				2.53*
Experimental Group	48	49.979	16.1615	

* Significant at 0.05 level (P<0.05).

Table 6.5 showed the data pertaining to significance of difference that existed in post-test mean achievement scores in history of students of control group and experimental group.

The calculated 't' value represented a significant difference (t=2.53, P<0.05) in post-test mean achievement scores in History of control group and experimental group. The mean score analysis showed that the achievement mean value of experimental group was at higher level (M= 49.979, SD=16.1615) than the control group (M=37.375, SD=15.056). Such finding confirms that it was the Super Learning Technique which created such difference in the mean achievement scores in favour of experimental group. Therefore, the hypothesis which stated "no significant difference between the experimental and control groups in their post-test mean achievement scores in History" was refuted at 0.05 level of confidence,

6.1.2 (c) Testing of Third Sub-Hypothesis [$H_{02(C)}$]

The third sub-hypothesis of the second hypothesis stated, "There was no significant difference between the experimental group and control group in their mean gain scores in achievement test in History".

The total sample was 96 having 48 students each in control group and experimental group. To get the gain scores in history of the students, the post-test scores in history obtained by students in their annual examination were subtracted from their respective pre-test scores in history, which were obtained from their half yearly examination marks. Then, the acquired gain scores of control group and experimental group were analysed by application of SE_D and 't' test. The calculated result is presented in Table 6.6.

TABLE 6.6
Significance of Difference in Mean Achievement Gain Scores in History of Control Group and Experimental Group

Group	*N*	*M*	*SD*	*t*
Control Group	48	9.1875	6.3562	
				3.3599**
Experimental Group	48	15.8125	12.0924	

** Significant at 0.01 level (P<0.01).

Table 6.6 showed the data relating significance of difference between the control group and experimental group in their mean achievement gain scores in history. The calculated data has given a significant difference in the mean gain scores in achievement of control group and experimental group (t=3.3599, P<0.01). Analysis of mean value also reported the higher level of experimental group (M=15.8125, SD=12.0924) over the control group (M= 9.1875, SD=6.3562) in mean and SD measures relating their achievement gain scores. Such findings made the fact confirmed that experimental group had gained significantly more than the control group in achievement in history. The result also made it sure that the Super Learning Teachnique (SLT) through which the experimental group was taught the history subject was more effective than the traditional method of teaching history in increasing achievement of students in concerned subject. Therefore, the third sub-hypothesis, which stated "no significant difference between experimental group and control group in their mean gain scores in achievement test in History" is rejected at 0.01 level of significance.

An overall analysis of all the three sub-hypotheses of second hypothesis determines the achievement of second objective of the study which wanted to find out the effect of Super Learning Technique on the achievement of students in History. Data obtained from the experiment was analysed in three phases—pre-test, post-test and gain score—to scientifically assertain whether SLT had some impact on achievement of students' in history. When pre-test analysis showed a non-significant result (t=0.6398, P>0.05), at that time, the post-test analysis had given significant difference (t=2.53, P<0.05). To see the scientificity of post-test result, when gain scores of achievement in history was analysed, the result was also found significant at 0.01 level (t=3.3599, P<0.01). Most specifically, the post-test and gain score analyses confirmed that the experimental group had a higher mean value in post-test (M=49.979, SD=16.1615) and also in gain score analysis (M=15.8125, SD=12.0924) than the mean values in post-test (M=37.375, SD=15.056) and gain scores (M=9.1875, SD=6.3562) of control group. Such higher gain of experimental group points at the successfulness of intervention programme, i.e., of Super

Learning Technique (SLT) in increasing achievement scores of students. From these analyses, it can be concluded that Super Learning Technique (SLT) has the potentiality of enhancing achievement of students in history.

The above finding of the study was supported by the Ostrander and Schroeder (1997), Ostrander (2002), Atkins (1992) and Fre (1992), who used different techniques of super learning in advancing learning. Robinson's (1998) report, that super learning makes learning 24% faster, found true here in this study when it was reported near about 12 point mean difference in post-test achievement scores in history of control group and experimental group. From the general view it was realized that learning History has created a phobia among the students. The students are treating the subject as load of information and it is very difficult to memorise all the dates, names and events. Now-a-days, it has been realised by the teachers and professors of history, that the student strength in history department of colleges and universities of Orissa and India has been decreasing day by day because of such subjectivity of this subject. In this regard the techniques of relaxation and mind calming which are practised by SLT seemed helpful for releasing tension from students' mind. Moreover, the process of memorisation with music and learning with rhythmic super learning music helped the learners in learning the themes easily and incorporating the presented themes in the memory (Hoffman, 2002; Tomatis, 2000). The sound therapy experiment of Jourdy (2002) also favours such finding like Prichard's (2000) study which showed that "superlearning (r) Mathematics" was effective in increasing the scores of secondary school students in geometry and trigonometry by overcoming the mathophobia from among the students. The SLT, here, was tried out and found successful in eliminating fear of learning history from students' mind and relaxing them for learning history more effectively. That is why, Ostrander and Schroeder (1979) reported that super learning not only produces super academic performance but also increases memory, remembering and recalling capacity which boost the academic performance.

At present, when cybernetic innovations and technological advancements have made the educational system post-modern, at that time, incorporation of super learning music of 60 beats and audio-visual teaching procedures in learning and remembring into SLT (Seki, 1983; lang, 1984) has revolutionised the present learning system in improving. the achievement of students. Moreover, SLT was proved to be most effective in developing scholastic achievement in social studies as it did in language (Wagner, 1984; Mahaney, 1989) and mathematics (Prichard, 2000).

On the other hand, scholastic achievement or academic performance is a variable which is variedly related to many other variables like intelligence, age, sex, motivation, maturation and creative thinking besides with that of teaching strategy (Passi, 1972; Bedi, 1974; Jarial, 1981; Tripathy, 1983; Kundu, 1984; Reddy, 1991; Kumari, 1992; Gautam, 1992; Srivastava and Srilatha, 1992; Jampole, Mathews and Konopak, 1994; Behera, 1995; Prusty, 1996; Sennelt and Ceci, 1996). But, the interpretation of experimental condition of present study exemplified that both the control group and experimental group were almost equal on the ground of age, sex, creative thinking and achievement at pre-test stage. On the ground of intelligence, both groups were matched with statistically insignificant difference. On these grounds there was no other variable than socio-economic standard and educational environment. As the experimental school was the school situated within the campus of Utkal University and 90% students were of university staff members and there were mixed group students in the sample, no such significant difference was expected among those students on SES and environmental condition. The only factor which was suspected to have exerted some impact on students' achievement was educational factor. Further, when control and experimental groups were almost equal in their pre-test achievement scores and control group was taught through that conventional method producing no significant difference in post-test achievement score and achievement gain score than the experimental group, which was taught through SLT, it was fully confirmed that whatever difference was seen in the achievement of experimental group was only because of the effect of intervention programme, i.e., Super Learning Technique.

From the above interpretation, it is crystal clear that the super learning technique (SLT) has maximum potentiality of increasing scholastic performance of students in History. It makes history learning stressfree and increases memorisation through use of audio-visual aids and other mind calming and memory processes. Therefore, the second objective of the study, which wanted to know the effect of SLT on academic achievement in history, was verified with positive result. In nutshell, the Super Learning Technique (SLT) was found effective in developing achievement of students in history.

6.1.3 Development of Creative Thinking and Level of Intelligence—An Impact Analysis

Every personality variable of the organism, in somehow or other, is related to other personality variables. Accordingly, from the scientific study of creative thinking with Guilford's morphological model of intelligence (1950) and relationship analysis between creative thinking and intelligence by Getzel and Jackson (1962) till now, the relation between these two variables remained as a point of great interest among investigators (Passi, 1998). Studies of Guilford and Christensen (1956), Yamamoto (1964), Soloman (1968), Massad (1969), Davis and Belcher (1971), Milgram (1984), Chadha and Chandna (1990), Freeman (1995), Runco and Nemiro (1995), Dey (1984), Mishra (1993), Prusty (2002) reported a low degree of positive correlation between intelligence and creative thinking with 'r' value ranging from 0.10 to 0.40 and with a median of 0.30, which, when shared as common variance becomes 9%. Researches of Khire (1971), Gupta (1972), Mehdi (1973, 1977, 1979), Menon (1980), Chadha and Sen (1981) and Pandey (1981), reported non-significant and negative relation between these two variables. Interpreters speak of "threshold IQ", beyond which creative thinking and intelligence become independent; school atmosphere and method of teaching which increases intelligence and creative thinking; different type of creative thinking and their varied measures which create difference in relation of creative thinking and intelligence.

Such conflicting findings put a question mark before the interdependence of creative thinking and intelligence. When Guilford (1956) treated creative thinking as divergent thinking and intelligence as convergent thinking, relating their relation, he also stated a low correlation. But Getzel and Jackson's (1962) analysis of "threshold point" spoke of the cutoff point in intelligence up to which intelligence and creative thinking ware found to be passively related. That means upto that level a certain amount of intelligence is mostly required for a person to be creative (Anderson, 1960; Roe, 1960; Torrance and Associates, 1962). After that point both the variables seemed independent of each other. That means though there exists a high positive correlation between them, it can not be always seen that the highly creatives will be highly intelligent. Torrance (1962) accept this point arround 120 1Q beyond which the influence of intelligence decreases and the creative thinking factors becomes discriminatory. Such findings were substantiated more by the researches of Boersma and O' Bryan (1968), Comeron (1968), Soloman (1968), Masad (1969), Bruiniks and Feldman (1970), Weinstein and Bobko (1980) and Freeman (1995) those find negligible and no correlation between these two variables. Torrance's (1984) finding that only 30% students are intellectually and creatively gifted and Hall's (1985) finding of a little relationship between high creative and high IQ support the above finding. Still, Studies of Mc Cabe (1991), Mumford, Connelly, Baughman and Marks (1995) and Prusty (2003) found that high intelligence has high, positive and significant relation with high creative thinking. When some of the researchers point to the use of varied intelligence and creative thinking tests (Mille and Merrifield, 1962; Mc Nemar, 1964; Passi, 1998), others also suspect the influence of academic and environmental conditions or socio-cultural factors in bringing such difference between intelligence and creative thinking (Passi, 1998).

Under such circumstances, when a new method is thought of being applied to know the extent to which that works in bringing development in creative thinking keeping pace with intelligence, it becomes inperative to know the inter-variable influence and effect of the new method thereof. On the other hand, being the important personality and academic determinant, intelligence and creative thinking seen to have exerted some solid influence on any sort of method of teaching. Therefore, in the present study, when Super Learning Technique (SLT) was decided to be experimented as an independent variable, it was also decided to study the effect of SLT on development of creative thinking in relation to level of intelligence. So, accordingly, the third objective of the study intended to find out the relationship that existed between intelligence and development of creative thinking as an effect of Super Learning Technique (SLT).

In order to verify the above stated objective, the study had formulated three null hypotheses to test the significance of difference in creative thinking scores of high and low intelligence group of control group and experimental group at pre-test, post-test and also in gain score analyses as follows.

6.1.3 (a) Testing of First Sub-Hypothesis [$H_{03(a)}$]

The first sub-hypothesis of third hypothesis [$H_{03(a)}$] stated, "There was no significant difference in pre-test creative thinking mean scores of high intelligence group and low intelligence group of (1) control group and (2) experimental group." Two-way Analysis of Variance (2 × 2 ANOVA) was used to test the significance of the hypothesis.

Mehdi's Verbal Test of Creative Thinking and Tondon's Group Test of Intelligence (Verbal, 2/70) were used for obtaining scores in creative thinking and intelligence respectively. The total number of sample was 96. As the sample was small in number, it was seen that after finding out low and high intelligence groups the number of samples would be more smaller for application of parametric statistics. So it was decided to apply raw-score formula of finding out median of the data to divide the sample into high and low intelligence groups. During calculation of median, the sample which carried the median value was eliminated from the sample. After such calculation it was found that each group had 22 number of students (n = 22). Accordingly high intelligence group and low intelligence group were found from both control and experimental group. In total, four groups were formed as follows:

- High-Intelligence Control Group
- High-Intelligence Experimental Group
- Low-Intelligence Control Group
- Low-Intelligence Experimental Group

Equal cell method of 2 × 2 ANOVA was used for analysis

of data. There were 22 subjects in each cell (n = 22) and the total number of subject was 88 (n = 88). For such equalization some subjects were randomly eliminated. This procedure was same for all the three sub-hypotheses, of this third hypothesis.

As per the requirement of the first sub-hypothesis stated above, the pre-test creative thinking scores of high intelligence and low-intelligence groups of control group and experimental group were entered into the respective cells. Then the Raw Score Method was applied to find out 'F' ratio through two-way Analysis of Variance and to test the significance of the sub-hypothesis. Table 6.7 gives the data relating summary of 2 × 2 ANOVA on pre-test creative thinking mean scores of high-intelligence group and low-intelligence group of control and experimental groups.

TABLE 6.7

Summary of 2 × 2 ANOVA on Pre-test Creative Thinking Mean Scores of High-Intelligence and Low-Intelligence Groups of Control Group and Experimental Group

Source	*df*	*SSv*	*MSv*	*F*
Level of Intelligence	1	1746.18	1746.18	3.7042 n.s.
Group	1	0.72	0.72	0.0015 n.s.
Interaction	1	2383.69	2382.69	5. 0566*
Within	84	39597.73	471.4015	

n.s. = not significant * significant at 0.05 level.

Table 6.7 represented the data relating to summary of ANOVA on pre-test creative thinking scores of students belonging to different levels of intelligence of control group and experimental group. The result showed a non-significant effect of level of intelligence on the creative thinking scores of control and experimental groups ($F = 3.7042$, $df = 1$, $p < 0.05$). The impact of control group and experimental group was not found significant on creative thinking of students ($F = 0.0015$, $df = 1$, $p > 0.05$). But the interaction effect was found significant at 0.05 level of significance ($F = 5.0566$, $df = 1$, $P < 0.05$). It showed that there exist an interaction effect of different levels of intelligence and different groups in their creative thinking scores. As it is the analysis of pre-test result with relation to levels of intelligence and groups, further analysis was not undertaken with a view to see the variance at post-test and gain score analyses in the following hypotheses. Overall, it was confirmed that, at pre-test stage there was no difference in the creative thinking scores on the ground of control group-experimental group difference and also on the low-high intelligence levels.

6.1.3 (b) Testing of Second Sub-Hypothesis [$H_{03\ (b)}$]

The second sub-hypothesis of third hypothesis ($H_{03\ (b)}$] conjectured, "There was no significant difference in post-test creative thinking mean scores of high intelligence group and low intelligence group of (i) control group, and (ii) experimental group".

Two-way Analysis of Variance (2 × 2 AVOVA) was used as the means of verifying the sub-hypothesis. The same procedure that was followed in finding out different groups of students—low intelligence control group, low intelligence experimental group, high-intelligence control group and high-intelligence experimental group—for first sub-hypothesis, was also followed here in forming same groups for second sub-hypothesis. Accordingly, the post-test creative thinking scores of high intelligence group and low intelligence group of control group and experimental group were entered into the respective cells. Thenafter, the raw score method was applied to findout the F ratio and for testing the second sub-hypothesis. Table 6.8 gives the data relating summary of 2 × 2 ANOVA on Post-test creative thinking scores of high intelligence and low intelligence groups of control and experimental groups.

Table 6.8 showed the data relating summary of ANOVA on post-test mean creative thinking scores of different levels of intelligence (high and low) and of groups (control and experimental). The calculated data showed that the level of intelligence had exerted no significant effect on the creative thinking of students (F = 2.49, df = 1, $p \geq 0.05$). But the main effect of groups was found significant (F = 10.3808, df = 1, $p < 0.01$). A look into the mean creative thinking scores of different groups showed that in total mean creative thinking value, the control group was (M = 91.6363) very much lower than the mean creative thinking value of experimental group

TABLE 6.8
Summary of 2 × 2 ANOVA of Post-test Creative Thinking Mean Scores of High-Intelligence and Low-Intelligence Groups of Control and Experimental Groups

Source	*df*	*SSv*	*MSv*	*F*
Level of Intelligence	1	2542.84	2542.84	2.49 n.s.
Group	1	106116.24	106116.24	10.3808 **
Interaction	1	863.46	863.46	0.8446 n.s.
Within	84	85871.66	1022.2816	

n.s. = not significant ** significant at 0.01 (P> 0.01).

(M = 161.0909). Such supremacy of experimental group was also seen in the mean creative thinking scores of high-intelligence experimental group (M = 163.3636) and low intelligence experimental group (M = 158.818) over mean creative thinking value of high-intelligence control group (M = 100/363) and low intelligince control group (M = 83.1363). Such results confirmed that the experimental group had gained more than the control group from Super Learning Technique (SLT) in developing the creative thinking scores. Further, an in-depth analysis of the performance of high and low intelligence groups of experimental group relating development of creative thinking showed that though "F" ratio had not shown any significant difference in development of creative thinking on the ground of level of intelligence, the mean score analysis had put high-intelligence group at higher level than the low-intelligence group. Such finding was substantiated by the significant difference depicted in second sub-hypothesis of first hypothesis ($H_{01(b)}$] with 't' value of 10.3910 for composite creative thinking in favour of experimental group (M = 167.8749, SD = 44.682) putting control group at lower level (M = 94.041, SD = 20.664). Therefore, the sub-hypothesis which stated "no significant difference in post-test creative thinking mean scores of high-intelligence group and low-intelligence group of (i) control group, and (ii) experimental group" was rejected at 0.01 level of significance.

6.1.3 (c) Testing of Third Sub-Hypothesis [$H_{03(c)}$]

The third sub-hypothesis of the third hypothesis stated, "There was no significant difference in the gain scores in creative thinking of high-intelligence group and low-intelligence group of—(i) Control group, and (ii) Experimental group".

The above-stated hypothesis was tested by 2 × 2 ANOVA. After finding out the high-intelligence, low-intelligence groups of control and experimental groups their creative thinking gain scores were entered into respective cells. The raw score method was applied to find out "F" ratio to test the hypothesis. Table 6.9 represents the data relating summary of 2 × 2 ANOVA on creative thinking gain scores of high intelligence and low-intelligence groups of control group and experimental group.

Table 6.9
Summary of 2 × 2 ANOVA on Creative Thinking Gain Scores of High-Intelligence Group and Low Intelligence Group of Control and Experimental Groups

Source	*df*	*SSv*	*MSv*	*F*
Level of Intelligence	1	76.41	76.41	3.29 n. s.
Group	1	107800.00	107800.00	46.45**
Interaction	1	20.05	20.05	0.86 n.s.
Within	84	19949.64	23.21	

n.s. = not significant ** = significant at 0.01 level.

The data presented in Table 6.9 showed no significant effect of different levels of intelligence on the development of creative thinking ($F = 3.29$, $df = 1$, $p > 0.05$). But there was significant effect of groups on the development of creative thinking of students ($F = 46.45$, $df = 1$, $p < 0.01$). The analysis of mean gain scores in creative thinking showed that the experimental group was at higher level ($M = 70.68118$) than the control group ($M = 0.6818$). The result confirmed that the experimental group had gained more in creative thinking measures than control group and that was only because of the impact of Super Learning Technique (SLT). But the interaction effect was not found significant ($F = 0.86$, $df = 1$, $p > 0.05$). Such data reported equal effectiveness of SLT for low-intelligence and high-intelligence group in respect of increasing creative thinking.

An overall analysis of all the three sub hypotheses of the third hypothesis showed a clear picture of impact of super learning technique on development of creative thinking. The hypothesis also tried to establish the link between level of intelligence and development of creative thinking as a result of Super Learning Technique (SLT). The analyzed data showed that level of intelligence had not exerted any significant impact either in pre-test stage ($F= 3.7042$, $df = 1$, $p > 0.05$) or in post-test stage ($F = 2.49$, $df = 1$, $p > 0.05$) or in gain score analysis ($F = 3.29$, $df = 1$, $p > 0.05$) on the creative thinking scores of the samples. Such result confirmed that, Super Learning Technique (SLT) was proved equally beneficial both for low-intelligence and high-intelligence groups. In fact, level of intelligence has no impact on SLT in determining the creative thinking of students. In this regard, the positive and significant relation between creative thinking and intelligence as reported by Yamamoto (1964), Soloman (1968), Massad (1969), Milgram (1984), Chadha and Chandna (1990), Mishra (1993) and Prusty (2002) had not exerted any influence on the Super Learning Technique in excelling scores in creative thinking. On the other hand, the low correlation between these two variables as reported by Bruiniks and Feldman (1970), Weinstein and Bobko (1980), Torrance (1984), Freeman (1995) could not be a problem for low-intelligence group to acquire an equal amount of creative thinking scores with high intelligence group from SLT teaching strategy.

On the ground of group factor, the calculated 'F' value was always significant, except pre-test stage. At post-test stage the F value was 103.80 ($df = 1$, $p < 0.01$) and at gain score, the 'F' value was 46.45 ($df =1$, $p < 0.01$). At each stage of significant difference the experimental group was at higher level than control group in their creative thinking mean scores. At post-test stage, the mean value in creative thinking of experimental group was higher ($M = 161.0909$) than control group ($M = 91.6363$). In gain score in creative thinking also the experimental group (was also at higher level ($M = 70.6818$) than the control group ($M = 0.6818$). Such finding were also substantiated by the significant 't' value in the composite creative thinking scores of control and experimental groups at post-test stage ($t = 10.3910$, $p < 0.01$), as calculated in second sub-hypothesis of first hypothesis [$H_{01(b)}$]. In that situation also, experimental group had scored higher mean value (M = 167.8749) than the control group (M = 94.664). From all those analyses it was confirmed that Super Learning Technique (SLT) was proved highly beneficial in increasing creative thinking of students. The control group, which was taught through traditional method could not exert much more significant result as was done by SLT for experimental group. Thus, it can be concluded that SLT was proved as a sucessfull teaching strategy to develop creative thinking being equally effective for high and low-intelligence groups.

On the above ground, the third objective, which wanted to study the effect of SLT on development of creative thinking in relation to levels of intelligence was confirmed that, SLT increased creative thinking without being influenced by the levels of intelligence. The finding was corroborated in the findings of researches conducted by Lozanov (1979), Ostrander and Schroeder (1995), Jourdy (2000), Mahaney (1989), Adaman and Blancy (1995). Studies other than experiment of Super Learning Technique (SLT) conducted by Stasinos (1986), Torrance and Safter (1986), Patel (1987), Burns (1988), Buyer (1988), Joseph (1988), Ekuvall and Parnes (1989), Chislett (1995), Klauer (1996), Greer and Levine (1991), Coleman (1992), Prusty (2004) support the finding which went in favour of SLT.

6.1.4 Development of Academic Achievement and Levels of Intelligence—Impact Analysis of SLT

Relationship of academic achievement with that of intelligence is automatic and substantial. Though academic activities intend to bring up cognitive, affective and psychomotor abilities (Bloom, 1956; Karthawal, Bloom and Masia, 1964), in turn, such cognitive ability of the learner determines the extent of academic achievement. Intelligence refers to the capacity of reasoning, judging and drawing conclusion. It is the function of cerebral hemisphere preferably, the activity of left hemispheres (Rosen, Padilla and Hynd, 1984).

Researches reporting high, positive and significant correlation between intelligence and achievement are more than the studies reporting low correlation between these two variables. Cognitive field theory of Lewin, Cognitive thoery of Piaget and Morphological Analysis of Intelligence by Guilford have clearly stated the significance of intellectual growth and its impact on students' achievement. Binet, who pioneered the study and measurement of intelligence also tried to find out the relationship that exists between achievement and intelligence. The maximum number of studies report that high intelligence is the determining factor of better academic performance. When a person lacks intelligence he/she is called as idiot morone. As is seen in the case of retarded subjects, they fail to perform their own works because they lacked the due amount of intelligence.

Studies of Suri (1989), Garg (1988), Ramchandrachar (1989), Kumari (1986), Panda (1991), Mohanty (1991), Kumar, Dwivedi and Malik (2003) show a positive impact of intelligence on academic achievement of students. Guilford's structure of intellect (1957), Piaget's cognitive theory and Lewin's cognitive principles (Woolman, 1989) support such finding (Yadav, 1991). Still, there are studies which do not support the relationship. But it is clearly realised by every conscious person that there exist an interrelation between intelligence and achievement. Achievement of student is regulated by their intelligence. Therefore, the children, those have a low IQ, say below 30 or 20, are called as idiots or morone (Binet, 1934). The slow learners posses quite a below average IQ and the gifted those have IQ of 140 and above have excelled in their academic performance (Vyas, 1992).

Under such circumstances, it was asserted that as the perception, achievement motivation, analysis capacity, understanding and comprehension ability overall the mental function of intelligent students seem higher, It is so expected that they would be successful in performing any activity. On that consideration, it was conjectured that the intelligence of students could have benefited them in reaping success from super learning programme. Form the research studies of Yeng and Ying (1982), Master, Khatina and Praper (1988), Khatina and Torrance (1973), Brittain (1985), Katz (1985), Jausovei (1985), Hoppe (1988), Loye (1988), Suri (1990) it was clear that the left hemisphere of the individual's brain is endowed with intellectual abilities. But all these talents when get combined with the activities of right hemisphere activities, the creative talent get excelled. Such finding goes with the findings of Getzel and Jackson (1962), Torrance (1964) and of many others. But it is crystal clear that if such right-left hemispheric activities will be utilized in academic activities, the performance would be spectacular one. That was analysed when Guilford (1950) conceptualized creative thinking as divergent thinking and intelligence as convergent thinking and gave the concept of "threshold IQ" relating their interrelation. While analysing the concept of giftedness and creative talents and their relation with that of academic achievement Getzel and Jackson (1962) found the high IQ students at higher level in academic achievement than creative performance. Such result is also supported by Behera (1992), Pradhan (1994), Prusty (1996) and Mishra and Mishra (2002). It is because of the cut-off level relation between creative thinking and intelligence.

However, when Super Learning Technique (SLT) was used as a means of achieving super learning, an analysis is needed to know the effectiveness of SLT on development of achievement scores basing on the level of intelligence of the students. Therefore, the study had formulated three sub-hypothesis to study the effect at pre-test, post-test and in gain score analyses of required data. The analyses were presented below.

6.1.4 (a) Testing of First Sub-hypothesis [$H_{04\ (a)}$]

The first sub-hypothesis of the fourth hypothesis [$H_{04\ (a)}$] stated, "There was no significant difference in pre-test achievement mean scores in history of high-intelligence and low intelligence groups of: (i) experimental group, and (ii) control group".

Marks is History obtained by students in half yearly examination was considered as pre-test achievement score in history. On the other hand, scores obtained from Tondon's Group Verbal Test on Intelligence was accepted as intelligence score of the sample. Taking the intelligence scores of all the students, median was calculated and taking the median score of intelligence (Mdn = 39) the high intelligence groups and low intelligence groups were formed in control group and experimental group separately. In total, four groups—high-intelligence control group low-intelligence control group, high-intelligence experimental group and low intelligence experimental group—were found. Then the achievement mean scores of the samples of respective groups were found and data was analysed by application of Two-way ANOVA. Table 6.10 showed the data relating significance of difference in pre-test mean achievement scores in history of high intelligence and low intelligence groups.

TABLE 6.10
Summary of 2 × 2 ANOVA on Pre-test Mean Achievement Scores in History of High intelligence and Low-Intelligence Groups of Control and Experimental Groups

Source	*df*	*SSv*	*MSv*	*F*
Level of Intelligence	1	4118.23	4118.23	19.5377**
Group	1	1207.68	1207.68	5.7295*
Interaction	1	443.1827	443.1827	2.1025 n.s.
Within	84	17705.868	210.7841	

** = Significant at 0.01 level (p < 0.01), * = Significant at 0.05 level (p < 0.05), n.s. = not significant.

Table 6.10 represent the data relating significance of difference in achievement mean scores in history of high-intelligence group and low-intelligence group of control and experimental group at pre-test stage. The calculated result presented a significant 'F' value showing difference in level of intelligence relating pre-test achievement mean scores. It confirmed that at pre-test stage, level of intelligence had played a significant role in bringing difference in achievement scores of students ($F = 19.5377$, $df = 1$, $p < 0.01$). On the other hand, group effect was found significant at 0.05 level ($F = 5.7295$, $df = 1$, $p < 0.05$). But the interaction effect was not significant. An analysis of the mean score showed that high-intelligence group of both control group ($M = 50.1364$) and of experimental group ($M = 39.5$) had higher mean achievement value than the low-intelligence group of control group ($M = 33.2273$) and of experimental group ($M = 28.8181$). But since the high-intelligence group of control group and experimental group were at higher level, the combined group effect was found significant at 0.05 level. Further, a comparison of the achievement mean value of control and experimental groups showed a higher mean value of control group (M = 41.6818) than the experimental group (M = 34.1590). It signifies the predominance of control group over experimental group in pre-test mean achievement scores.

6.1.4(b) Testing of Second Sub-Hypothesis [$H_{04(b)}$]

The second sub-hypothesis of fourth hypothesis [$H_{04(b)}$] stated, "There was no significant difference in post-test achievement mean scores in history of high-intelligence and low-intelligence groups of—(i) control group and (ii) experimental group".

The total sample was 88 with 44 each in control and experimental groups. Both the high and low intelligence groups had their equal representation of 22 samples in both the groups. Therefore, like $H_{04\,(a)}$, this hypothesis had four sub-groups for analysis. The annual examination marks in history was considered as post-test achievement score in history and that mark was obtained relating samples of various groups. The obtained data was analysed by application of two-way ANOVA (2 × 2 ANOVA). The calculated result is presented in Table 6.11.

TABLE 6.11

Summary of 2 × 2 ANOVA on Post-test Mean Achievement Scores in History of High-Intelligence and Low-Intelligence Groups of Control Group and Experimental Group

Source	*df*	*SSv*	*MSv*	*F*
Level of Intelligence	1	3167.97	3167.97	34.8497**
Group	1	4596.54	4596.54	50.5649**
Interaction	1	192.08	192.08	2.1130n.s.
Within	84	8139.91	90.9037	

** = Significant at 0.01 level (P<0.01), n.s. = not significant.

Table 6.11 showed the 'F' values relating significance in post-test mean achievement scores in History of high-Intelligence group and low-Intelligence group of control group and experimental group. The result showed significant impact of level of intelligence on the post-test achievement scores of students with a significant 'F' value (F = 34.8497, df = 1, P >0.01). The impact of group was also found significant (F = 50.5649, df = 1, p > 0.01). But the interactions effect was not significant. The significant difference that was reported relating levels of intelligence was studied on the ground of the mean values of different levels of intelligence. The mean value of high-intelligence group of control group (M = 44.5) was higher than the mean value of low-intelligence group of control group (M = 29.5454). On the other hand, the high-intelligence group of Experimental group was also at higher level in mean value (M = 56.00) than the mean values of low intelligence group (M = 46.9545). This result showed that the high-intelligence groups of both the groups scored more in their post-test mean achievement scores. Therefore, it was confirmed that high intelligence had benefitted the students more in achieving greater achievement score in history as a result of Super Learning Technique (SLT). It was also seen that the group effect was also reported as significant with higher mean achievement score of experimental group (M = 51.4772) over the control group mean achievement scores (M = 37.0227). Such finding confirmed that the experimental group had achieved such higher significant achievement scores in history only due to the effect of SLT.

But since both the pre-test and post-test results showed significant 'F' values of levels of intelligence and groups, it was not clear whether those significant differences were due to the effect of SLT or because of pre-test stage carry over impact. To confirm such influence, the gain score in achievement in history of experimental group only was analysed through the following hypothesis.

6.1.4 (c) Testing of Third Sub-Hypothesis [$H_{04\ (c)}$]

The third sub-hypothesis of the fourth hypothesis ($H_{04\ (c)}$] stated, "There was no significant difference in mean achievement gain scores of high-intelligence and low intelligence groups of experimental group".

Though there were 48 subjects in experimental group from the beginning of the study, in the process of finding out the high-low intelligence groups some samples were kept out of the analysis of this hypothesis either for equalization of the groups or for the median value acquired by the subjects. However, in the analysis of this sub-hypothesis [$H_{04(c)}$] the total sample of the experimental group was 44 having 22 samples each in high-intelligence and low-intelligence groups. The median was calculated to determine the score of difference between high and low intelligence groups. The gain score in achievement of history was calculated by subtracting the post-test achievement score in history from pre-test achievement score in history. The half yearly examination marks in history was treated as pre-test achievement score whereas the annual examination marks in history was considered as the post-test achievement marks in history. The obtained data was analysed by application of One-way Analysis of Variance (One-way ANOVA). The analysed data is presented in Table 6.12.

TABLE 6.12
Summary of One-way ANOVA on Mean Achievement Gain Scores in History of High-Intelligence Group and Low-Intelligence Group of Experimental Group

Source	*df*	*SSv*	*MSv*	*F*
Between	1	134.75	134.75	3.7604 n.s.
Within	42	1505.682	35.833	

n.s.= not significant at 0.05 level.

Table 6.12 showed the data relating mean achievement gain scores in history of high intelligence and low-intelligence groups of experimental group. The analysed data showed a non-significant 'F' ratio (F = 3.7604, df = 1, p >.0.05) which confirmed that level of intelligence had not produced any significant difference in achievement gain scores of experimental group. It had been proved by second hypothesis of study [$H_{02\ (a)}$, $H_{02\ (b)}$ and $H_{02\ (c)}$] that experimental group had benefitted more in gaining better achievement scores (at post-test and gain score results) than the control group. But the analysis of third sub-hypothesis of fourth hypothesis [$H_{04\ (c)}$] in contrast to the first and second sub-hypothesis of fourth hypothesis [$H_{04\ (a)}$ and $H_{04\ (b)}$] showed that Super Learning

Technique (SLT), though was proved effective in developing achievement scores of students, was not affected by levels of intelligence. It was reported that both high intelligence and low-intelligence groups were equally benefitted from SLT. From the finding it was confirmed that the post-test analysis of mean achievement test scores of high and low intelligence groups was found effective, only because of their pre-test differences which was very much high.

An overall analysis shows that the analysis reported by the studies conducted by Ostrander and Schroeder (1979, 1995 & 1997), Mahaney (1989), Jorudy (2000), Curtis (1984) and Lang (1986) also found the same result. However, it was seen that though SLT had not found any significant effect of level of intelligence on development of academic achievement of students, the technique accepts that some amount of intelligence had became a necessary factor of developing academic excellence through SLT. In many studies, it was also seen that SLT had increased IQ of students to 10 to 15 points (Atkins, 1992, Fre, 1992). In this regard, it was asserted that SLT was very fruitful in developing achievement but the levels of intelligence had not influenced the result significantly. Therefore, it was concluded that SLT was found equally effective for high and low intelligence groups in developing their academic achievement in History.

6.1.5 Development of Creative Thinking and Academic Achievement—A Comparative Analysis

From the analysis of above stated four hypothesis (from H_{01} to H_{04}), it was clear that Super Learning Technique (SLT) was very much effective in developing the creative thinking and academic achievement of students of secondary level. But here attempt was made to analyse the rate of development of these two variables as an impact of Super Learning Technique (SLT).

The positive and significant relationship that existed between creative thinking and academic achievement was reported by Torrance (1959), Bentley (1966), Carey (1966), Mayhon (1966), Gilchrist (1970), Rechardson (1989), Mc Cabe (1991), Carroll and Howieson (1992), Bewa and Pandy (1992), Kour (1992), Hota (1993), Padhi (1995) and Prusty (2002). Inspite of the non-significant relationship that was reported by Holland (1961), Pathak (1962), Flescher (1963), Jacobson (1966), Dewing (1970), Paramesh (1973), Sharma (1981), Dey (1984), Chadha and Chandana (1990), Toth and Baker (1990), Freeman (1995) and Kapoor (1996), these two attributes seemed influensive on each other. It was also revealed that, the person who had creative thinking ability had also done better in academic achievement. There was differences relating type of creative thinking, such as, artistic creativity, mathematical creativity, scientific creativity, technical creativity (Sharma, 2000). It is also reported that some creative thinking packages have brought development of a specific type of creative thinking (Passi, 1998). Some studies showed that specific method has proved effective in developing either fluency, flexibility, originality and elaboration altogether or in any specific factor. Prusty (2004) reported a moderate, positive and significant relationship between creative thinking and achievement ($r = + 0.4959$, $t = 6.1849$, $p < 0.01$). The Creative Method of Teaching English (CMTE), developed and experimented by Prusty (1999), was reported to be effective in developing creative thinking and academic achievement of students. The study reported positive and significant relation between development of creative thinking and academic achievement ($r = + 0.5332$, $t = 9.1675$, $p < 0.01$). In the analysis of creative thinking gain scores and achievement gain scores. Such findings were supported by hemispheric synchronisation or left-right brain combination as reportest by Yeng and Ying (1982), Master, Joe and Paper (1988), Brittain (1985), Katz (1985), Jousovei (1985), Loye (1988), Hoppe and Kyle (1987) and Suri (1990). But these personality variables influence the achievement of students in great extent. In day-to-day observations, it was seen that the highly creative persons have achieved everything in their life including academic excellence.

In this study, attempt was made to know the relationship that was existing between rate of change in achievement and in creative thinking as an impact of Super Learning Technique (SLT). To test this objective there, hypotheses formulated in the study were related to the analysis of gain scores in creative thinking and academic achievement. Before knowing the rate of increment in creative thinking and achievement of students it was imperative to know their interrelationship. So the first two sub-hypothesis dealt with their relationship and the third one was on their rate of increment.

6.1.5 (a) Testing of First Sub-Hypothesis [$H_{05\ (a)}$]

The first sub-hypothesis of the fifth hypothesis of the study stated, "There was no significant difference in mean creative thinking gain scores of high-achievers and low-achievers in history achievement test scores of the experimental group."

Taking median value of achievement as the point of difference, high-achievement and low-achievement groups were formed. The creative thinking gain scores were obtained and placed for analysis. The data was analysed by application of one-way ANOVA. There were two groups of samples—high-achievement group and low-achievement group. Each group had 22 subjects taking the total sample strength to 44. The analysed data was presented in Table 6.13.

TABLE 6.13

Summary of One-way ANOVA Relating Significance of Difference in Mean Creative Thinking Gain Scores of High-Achievers and Low-Achievers of Experimental Group

Source	*df*	*SSv*	*MSv*	*F*
Between	1	141.84	141.84	0.1976 n. s.
Within	42	30152.92	717.9276	

n. s. = not significant at 0.05 level.

Table 6.13 showed significance of mean creative thinking gain scores of high achievers and low-achievers of experimental group in history achievement test scores. The analysed data showed a non-significant 'F' value ($F = 0.1976$, $df = 1$, $p > 0.05$), which confirmed that level of achievement had not influenced the creative thinking of students. Both high and low achievers had scored almost equal scores in creative thinking gain scores.

6.1.5 (b) Testing of Second Sub-Hypothesis [$H_{05(b)}$]

The second sub-hypothesis of fifth hypothesis [$H_{05(b)}$]

stated, "There was no significant difference in mean achievement gain scores of high-creative group and low-creative groups of experimental group.

To test the above sub-hypothesis, the high creative and low creative groups were formed by finding out median value of overall creative thinking scores. In total, there were 44 subjects in both the groups with 22 subjects in each group. Their mean achievement gain scores were obtained by subtracting the post-test achievement scores from pre-test achievement scores. The scores were plotted in two groups such as high creative and low-creative groups. The obtained data was analysed by application of One-way ANOVA. Table 6.14 presented the data relating the significance of difference in mean achievement gain scores of high-creative group and low-creative groups of experimental group.

TABLE 6.14
Summary of One-way ANOVA on Significance of Difference in Mean Achievement Gain Scores of High Creative and Low Creative Groups of Experimental Group

Source	*df*	*SSv*	*MSv*	*F*
Between	1	29.454	29.454	0.9727 n. s.
Within	42	1271.728	30.2792	

n.s. = not significant at 0.05 level.

Table 6.14 showed the data relating significance of difference in mean achievement gain score of high-creative and low-creative groups of experimental group. The calculated data showed a non-significant 'F' value (F = 0.9727, df = 1, p > 0.05), which represented the equal achievement gain scores of high-creative and low-creative groups. It clearly showed that levels of creative thinking was not a factor to influence students' achievement in history. Therefore, the hypothesis which stated "no significant difference in mean achievement gain scores in history of high-creative and low creative groups of experimental group" was retained at 0.05 level of significance.

6.1.5 (c) Testing of Third Sub-Hypothesis [$H_{05(c)}$]

The third sub-hypothesis of fifth hypothesis [$H_{05(c)}$] stated, "There was no significant correlation between creative thinking gain scores and achievement gain scores".

When studies of Torrance (1959), Carey (1966), Mayhon (1966), Gilchrist (1970), Rechardson (1989), Pandey (1992), Kaur (1992), Prusty (2002) reported positive relation between creative thinking and academic achievement, at the same time studies also signified low or no relation between them (Pathak, 1962; Flescher, 1963; Jacobson, 1966; Chadha and Chandana, 1990; Kapoor, 1996). Such analysis favours contrastic view points relating growth of creative thinking and academic achievement. Under such controversial findings, the present study, when was found significant in increasing creative thinking and academic achievement of students, it was felt imperative to know whether there existed some relation between the development of those two variables as an effect of Super Learning Technique (SLT).

To analyse such relationship between the rate of development of creative thinking and rate of increment in academic achievement, the above-stated hypothesis [$H_{05\,(c)}$] was formulated. To test the hypothesis creative thinking gain scores and academic achievement gain scores in history were obtained by subtracting the respective post-test scores from pre-test scores. The obtained data was analysed by application of scattergram correlation. The calculated coefficient of correlation was stated in Table 6.15.

TABLE 6.15

Co-efficient Correlation between Achievement Gain Scores in History and Creative Thinking Gain Scores

Variables	*Correlation*	*t-value*
Achievement Gain Score Creative Thinking Gain Score	+0.62	7.6650**

** = Significant at 0.01 level ($p < 0.01$).

Appendix-H showed the scattergram table and according to the values plotted in that table, following calculation was made. The calculation gave the above result. The scattergram correlation was calculated by applying the following formula:

$$r = \frac{\Sigma fxy - \frac{(\Sigma fx)(\Sigma fy)}{N}}{\sqrt{\Sigma fx^2 - \frac{(\Sigma fx)^2}{N}} \times \sqrt{\Sigma fy^2 - \frac{(\Sigma fy)^2}{N}}} \quad \text{...........(Aggarwal, 1993)}$$

$$= \frac{571 - \frac{(81)(230)}{-96}}{\sqrt{543 - \frac{(81)^2}{96}} \times \sqrt{1332 - \frac{(230)^2}{96}}}$$

$$= + 0.62$$

$$t = \frac{r}{\sqrt{1 - r^2}} \times \sqrt{N - 2}$$

$$= \frac{0.62}{\sqrt{1 - .3844}} \times \sqrt{94}$$

$$= 7.6650^{**} \ (p < 0.01)$$

The calculated result showed high, positive and significant relationship ($r = + 0.62$, $t = 7.6650$, $p < 0.01$) between creative thinking gain scores and achievement gain scores in history. The analysed result confirmed that development of creative thinking and achievement in history progressed in equal pace and in an increment of high and significant coefficient of correlation. The result also substantiated the effectiveness of Super Learning Technique (SLT) in developing creative thinking and achievement in history of students at almost an equal rate. The result went with the findings of Ostrander and Schroeder (1995), Mahancy (1989), Lang (1984) and Curtis (1984) who had experimented super learning in various levels of education and found the technique substantial in increasing students' achievement, creative thinking and intelligence (www Superlearning.com). The Creative Method of Teaching English (CMTE) developed and experimented by Prusty (2004) and creative method of Teaching science by Pradhan (1994) though were based an Gordon's synectics, were also found effective in developing both creative thinking and achievement. They reported the development of achievement as nurturant effect. Still, it could be concluded that like all those methods, SLT was proved to be effective in developing students creative thinking and academic achievement in History.

6.1.6 Development of Creative Thinking of Boys and Girls

Sex has been regarded as an important variables whose influence on creative thinking has been extensively studied. But researches carried out both in India and in the west seem contradictory in determining the relation of sex with that of creative thinking. Studies conducted on sex difference in creative thinking revealed not only "no sex difference" between males and females, but there occurred significant differences between them and in some aspects of creative thinking at a certain period of life the males excelled the females whereas, in other aspects, at another period, the females surpassed males significantly (Sharma, 2000). It was early part of twentieth century, when the percentage of contribution of female towards active creative social condition was negligible. Cattle (1903) reported 33 active females out of 1000 people, and Ellis (1904) recorded excellence of 55 females out of 1030 highly eminent British geniuses. Castle (1913) identified only 868 women who were noted for their creative contribution.

By today, the time has changed the situation a lot. Democratic consciousness, development of progressive outlook among people of the world, knowledge explosion, influence of electronic and print media, changing socio-cultural, religious, economic and political environment has brought a tremendous change in the outlook, status, temperament and in aspiration of female folk of the world. Such factors have also instigated the female mass to bring out their inherent potentialities. No doubt, the freedom and liberty given to the women mass of our society has been proved effective in producing ladies like Mother Teresa, Margaret Thacher, Yan San Su ki, Indira Gandhi, Kalpana Chawla and many others. They have been proving themselves as able scientist, administrator, engineer, doctor, astronounts and philosopher. Therefore, the research study of

Jarial (1983) which had reviewed 127 studies found 49 studies those reported the supremacy of females over males in creative thinking ability. Torrance (1961, 1962, 1963 and 1965) found that girls excell in verbal fluency, flexibility and originality (Gregor, 1965; Naufield, 1965; Ogletree, 1968; Soloman, 1968; Singh, 1978; Sajid and Hussain, 1984; Ramkrishna, 1986; Richardson, 1986; Behera, 1993; Hota, 1993; Pandey and Rai, 1995; Prusty, 2003).

Still, some study report the excellence of boys over girls in their creative thinking. Though there were difference relating sample, environmental factor, type of tests and statistical techniques used for analysis of obtained data, the result of studies conducted by Raina (1969), Mari (1973), Nayana (1981), Akinbye (1982), Vora (1984), Hussain (1985), Lutzer (1991), Hota (1993), Gelade (1995), Kapoor (1996), Joyce (1997), Dorothy (2000) substantially reported the higher creative ability of boys than the girls.

Such relation becomes more critical to arrive at an acceptable conclusion when researches of Pathak (1962), Pogue (1965), Singh (1986), Rao (1988), Sharma and Bhatia (1988), Mukhopadhyay, Chakrabarti and Kundu (1990), Behera (1993), Pandey and Rai (1995) reported "no relationship" between sex and creative thinking.

Under such contradictory relation which exist between creative thinking and sex, Super Learning Technique (SLT) was used in teaching history to secondary school students. Therefore, their relation is to be verified meticulously to know how far boys and girls had benefitted and what relation was existing there in development of creative thinking of boys and girls. Accordingly, the objective of the study was set "to find out the difference in creative thinking scores of boys and girls as an impact of super learning technique.

To verify the above stated objective, three null hypotheses were formed to test the significance of difference in three stages—pre-test stage, post-test stage and in gain score analysis. Scores obtained through Mehdi's Test on Creative Thinking before and after intervention programme were treated as pre-test and post-test scores in creative thinking respectively. The difference between pre-test and post-test creative thinking scores gave the creative thinking gain score. The three hypotheses were verified as follows.

6.1.6 (a) Testing of First Sub-Hypothesis [$H_{06\ (a)}$]

The first sub-hypothesis of sixth hypothesis [$H_{06(a)}$] stated, "There was no significant difference between boys and girls in their mean creatieve thinking scores at pre-test stage".

As the study had followed equal group design, there were 48 boys and 48 girls in total, having 24 each from boys and girls in both control and experimental groups. The obtained pre-test creative thinking scores of boys and girls was analysed by SE_D and 't' test. The calculated result is presented in Table 6.16

TABLE 6.16

Significance of Difference in Pre-test Creative thinking Mean Scores of Boys and Girls

Sex	*N*	*M*	*SD*	*t*
Boys	48	113.5	21.31	7.1560**
Girls	48	84.458	18.342	

** = significant at 0.01 level ($p < 0.01$).

Table 6.16 showed the calculated data relating significance of difference that exist between boys and girls in pre-test mean creative thinking scores. The data showed a significant difference ($t = 7.1560$, $p < 0.01$) with a higher mean creative thinking score of boys ($M = 113.5$, $SD = 21.311$) over the girls ($M = 84.458$, $SD = 18.342$). It confirmed that the boys were superior to girls in their pre-test mean creative thinking scores. Therefore, the first sub-hypothesis, which stated "no significant difference between boys and girls in their mean creative thinking scores at pre-test stage was rejected at 0.01 level of confidence.

Such finding was supported by the studies conducted by Kely (1965), Straus and Straus (1968), Sajid (1984), Lutzer (1991), Gelade (1995) and Kapoor (1996). But the research findings of Torrance (1961), Naufield (1965), Ogletree (1968), Richmond (1971), Singh (1978), and Behera (1993) went against such finding.

6.1.6 (b) Testing of Second Sub-Hypothesis [$H_{06\ (b)}$]

The second sub-hypothesis of sixth hypothesis of the study stated, "There was no significant difference between boys and girls in their mean creative thinking scores at post-test stage".

After the pre-test, the control group was taught the history subject through traditional method and the experimental group was taught the same subject through Super Learning Technique (SLT). Just after the intervention programme Mehdi's Test on Creative Thinking was administered to both the groups to get the post-test creative thinking scores. The obtained scores were analysed by application of SE_D and 't' test. Table 6.17 represents the data relating the significance of sex difference in post-test creative thinking mean scores.

TABLE 6.17

Significance of Difference in Post-Test Mean Creative Thinking Scores of Boys and Girls

Sex	*N*	*M*	*SD*	*t*
Boys	48	141.75	51.866	3.1004**
Girls	48	116.00	24.917	

** = Significant at 0.01 level ($p < 0.01$).

Table 6.17 showed the data relating significance of difference in post-test mean creative thinking scores of boys and girls. The calculated result gave a significant difference ($t = 3.1004$, $p < 0.01$) between boys and girls in their post-test creative thinking mean scores. The analysis of mean values of creative thinking showed that the boys were at higher level (M = 141.75, SD = 51.866) than the girls (M = 116.00, SD = 24.917). On the basis of the above finding it can be interpreted that the hypothesis which stated "no significant difference in post-test mean creative thinking scores of boys and girls" was rejected at 0.01 level of significance. The result exemplified that the boys had succeeded to acquire better creative thinking ability at post-test stage. But the difference was made very clear in analysis of third sub-hypothesis which was related to gain scores in creative thinking. A comparative frequency polygone on the pre-test and post-test creative thinking scores of girls and boys of experimental group are given in Figure 6.1 and Figure 6.2 respectively.

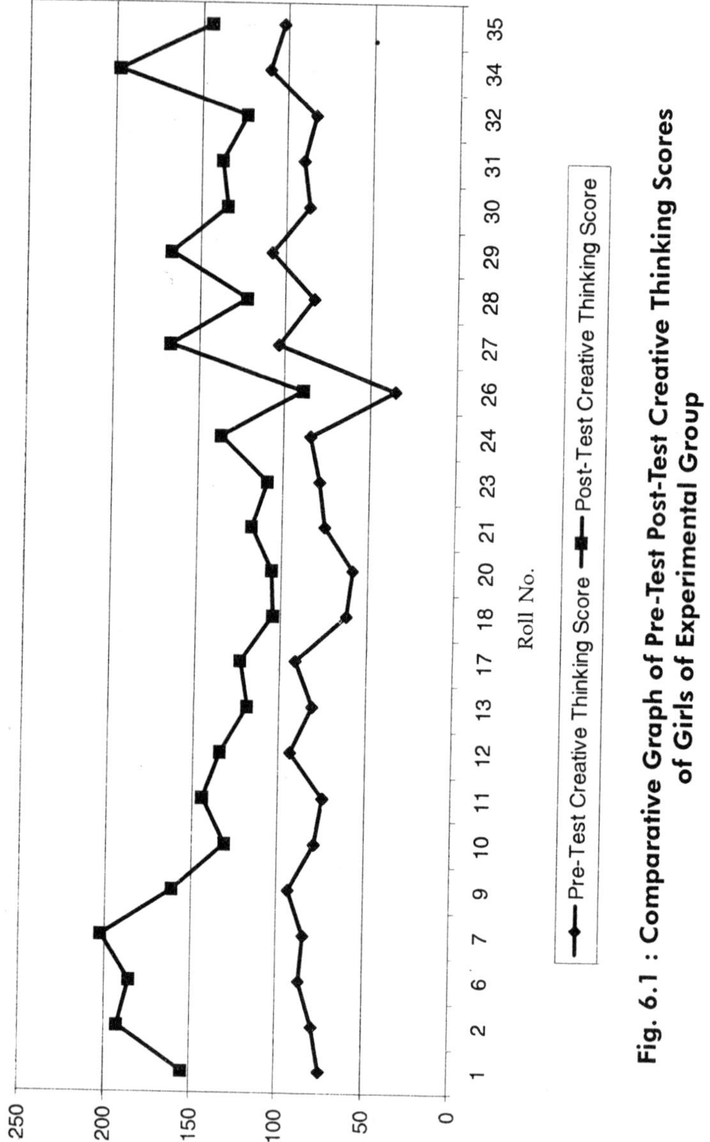

Fig. 6.1 : Comparative Graph of Pre-Test Post-Test Creative Thinking Scores of Girls of Experimental Group

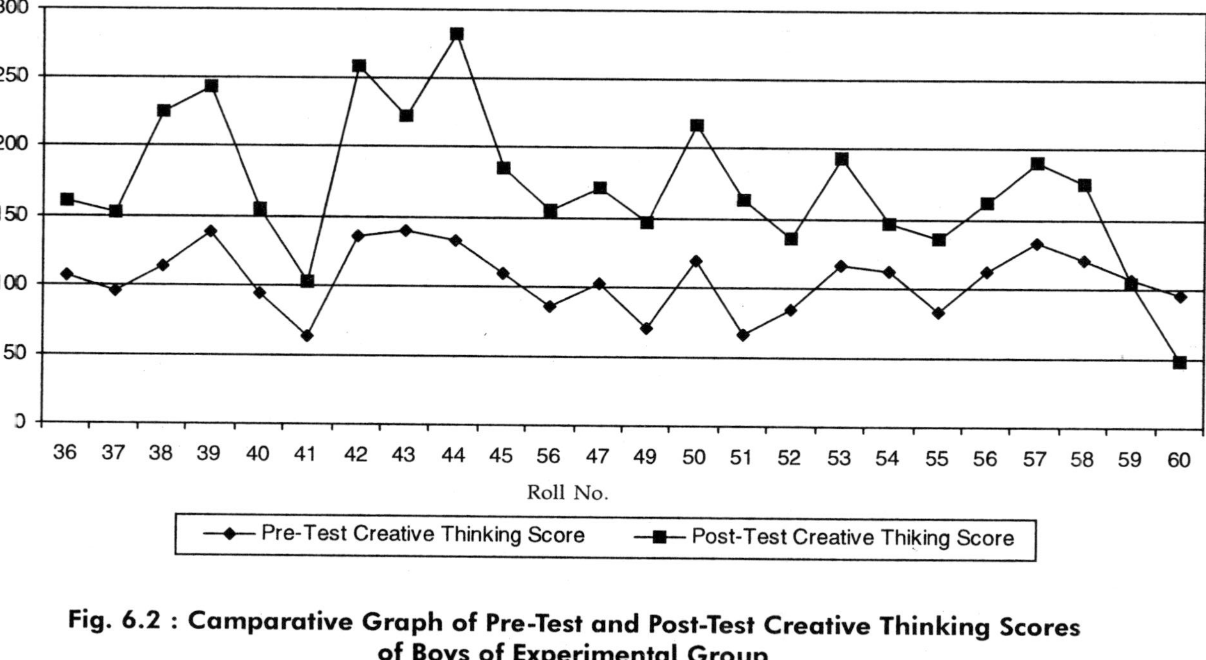

Fig. 6.2 : Camparative Graph of Pre-Test and Post-Test Creative Thinking Scores of Boys of Experimental Group

6.1.6 (c) Testing Third Sub-Hypothesis [$H_{06(c)}$]

The third sub-hypothesis of the sixth hypothesis stated, "There was no significant difference between the boys and girls of experimental group in their gain scores in creative thinking".

The experimental group was consisted of 48 subjects with equal representation of boys and girls (B-24, G-24). Gain scores of creative thinking was obtained by subtracting post-test score of creative thinking from pre-test creative thinking scores, acquired by the students. The obtained data was calculated by application of SE_D and 't' test. The calculated data is presented below in Table 6.18.

TABLE 6.18

Significance of Difference in Mean Creative Thinking Gain Scores of Boys and Girls of Experimental Group

Sex	*N*	*M*	*SD*	*t*
Boys	24	73.33	27.976	1.3030 n. s.
Girls	24	64.5	24.152	

n. s. = not significant at 0.05 level.

Table 6.18 showed the data relating significance of difference that existed between boys and girls in their creative thinking gain scores. The pre-test and post-test creative thinking score analysis represented the significant difference in favour of boys. But both the analyses were conducted taking the boys and girls of both the groups. Their significant difference though confirmed that the boys had surpassed the girls in their pre-test and post-test creative thinking scores, it could not be confirmed whether the difference in post-test creative thinking score was due to super learning technique or for something else. Therefore, the third sub-hypothesis tried to study the gain scores of boys and girls of experimental group only. However, the calculated result stated a non-significant difference, ($t=1.3030$, $p > 0.05$) in the mean creative thinking gain scores of boys and girls. It showed that boys and girls had equally benefitted from the SLT in developing their creative thinking. From such finding it was concluded that the SLT was equally effective for boys and girls relating development of their creative thinking.

Still, the finding of second sub-hypothesis which was related to post-test creative thinking scores of boys and girls was not so clear to land in any scientific conclusion. It was because of the significant difference between boys and girls in pre-test creative thinking scores (t = 7.1560, p < 0.01). In that analysis boys were at higher degree in their mean creative thinking values (M = 113.5, SD = 21. 311) than the girls (M = 84. 458, SD = 18.342). On the other hand, the significant result of post-test (t = 3.1004, p < 0.01) gave a higher mean value of boys (M = 141.75, SD = 51. 86) than girls (M = 116.00, SD = 24.917). An analysis of the pre-post test creative thinking mean value difference of boys and girls showed that the girls had acquired more (mean value difference = 31.515) than the boys (mean value difference = 28.25). Such difference showed that the rate of increment in creative thinking scores of boys, from pre-test stage to the post-test stage, was lower than the girls. This difference is clearly shown in Figure 6.3, which confirms a visible and significant rise of creative thinking scores of girls over boys from pre-test stage to post-test stage. Though the gain score analysis showed non-significant difference between boys and girls in mean creative gain scores, still it was seen that girls had benefitted something more than the boys. But that difference was not found statistically significant in gain score analysis. Therefore, it was concluded that there was no significant difference in development of creative thinking of boys and girls as an impact of Super Learning Technique (SLT). Such finding was substantiated by the findings of Pathak (1962) when he used circles test and incomplete figure test of TTCT; of Pogue (1965) and Mayhon (1966), who used Minnesota Test of Creative Thinking. When Katiyar and Jarial (1985) had experimented their self-devised Verbal Creative Development Programme (VCDP) and Non-verbal Creative Development Programme (NCDP) and found both the technique effective in developing creative thinking, was surprised in seeing no significant effect of sex on development of creative thinking as an impact of VCDP and NCDP. Accordingly, the result of studies conducted by Singh (1986), Rao (1988), Mukhopadhyay, Chakrabarti and Kundu (1990), Behera (1993) and Pandey & Rai (1995) support the finding. It was the influence of education, social development, economic self-sufficiency, development of democratic and political outlook and cultural transmission done through mass media which have had changed the temperament of girls. They are trying to unfold their inherent potentialities for full fledged development of their personality. Probably, the visualization and affirmation—the two important steps of SLT had worked much in increasing self-confidence among girls. The stresses those were succumbed by the girls of first part of twentieth century were because of partial influence of the then society. Those, though are not seen in our post-modern society, still our girls are not free from their mental agony. Humane treatment is less available to them. Their participation in developmental activities are still not significant. Most of the parents do not prefer to send their girls to co-educational institutions. Under such circumstances the relaxation activities of Super Learning Techniques (SLT) seemed to had a spectacular influence on girls to come to par with boys.

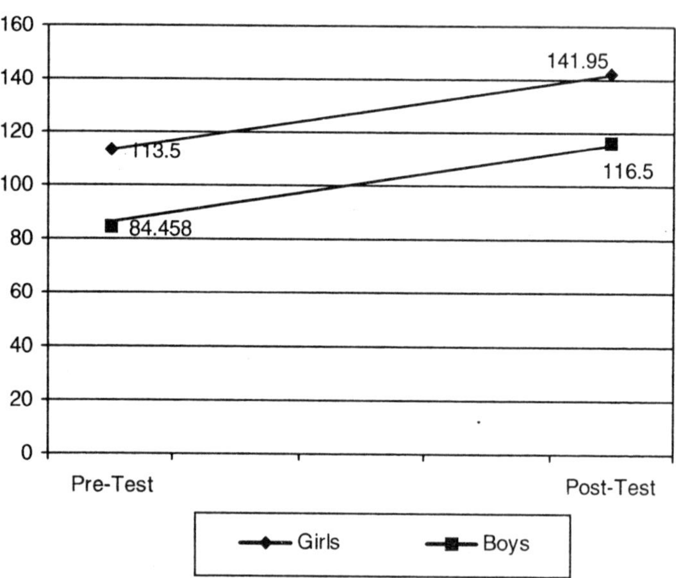

Fig. 6.3 : Comparative Graph on Mean Creative Thinking Scores of Boys and Girls at Pre-Test and Post-Test Stages

6.1.7 Development of Academic Achievement of Boys and Girls

Academic achievement is a variable which is always influenced by sex. Such variance also differs on the basis of different subjects. Sometimes boys excelled the girls in their academic achievement whereas, in another time, girls excelled the boys (Mathur, 1992; Behera, 1993; Prusty, 2001; Menon, 1990; Mohanty, 1992; Muthumnikam, 1992). But the most interesting findings were reported by Nair (1984), Nagilankim (1991), Pradhan (1990), Pradhan (1989), Behera (1992) and Prusty (2002) which exemplified no such significant effect of sex on achievement.

The causes of such contradictory research findings was that academic achievement is a variable related with various behavioural variables such as intelligence, socio-economic status, sex, birth order, motivation, attitude, aptitude and many others. Since, sex is one of those variables, its independent effect can't be studied. There are studies those studied the impact of sex as an independent variable through multiple coefficient of correlation. But in behavioural science its impact as a single variable is very difficult to be studied. Even replications also differed in their result.

Under such circumstances, the present study which had found Super Learning Technique (SLT) effective for developing creative thinking and academic achievement and also equally effective for boys and girls in developing creative thinking, was also studied the role of sex in developing academic achievement in History. Therefore, the seventh objective of the study intended to find out the difference in academic achievement of boys and girls as an effect of Super Learning Technique (SLT). In order to realize the above stated objective three null hypotheses were formulated to test the significance of difference in academic achievement of boys and girls at three stages—pre-test, post-test and gain score stages.

6.1.7 (a) Testing of First Sub-Hypothesis [$H_{07\ (a)}$]

The first sub-hypothesis of the study [$H_{07\ (a)}$] state, "There was no significant difference in mean achievement scores in history of boys and girls at pre-test stage".

There were 96 samples in total with equal representation of 48 boys and 48 girls. Half yearly examination marks in history was considered as the pre-test achievement scores in History of the students. The obtained data was analyzed by application of SE_D and 't' test. The analysed result is presented in Table 6.19.

TABLE 6.19
Significance of Difference in Mean Academic Achievement Scores of Boys and Girls at Pre-test Stage

Group	*N*	*M*	*SD*	*t*
Boys	48	44.1666	9.4504	
				2.9437**
Girls	48	37.3333	18.6540	

** = Significant at 0.05 level (P < 0.01).

Table 6.19 showed the result of analysis of data relating significance of difference in pre-test academic achievement scores of boys and girls. The analysed result showed a significant difference ($t = 2.9437$, $p < 0.01$). Such significant result had showed a higher mean value of boys (M = 4.1666, SD = 9.4504) than the girls (M = 37.3333, SD = 18.6540). The analysis showed that the hypothesis which state, "no significant difference in mean achievement scores in history of boys and girls at pre-test stage " was rejected at 0.01 level of significance.

6.1.7 (b) Testing of Second Sub-Hypothesis [$H_{07(b)}$]

The second sub-hypothesis of seventh hypothesis of the study [$H_{07(b)}$] stated, "There was no significant difference in mean achievement scores in history of boys and girls at post-test stage."

There were 96 students in total with 48 each in both the sexes. There were 48 boys and 48 girls, Marks obtained in history by students in Annual Examination of Class-IX was treated as post-test achievement score in history. The obtained data was analysed by application of SE_D and 't' test. Table 6.20 showed significance of difference in mean academic achievement scores of boys and girls at post-test stage.

TABLE 6.20
Significance of Difference in Mean Achievement Scores of Boys and Girls at Post-test Stage

Group	*N*	*M*	*SD*	*t*
Boys	48	45.833	14.8837	
				2.3563*
Girls	48	42.75	18.7776	

* = Significance at 0.05 ($p < 0.05$).

Table 6.20 showed the significance of difference in mean achievement scores in history of boys and girls at post-test stage. The result gave a significant difference between boys and girls in their post-test mean achievement gain scores ($t = 2.3563$, $p < 0.05$). The result also showed that the boys were at higher level in their post-test mean achievement scores in history (M = 45.8333, SD = 14. 8837) than the girls (M = 42.75, SD = 18.776). But such analysis with reference to the analysis at pre-test stage points at the exact impact of Super Learning Technique (SLT) on development of academic achievement in history. Therefore, the second sub- hypothesis of seventh hypothesis which stated, "no significant difference in mean achievement score in history of boys and girls at post-test stage" was refuted at 0.05 level of singnificance. Figure 6.4 and Figure 6.5 have given a comparative graph on the pre-post achievement scores of boys and girls of experimental group. But to see the actual impact, the gain score analysis needed alongwith graphical interpretation which are stated in Figure 6.4 and 6.5.

6.1.7 (c) Testing of Third Sub-Hypothesis [$H_{07(c)}$]

The third sub-hypothesis of seventh hypothesis [$H_{07(c)}$] stated, "There was no significant difference between boys and girls in their gain scores in academic achievement in History".

When it was seen that the pre-test and post-test results were found significant at 0.01 and 0.05 levels respectively, it was decided to find out the difference in gain scores of experimental group only. There were 48 subjects in experimental group having 24 boys and 24 girls. Their achievement gain scores were obtained by subtracting their annual marks in history from the

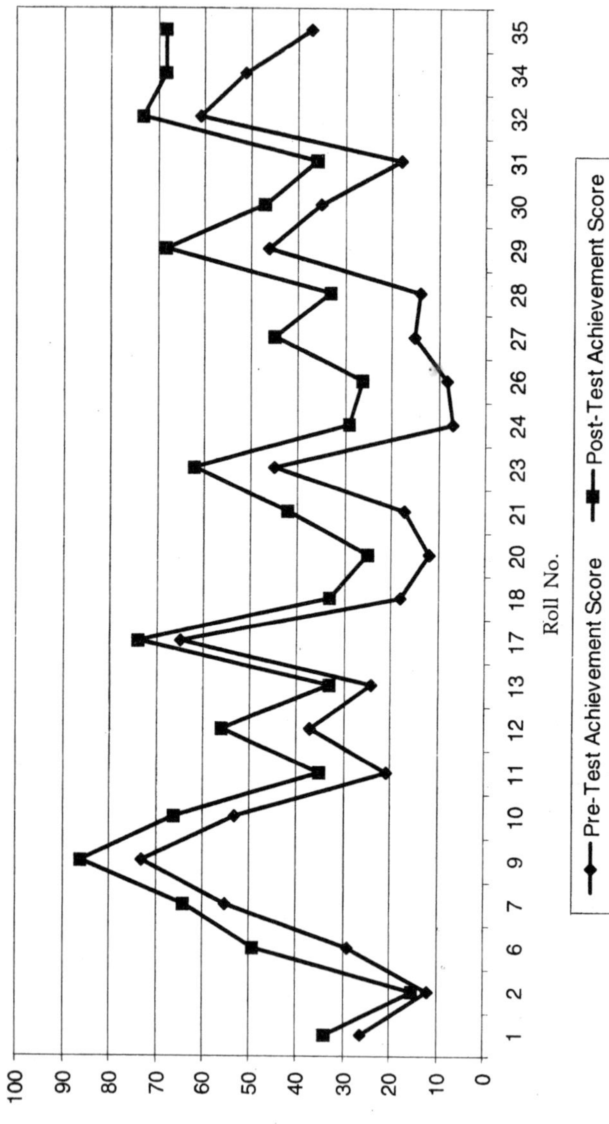

Fig. 6.4 : Comparative Graph on Pre-test and Post-test Achievement Scores of Girls of Experimental Group

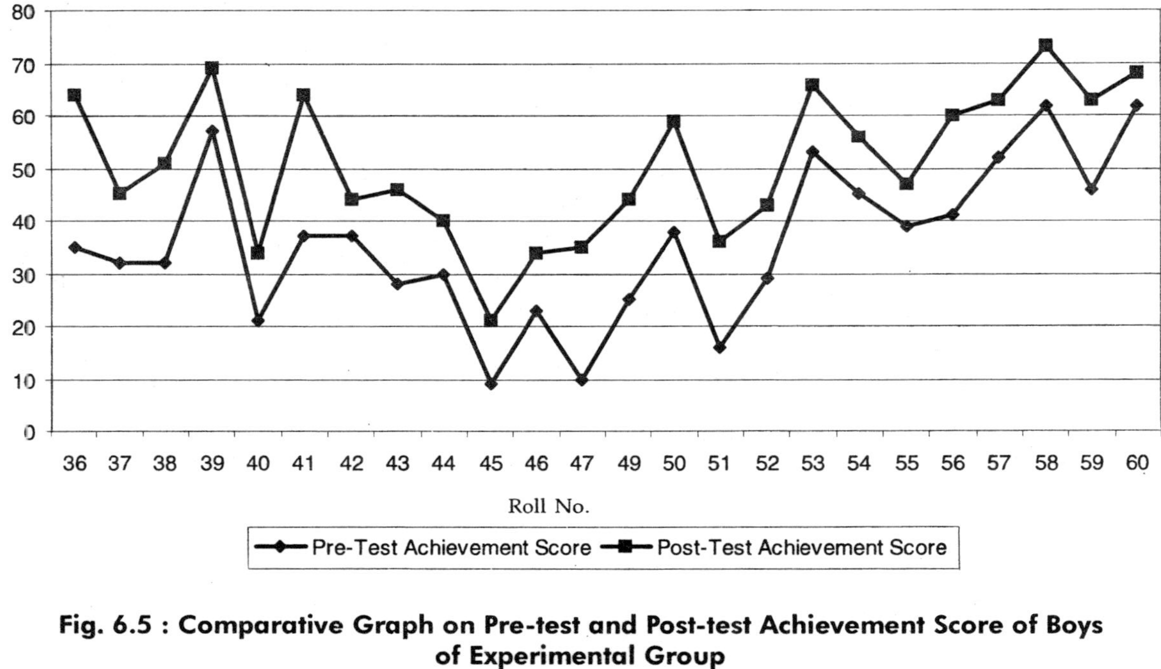

Fig. 6.5 : Comparative Graph on Pre-test and Post-test Achievement Score of Boys of Experimental Group

half yearly examination marks in history. The obtained gain scores were analysed by application of SE_D and 't' test. Table 6.21 represents the analysed data relating the significance of difference in mean gain scores in history of boys and girls of experimental group.

TABLE 6.21
Singnificance of Difference in Mean Achievement Gain Scores in History of Boys and Girls

Group	*N*	*M*	*SD*	*t*
Boys	24	16.7501	6.3069	
				5.7468**
Girls	24	15.1249	6.1527	

** = Significant at 0.01 level ($p < 0.01$).

Table 6.21 showed the significance of difference in mean achievement gain scores in history of boys and girls of experimental group. The calculated result showed a significant difference ($t = 5.7468$, $p < 0.01$) in gain scores in achievements of boys and girls. Analysis of mean value showed the higher mean value of boys (M =16.7501, SD = 6.3069) over the girls (M = 15.1249, SD = 6.1527) in their mean achievement gain scores. Such finding confirmed that the Super Learning Technique (SLT) which was found statistically significant in developing achievement in history, reported that the boys had scored better in achievement in history than the girls. Such higher achievement of boys was subtantiated by the analysis of pre-test and post-test results those stated significant difference in their respective achievement scores with higher mean values of boys. Therefore, this finding refuted the sub-hypothesis which state, "no significant difference between boys and girls in their gain scores in academic achievement in history".

An overall analysis confirmed the significant development of academic achievement in history by Super Learning Technique (SLT). Further, it also confirmed that there were significant differences in pre-test and post-test results of achievement in history and those significant result had put boys at higher level in mean values in achievement. The gain score

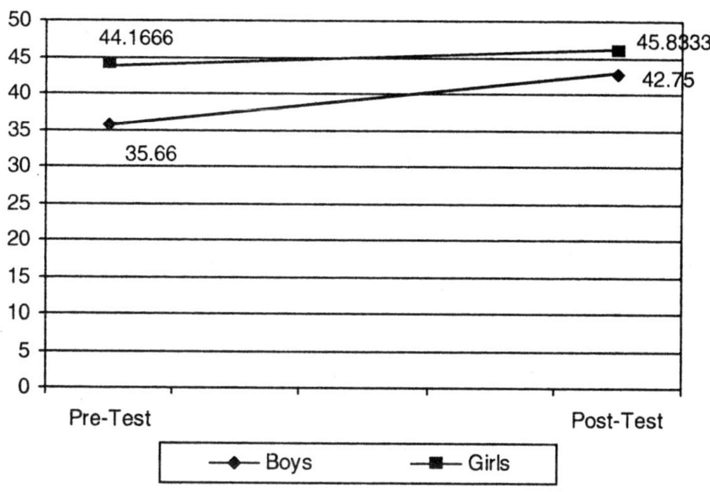

Fig. 6.6 : Comparative Graph on Achievement Scores in History of Boys and Girls at Pre-test and Post-test stages

analysis which gave a significant difference ($t = 5.7468$, $p < 0.01$) also showed the higher mean value of boys ($M = 45.8333$) over girls ($M = 42.75$). But in every case the SD value of girls were higher than the boys. On the other hand, significant pre-test result on achievement mean scores also exerted some influence on post-test and gain score analysis. Since the boys were at higher degree in their academic achievement in history than the girls at pre-test stage, such effect seemed to influence the result at post-test and gain scores by putting the boys at higher degree than girls. But Figure 6.6, which graphically represented the increment of achievement mean scores of boys and girls form pre-test level to post-test level showed higher difference in mean value of girls (Mean value difference = 5.1667) over the mean value difference of boys (mean value difference = 1.6667). Similar finding was reported relating mean creative thinking development of boys and girls (Figure 6.1). Taking both the findings into consideration comparative frequency polygon were drawn on the individual achievement and creative thinking scores of girls and boys in Figure 6.7 and 6.8 respectively.

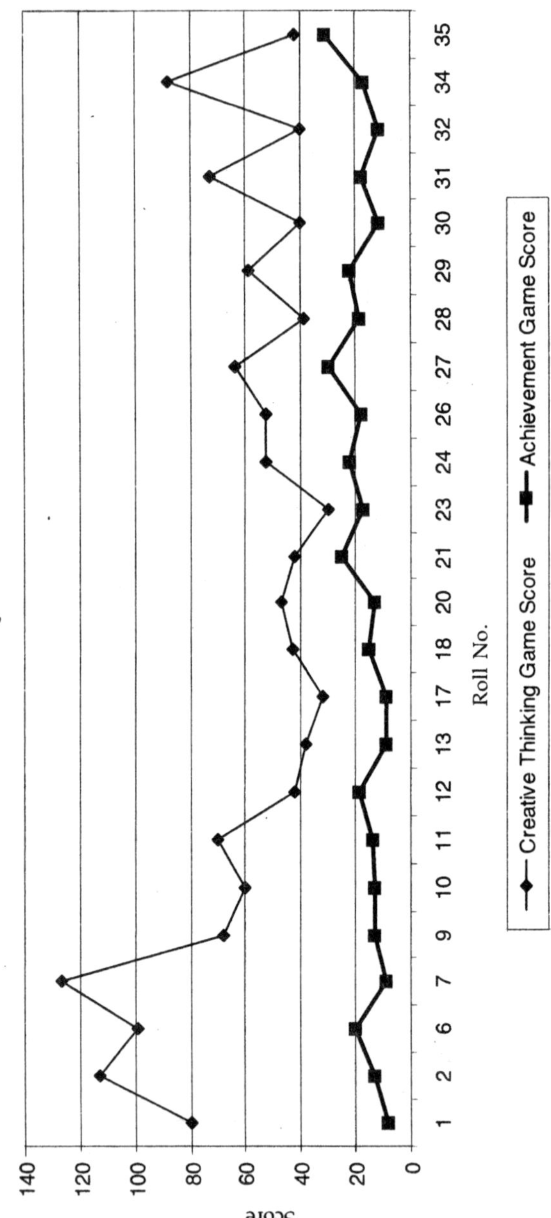

Fig. 6.7 : Comparative Graph on Gain Scores of Creative Thinking and Academic Achievement of Girls

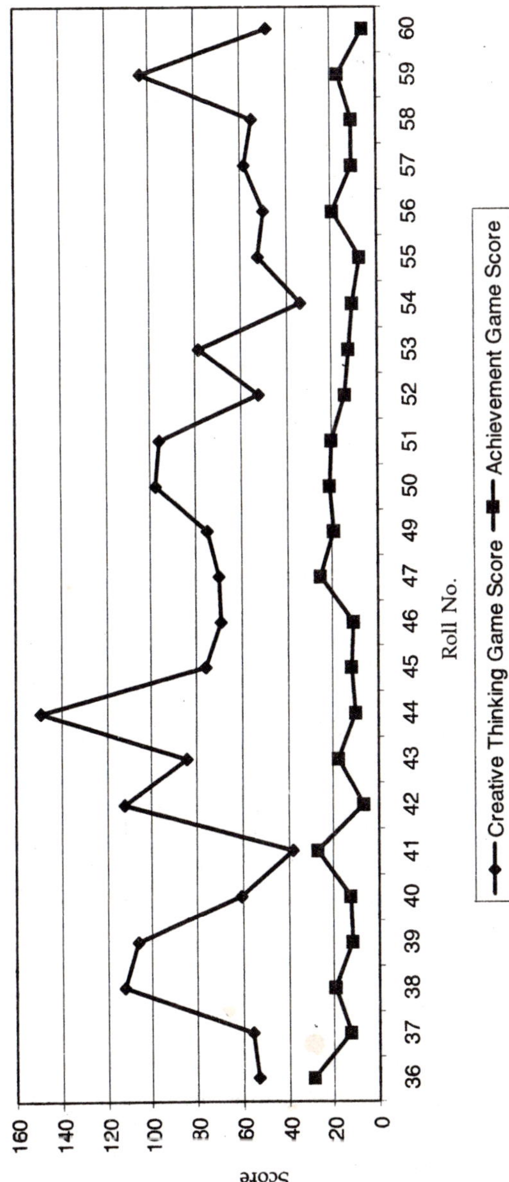

Fig. 6.8 : Comparative Graph on Gain Scores of Creative Thinking and Academic Achievement of Boys

6.2 FINDINGS OF THE STUDY

From the above analysis and testing of all the hypotheses of study the following findings were obtained:

6.2.1 There was no significant difference between control group and experimental group in their pre-test mean scores in fluency ($t = 0.5733$, $p < 0.05$), flexibility ($t = 1.9288$, $p < 0.05$), originality ($t = 1.6327$, $p < 0.05$) and in composite creative thinking mean scores ($t = 0.1823$, $p < 0.05$).

6.2.2 Control group and experimental group differed significantly in their post-test mean scores in fluency ($t = 7.2627$, $p < 0.01$), flexibility ($t = 12.7327$, $p < 0.01$), originality ($t = 2.6100$, $P < 0.05$) and in composite creative thinking scores ($t = 10.3910$, $p > 0.01$).

6.2.3 There was significant difference between control group and experimental group in their mean gain scores in creative thinking ($t = 16.3698$, $p < 0.01$). The experimental group was at higher level in mean creative thinking gain score ($M = 68.0416$, $SD = 27.4993$) than the control group ($M = 0.8334$, $SD = 27.25$). Such result confirmed that Super Learning Technique (SLT) was a successful technique of teaching and learning through which creative thinking can be enhanced.

6.2.4 The control group and experimental group had a non-significant difference in mean achievement scores in history at pre-test stage ($t = 0.06398$, $P > 0.05$).

6.2.5 There was significant difference in mean achievement scores in history of control group a experimental group at post-test level ($t = 2.53$, $p < 0.01$). The experimental group had a greater mean value ($M = 49.979$, $SD = 16.1615$) than the control group ($M = 37.375$, $SD = 15.056$).

6.2.6 The experimental group and control group differed significantly from each other in their mean gain scores in academic achievement in history ($t = 3.3599$, $p < 0.01$). The mean value in academic achievement gain scores of experimental group ($M=15.8125$, $SD = 12.0924$) was at higher level than the control group mean achievement gain scores ($M = 9.1875$, $SD = 6.3562$). Such finding confirmed that Super Learning Technique (SLT) was quite beneficial for developing academic achievement in History.

6.2.7 There was no significant difference in creative thinking mean scores of high-intelligence and low-intelligence group ($F = 3.7042$, $df = 1$, $p > 0.05$) and of control group and experimental group ($F = 0.0015$, $df = 1$, $p > 0.05$) at pre-test stage.

6.2.8 There was no significant difference in post-test creative thinking mean scores of high-intelligence and low intelligence group ($F = 2.49$, $df = 1$, $p > 0.05$). The control group and experimental group differed significantly from each other ($F= 103.80$, $df = 1$, $p < 0.01$) in their post-test creative thinking mean scores with higher mean value of control group ($M = 91.6363$)

6.2.9 On the ground of gain scores in creative thinking, there existed no significant difference between high intelligence group and low intelligence group ($F = 3.29$, $df = 1$, $p > 0.05$). The group had exerted significant effect on creative thinking gain score ($F = 46.45$, $df = 1$, $p < 0.01$) with higher mean value of experimental group ($M = 70.6818$) than the mean value of control group ($M = 0.06818$). The result showed that level of intelligence had no impact on Super Learning Technique (SLT) in developing creative thinking. SLT, thus was proved equally beneficial for high and low intelligence groups in increasing their creative thinking.

6.2.10 There was significant influence of levels of intelligence on pre-test achievement mean scores in history of control and experimental groups ($F = 5.7295$, $df = 1$, $p < 0.05$) at pre-test stage. There was an insignificant interaction effect on pre-test achievement scores of high intelligence and low intelligence groups of control and experimental groups ($F = 2.1025$, $df = 1$, $p > 0.05$).

6.2.11 Both levels of intelligence and group had exerted significant effect on the post-test achievement mean scores of students. There was a significant effect of intelligence on the post-test achievement scores of students ($F = 34.8497$, $df = 1$, $p < 0.01$). The mean value of high intelligence group of experimental group ($M = 56.50$) and control group ($M = 44.5$) were higher then their low intelligence groups ($M = 46.9545$ and $M = 29.5454$) respectively. Accordingly, the control and experimental groups differred significantly in their post-test mean achievement scores in history ($F = 50.5649$, $df = 1$, p < 0.01). The experimental group was at higher level in post-test mean achievement gain scores (M = 51.4772) than the post-test mean achievement scores of control group (M = 37.0227). The interaction effect was not significant (F = 2.1130, df = 1, p > 0.05).

6.2.12 There was no significant difference in mean achievement gain scores in history of high intelligence and low-intelligence groups of experimental group (F = 3.7604, df = 1, p < 0.05). The result confirmed that the Super Learning. Technique (SLT) was equally beneficial for high and low intelligence groups in developing their academic achievement in history.

6.2.13 The difference in mean creative thinking gain scores of high achievers and low achievers of experimental group was not significant (F = 0.1976, df = 1, p > 0.05).

6.2.14 There was no significant difference in mean achievement gain scores of high-creative and low-creative groups of experimental group (F = 0.9727, df = 1, p > 0.05).

6.2.15 There was high, positive and significant relationship in the rate of growth of creative thinking and development of academic achievement in History with coefficient of correlation of + 0.62 and 't' value of 7.6650 (p < 0.01) as an impact of Super Learning Technique (SLT). The result confirmed that SLT was equally and significantly beneficial for development of creative thinking and academic achievement in history of students. Thus, SLT was effective for development of creatives thinking and academic achievement.

6.2.16 There was significant difference in pre-test mean creative thinking scores of boys and girls (t = 7.1560, p < 0.01). The boys were at higher mean value (M = 113.5, SD = 21.31) than the girls (M = 84.458, p > 0.05).

6.2.17 The boys and girls differed significantly in their post-test mean creative thinking scores (t = 3.1004, p < 0.01) with higher mean value of boys (M = 141.75, SD = 51.866) over the girls (M = 116.00, SD = 24.917).

6.2.18 There was non-significant difference in mean creative thinking gain scores of boys and girls (t =1.3030, p > 0.05). But an overall analysis showed almost same rate of development of creative thinking of boys and girls.

6.2.19 There was significant difference in mean academic achievement scores in history of boys and girls ($t = 2.9437$, $p < 0.01$) at pre-test stage. The boys were at higher degree in their mean values ($M = 44.1666$) than the girls ($M = 37.3333$).

6.2.20 The Boys and girls differed significantly in their post-test mean achievement scores in history ($t = 2.3563$, $p < 0.05$). The boys were at higher level in post-test achievement mean value (M = 45. 833) than the girls ($M = 42.75$)

6.2.21 In gain score analysis of academic achievement in history of boys and girls, the result showed a significant difference at 0.01 level of confidence ($t = 5.7468$, $p < 0.01$). The boys had a greater mean value ($M = 16.7501$) than the girls ($M = 15.1249$). The result confirmed that the boys had benefitted more from Super Learning Technique (SLT) than the girls in respect of developing their academic achievement in history.

7 SUMMARY AND RECOMMENDATIONS

SUMMARY AND RECOMMENDATIONS

7.1 EXECUTIVE SUMMARY

Human organism is an epitome of manifold possibilities. Freud (1971) defined the exposed abilities as 1/10th of hidden propensities of the individual. There have been ceaseless endeavour to find out the means of unfolding the untapped brilliance. Sri Aurobindo (1920) tried to bring integrated development of beings to attain the state of "Super Man". Freud (1969) accepted that state as state of "super-consciousness". Vedic Indian tradition had also the belief of prefound hidden propensities of human being and had accordingly by recommended yoga, mediation and allied process to unfold those calibre. Psychologists and educationists had also developed many techniques and methods of teaching and learning so that the prevailing educational system could have potentiality of developing the inner abilities of the individual. Many others are in tryst with searching better means for the educational system to develop cognitive, affective and psychomotor domains of the individual.

Under such circumstances, Lozanov's (1979) Super Learning Technique is a landmark in bringing multidimensional development of human potentialities. Georgi Lozanav, the famous Bulgarian physician developed this technique on the basis of Raja Yoga of India and of some Bulgarian Yogic principles. The development of Super Learning Technique (SLT), from the very time of its application, has been revolutionized the system of learning. It speaks of a supra-method of energizing the human organism to bring mental smartness and physical boldness. This new method acts on a "super food" in eradicating mental poverty from the individual and consolidates the mind-set for better and self-sufficient self-concept. The multi-dimensional fruitfulness of SLT has been reported by numerous educationists, psychologists, businessmen, scientists, students, teachers, technocrats, astronauts, military or defence personnel, agriculturist and by many others (Ostrander and Schroeder, 1997). However, SLT is a technique which speeds up learning in manifold (Passi and Prabhu, 1997). It believes on left-right brain synchronization and takes the mind to alpha level. Scientists and educationists of all over the world have been experimenting with Super Learning Technique (SLT) in varied fields. In this regard, studies of Krilian (1981), Lozanov (1979), Ostrander and Schroeder (1979, 1995, 1997, 2002), Bay (1984), Abrezol (1990), Wagner (1984), Herrenberg and Heidenhain (1982), Atkins (1992), Fre (1992) and several others have reported significant effect of super-learning means on varied fields of activity.

India, though was the source of development of such super learning technique, till yet she possesses no such significant research study. On the other hand, the yoga and meditation tradition of India though had a good deal of strong theoretical expressions and personal experiences, lack of observable and scientific data which has been done in Western countries. Super learning, which has a significant contribution in many fields, needed to be studied in Indian context, most significantly in the field of education. Creative thinking, which is the most important behavioural characteristic of the individual and which brings unparallel social development needed to be studied in relation to Super Learning Technique (SLT). Taking all those considerations into account, it was decided to experiment the effect of SLT on development of creative thinking and achievement. So the study was stated as, "EFFECT OF SUPER LEARNING TECHNIQUE (SLT) ON DEVELOPMENT OF CREATIVE THINKING".

7.1.1 Objectives

The study intended to achieve the following objectives:

(i) To find out the effect of Super Learning Technique (SLT) on development of creative thinking.
(ii) To find out the effect of SLT on students' academic achievement in history.
(iii) To find out the relationship that existed between intelligence and development of creative thinking as an effect of SLT.
(iv) To study the rate of development of achievement scores in history in relation to levels of intelligence as an impact of SLT.
(v) To find out the relationship between change in creative thinking scores and change in achievement test scores as an effect of SLT.
(vi) To find out the difference in creative thinking scores of boys and girls as an effect of SLT.
(vii) To find out difference in academic achievement scores of boys and girls as an effect of SLT.

7.1.2 Hypotheses

Above stated each objective was studied through respective verifiable null hypotheses. The hypotheses of the study were as follows:

H_{01}(a) There was no significant difference between the experimental group and control group in their pre-test creative thinking scores.

(b) There was no significant difference between the experimental group and control group in their post-test creative thinking scores.

(c) There was no significant difference between the experimental group and control group in their mean gain scores in creative thinking.

H_{02}(a) There was no significant difference between the experimental and control groups in their pre-test mean achievement scores in history.

(b) There was no significant difference between the experimental group and control group in their post-test mean achievement scores in history.

(c) There was no significant difference between the experimental group and control group in their mean achievement gain scores in history.

H_{03}(a) There was no significant difference in pre-test creative thinking mean score of high-intelligence group and low-intelligence group of:
(i) Control Group, and (ii) Experimental Group.

(b) There was no significant difference in post-test creative thinking mean scores of high-intelligence group and low-intelligence group of : (i) Control Group, and (ii) Experimental Group.

(c) There was no significant differences in the gain scores in creative thinking of high-intelligence group and low-intelligence group of :
(i) Control Group and (ii) Experimental Group.

H_{04}(a) There was no significant difference in the pre-test achievement mean scores in history of high intelligence group of low-intelligence groups of:
(i) Experimental Group, and (ii) Control Group.

(b) There was no significant difference in post-test achievement mean scores in history of high-intelligence group and low-intelligence group of:
(i) Experimental Group, and (ii) Control Group.

(c) There was no significant difference in mean achievement gain scores of high-intelligence and low intelligence groups of experimental group.

H_{05}(a) There was no significant difference in mean creative thinking gain scores of high-achievers and low-achievers in history achievement test scores of the experimental group.

(b) There was no significant difference in mean achievement gain scores in history of high creative and low creative groups of experimental group.

(c) There was no significant correlation between creative thinking gain scores and achievement gain scores in history.

H_{06}(a) There was no significant difference between boys and girls in their mean creative thinking scores at pre-test stage.

(b) There was no significant difference between boys and girls in their mean creative thinking scores at post-test stage.

(c) There was no significant difference between the boys and girls of the experimental group in their gain scores in creative thinking tests.

H_{07}(a) There was no significant difference in mean achievement scores in history of boys and girls at pre-test stage.

(b) There was no significant difference in mean achievement scores in history of boys and girls at post-test stage.

(c) There was no significant difference between boys and girls in their gain scores in academic achievement in history.

7.1.3 Design

The Study had followed two designs—one for pilot study and the other was for research study. For the pilot study, One group Pre-test Post-test design was followed to find out the pitfalls of the SLT and to develop remedial measures thereof. The pilot study reported significant result of SLT in developing creative thinking. Pilot study also brought some changes in SLT programme for better effectiveness. Taking the changes into consideration and the significant difference between pre-test and post-test creative thinking result of the pilot study ($t = 5.8976$, $p < 0.01$), the true experimental design was proposed to be used in the research study.

Randomized Matched Groups Pre-test Post-test Design was followed for the research study. SLT was accepted as independent variable, effect of which was studied on dependent variables such as creative thinking and academic achievement in history. Sex, age and intelligence were regarded as extraneous variables which were controlled on different grounds. There were equal number of subjects in experimental group and control group. Both the groups were matched on intelligence and creative thinking. Experimental group was taught history subject through SLT whereas, the control group was taught through traditional method.

The final sample of the study was constituted with 96 subjects with 48 each in control and experimental groups and with equal representation of boys and girls (B = 48, G = 48). Mehdi's Verbal test on Creative Thinking and Tondon's Verbal Test on Intelligence (verbal 2/70), were used as measures of creative thinking and intelligence. Half-yearly examination marks in history was considered as pre-test achievement score and the annual examination marks in History was taken as post-test achievement scores. Tests on creative thinking and intelligence were administered at pre-test and post-test stages to obtain pre-test and post-test scores on respective variables. The experimental group was taught the history topics through SLT for about two months and the control group was taught the topics of same subject through traditional method. Both the groups were taught by the investigator. The duration of intervention programme lasted for two months and after intervention, the experimental and control groups were administered the tests on creative thinking and achievement.

The Super Learning Technique, the intervention programme of the study had two phases of activities. The first phase was known as mind calming session which included the activities like relaxation, visualization, affirmation and breathing exercises. The second phase which was known as memory session included learning and memorization through music. A 50 minute class was divided into different activities with alloted time. Teaching and memory activities included different activities of Super Learning Frame. The themes of the frame included statement of instructional objectives, stating major and minor themes, synchronized presentation of learning themes with and without music, memorisation of learned material with music, feedback presentation and evaluation and feedback review.

The data collected from control group and experimental group were analysed by application of parametric statistics such as coefficient of correlation, significance of difference between means, 't' test and ANOVA. The results were analysed and interpreted with reference to the related studies, empirical analysis and personal experiences. However, the interpretation of the result reported the following major findings:

7.2 MAJOR FINDINGS

The analysed and interpreted results reported the following major findings. The major findings were stated according to the objectives of the study.

7.2.1 Super Learning Technique (SLT) was effective enough in developing creative thinking of secondary school students.

7.2.2 Super Learning Technique (SLT) was very much effective in increasing academic achievement of students in history.

7.2.3 Super Learning Technique (SLT) was equally effective for high-intelligence and low-intelligence groups in developing their creative thinking. Level of intelligence had no significant impact on development of creative thinking as an impact of SLT.

7.2.4 Super Learning Technique (SLT) was not affected by levels of intelligence in developing students' academic achievement. Thus, SLT is equally effective for high intelligence and low intelligence groups in increasing their academic achievement in history.

7.2.5 The effect of Super Learning Technique (SLT) on development of creative thinking and academic achievement was almost equal and significant. The rate of growth of creative thinking and academic achievement as an effect of SLT was at same sequence. The relationship of such growth was high positive and significant.

7.2.6 Boys and girls both were equally benefitted from SLT in developing their creative thinking.

7.2.7 Boys were benefitted more than girls from Super Learning Technique (SLT) in developing their academic achievement in history.

7.3 IMPLICATIONS OF THE RESEARCH FINDINGS

There is a unanimous agreement on the contribution of

creative thinking in developing creativogenic society (Arieti, 1976). Formal education has become a major means of generating creative thinking among students through teaching various subjects. Accordingly, psychologists and educationists have developed several methods of teaching for development of creative thinking. Like Gordon's Synectics (1961), Osborn's Brainsterming (1957), Taylor's PAKSA (1961), Lozanov's Super Learning Technique (SLT) has been proved its effectiveness in varied fields and in almost all western countries. The major findings of the present study reported the significance of SLT in developing creative thinking and academic achievement. It has also reported the significant influence of sex as a variable to influence SLT to be more effective for boys in developing academic achievement. Therefore, on the ground of above findings, the following implications were suggested on the study.

7.3.1 Super learning Technique (SLT) can be used at secondary level of any school of urban area to develop creative thinking of students. Since the school, where SLT was experimented fulfils all characteristics of every type of school SLT can be used in all the schools with full success. Therefore, the secondary school teachers, educational administrators and planners should try to use SLT at secondary level.

7.3.2 At the present time, when learning history has created a sort of phobia among students and history departments of Orissa has been experiencing a desert-like situation, effectiveness of super learning on history has given the solace. Therefore, Super Learning Technique of learning history should be widely used in secondary schools of India, so that students' achievement will be increased and a sort of moral courage will be boosted among them to learn history with high sportiveness.

7.3.3 Innovative learning materials should be used at maximum rate and those should be made in eye-catching formula to create an impression in memory of the students. So, the teachers should be trained in that line to make SLT more effective in developing supra learning ability among learners.

7.3.4 Since 60 beats super learning music was found very much effective for rhythmic presentation and memorisation of information and learning themes and our Indian schools are practising prayer classes and some specific schools are practising meditation and alike activities, more stress be given on mass prayer and rhythmic presentation of learning matters with music. If tryst will be made to develop topic-based presentation of learning themes with music that would exert significant effect on learning of students.

7.3.5 Teachers, parents, educational supervisors should take due care to create a strong self-concept or self-confidence of attaining everything. Inspite of their failure, they should be encouraged positively and at everytime teacher should have motivating and encouraging attitude and interest to develop a positive and optimistic mental-set among learners. A positive mental set always develops a wining personality, i.e., the need of SLT.

7.3.6 At no cost, students should be left tension-ridden either physically or mentally. So teachers, parents, siblings and counsellors should work hard to release such tensions through simple physical exercises and with visualization of peaceful, calm and energizing situations. The prayer classes or just before the starting of classes of the day breathing exercise at least of five minutes alongwith meditation with slow baroque music/ slow music of flute would be profitable for releasing tension and increasing concentration, those are required for super learning.

7.3.7 Teachers should be trained relating development of super learning frame and converting the conventional topics into super learning frames with clear statement of learning objectives and major and minor learning themes thereof. Teacher Training Institutions, Institutes of Advanced Studied in Education, Regional Institutes of Education, NCERT, etc. should take initiative in developing super learning packages and developing training packages on super learning.

7.3.8 Curriculum constructors of teacher training courses should include SLT in teacher training courses of study and curriculum planners of school education should be trained on the line of super learning by which they will include topics in that direction.

7.3.9 Students, Teachers, Teachers' Council, Parent-Teacher Association (PTA), Mother-Teacher Association (MTA), Village Education Committee (VEC), the counsellors and Inspectors of Education need to be made aware first of the significance of SLT, so that the congenial environment would be available for application of SLT in the classroom. It is because, a fertile soil always infuses greater success for SLT.

7.3.10 Student—teacher relationship should be cordial, democratic and motivating. Students should be given immence freedom for expressing their open-ended thoughts and teacher should be in positive mind to organise the ill-organised thoughts of students. Teacher should provide free, encouraging, playful and failure-bearing teaching-learning environment to facilitate the effectiveness of SLT.

7.3.11 Super learning is not influenced by students' levels of intelligence in developing creative thinking and achievement in history. Therefore, the teacher should not be worried much for the low-intelligent students. But some care be taken for high-intelligent group if they need to excel their performance.

7.3.12 Both boys and girls performed equally in developing their creative thinking being influenced by SLT. So teacher should not be discriminative inside the class on the ground of sex. But when boys scored better in academic achievement than girls, it is required for the teacher to be careful for girls on the ground of achievement. Therefore, during teaching some care must be taken by the teacher in treating boys and girls. Overall, teachers should be impartial and democratic for both the sexes.

7.3.13 Overall tryst be made by the teachers to use SLT in perfect manner so that students learning will be progressed with super speed. Teachers should be involved in to feedback and feedback review activities of learning session which will rectify students' faults and lead their learning to success.

7.4 RECOMMENDATIONS FOR FURTHER RESEARCH

It has been stated in rationale of the study that though super learning has been widely and profitably used all over the world, in India, it has no use in its original form. But India has an old tradition of yoga and meditation which is the base of super learning technique. Now-a-days we also have a number of institutions those have made meditative practices the part and parcel of their educational activities. Still India lacked the materialistic use of the yogic technique. In this regard this study is an attempt of initiating research on Super Learning Technique

(SLT) in India. Being successful in proving effectiveness of SLT in developing creative thinking and academic achievement, the present research has opened the divergent fields of possibilities where research may be conducted.

7.4.1 Super Learning Technique (SLT) can be experimented on small group of students in the learning of few topics in one or two subjects.

7.4.2 The effect of SLT can be studied on any school subject or on a number of school subjects through learning those subjects by SLT.

7.4.3 Super learning may be tried out at different levels of education starting from primary through higher education.

7.4.4 It may be studied on different types of education such as, general, technical, professional, medical, defence, etc.

7.4.5 Super Learning Technique can be used on development of learning of children of special needs and exceptional qualities like handicaps, learning disables, gifted, mentally retarded, slow learners, etc.

7.4.6 Super Learning Technique may be used to enhance managerial competency of educational administrators—Headmaster, Principals, Vice-Chancellors, Directors, etc. to bring solution to increasing problems of the system.

7.4.7 Comparative studies may be undertaken on the system of group prayer and other religious practices and super learning technique (SLT) at any level of education.

7.4.8 As an extension of the present study, such effectiveness of SLT can be measured in relation to development of achievement scores of other subjects.

7.4.9 Repeated Measures Design, Replications and multigroup designs may be used to study the effectiveness of SLT on achievement in specific subject or on a number of subjects.

7.4.10 The effect of Super Learning Technique (SLT) may be studied on different behavioural characteristics of the person.

7.4.11 Cross-cultural studies may be conducted to compare the effectiveness of SLT in varied situations and also on different or same subjects and levels.

7.4.12 Effect of Super Learning Technique (SLT) may be studied on development of memory, retention, intelligence, attitude, cognitive abilities, perception and related psycho-educational variables.

7.4.13 Effect of Supper Learning Technique can be compared with the effect of other techniques like brain storming, synectics, PAKSA, Reverse learning, CMTE, CMTS, etc., to ascertain their level of effectiveness.

7.4.14 Effect of Super Learning Technique (SLT) may be compared between performances of urban and rural students and between different types of schools under varied administration.

7.4.15 The relation of SLT with that of students' examination stress and development of academic performance can also be studied at different levels of education and on the basis of achievement on different subjects.

APPENDICES

Appendix - A	Tondon's Verbal Group Test on Intelligence (2/70)
Appendix - B	Scoring Key of Verbal Group Test on Intelligence
Appendix - C	Mehdi's Verbal Test on Creative Thinking
Appendix - D	Scoring Sheet of Mehdi's Verbal Test on Creative Thinking
Appendix - E	A Model of Super Learning Lession
Appendix - F	Scattergram Correlation between Achievement Gain Score and Creative Thinking Gain Score

APPENDIX A

Confidential

VERBAL GROUP TEST OF INTELLIGENCE (2/70)
(BY DR. R.K. TONDON)

Do not write and mark anything on this test. All answers are to be written in the answer paper attached at the end of the test.

XX XXX XXX XXX

INSTRUCTION

It is a simple mental ability test. There are 91 questions in five pages which are to be answered within twenty minutes. All questions are written in simple language. You are to find out the correct answer and write the number of answers in the answer paper. Likewise answer of all questions are to be given in numbers. So writing is very less here. In each question there is a correct answer and every answer has a number or numeral. As there is less time it may not be possible for a person to answer all questions. So answer the questions as quick as possible. If any questions seems more difficult. It is better to switch over to another question without wasting time in that.

You will start answering when instruction will be given to do so and will try to answer as quick as possible.

Writing or marking on the test is not allowed.

Now turn over the page and read the questions given for practice.

EXAMPLE FOR PRACTICE

Answers are given in Answer sheet (See the Practice column).

The following questions are like the questions given in the test. Answers of these practice questions are given in the answer sheet. Now we will try to answer those questions.

1. 1, 2, 3, 4, 5, 6,..... write the next number in serial
   (1) 8, (2) 9, (3) 6, (4) 10, (5) 7
2. 5, 10, 15, 20, ... Write next number in serial
   (1) 7, (2) 25, (3) 35, (4) 30, (5) 4
3. Fan is useful for us, because—
   (1) It is costly, (2) It given us air, (3) It looks nice, (4) Everyone can use it easily
4. Mouse is dangerous, because—
   (1) It spreads plague, (2) It frightens in night, (3) They are found in houses, (4) It looks ugly
5. Meaning of the word "Rich" is—
   (1) Kindness, (2) Healthy, (3) Big, (4) Welwisher, (4) Wealthy
6. Meaning of word "Mother" is—
   (1) Friend, (2) Enemy, (3) Relative, (4) Brother, (5) 'Ma'
7. Opposite of Black colour is—
   (1) Dark, (2) Day, (3) White (4) Night, (5) Light
8. Opposite of the word "Life" is—
   (1) End, (2) Death, (3) Pessimism, (4) Pleasure, (4) Soil
9. Cow : Calf :: Goat :
   (1) Horse, (3) Sheep, (3) Kitten, (4) Kid, (5) Dog
10. Lion : Lioness : : King :
    (1) Owner, (2) Maid servant, (3) Queen, (4) Palace, (5) State
11. Ram is sitting in right side of Mahesh and Ramesh in left side of Mahesh. So who is in the middle?
    (1) Ram, (3) Ramesh, (3) Mahesh.
12. If Rita is taller than Rama, Prava is shorter than sita and Rita is taller than Prava. So who is shortest among all?
    (1) Rama, (2) Rita, (3) Sita, (4) Prava.

13. Which word is different from others ?
    (1) Dog, (2) Cat, (3) Monkey, (4) Cow, (5) Rat
14. Which word is different from others?
    (1) Wool, (2) Cartoon, (3) Gum, (4) Silk, (5) Velvet

(If you have any doubt on above questions, you can ask and clear your doubts).

(Do not turn over the Page Until you are told to do so).

QUESTIONS FOR THE TEST

(Write the answers of following questions of this page in column–01 of Page-01 of the answer sheet).

1. What is the meaning of millionnaire—
   (1) Big, (2) Healthy, (3) Rich, (4) Full, (5) Old
2. We wear cotton dresses, because—
   (1) If looks beautiful, (2) It is produced in India in large numbers, (3) It is colourful, (4) It protects the body.
3. Ram is Thiner than Mohan. Kamala is thiner than Rama. Who is the thinest one—
   (1) Ram, (2) Mohan, (3) Kamala
4. Meaning of flower is—
   (1) Tree, (2) wasp, (3) bud, (4) Sunshine, (5) Dust
5. We drink milk because—
   (1) It is tasteful, (2) It is white, (3) Sugar is easily mixed in it, (4) It is useful for health.
6. Opposite of word cold is—
   (1) Hot, (2) Cold, (3) Ice, (4) Water, (5) Fire
7. Tree is helpful for us, because—
   (1) It has leaves, (2) It is dense, (3) It gives us wood, (5) Birds live here.
8. 16, 17, 18, 19, 20, ... Write the next number—
   (1) 22, (2) 25, (3) 14, (4) 21, (5) 23.
9. The meaning of Labourious means—
   (1) Good, (2) Industrious, (3) Lazy, (4) Happy, (5) Cleaver
10. Air is useful. Because—
    (1) It is found in atmosphere, (2) It protects from heat, (3) Cold air is comefortable, (4) It helps in making live.
11. Opposite of word "Friend" is—
    (1) Brother, (2) Relation, (3) Enemy, (4) Own family member, (5) Distance relation
12. Eye : See : : Ear :
    (1) Speak, (2) Smell, (3) Cut, (4) Listen, (5) Walk
13. Water is useful for us, because—
    (1) It helps in washing, (2) We drink it, (3) It is easily available, (3) Mix easily with milk.
14. 6, 7, 12, 13, 18, ... which is the next serial number—
    (1) 14, (2) 10, (3) 15, (4) 19, (5) 25
15. Meaning of word powerless is—
    (1) Sick, (2) patient, (3) strong, (4) weak, (5) sorrowful

16. Rakesh born before Ramesh, Krushna born before Rakesh, so who is youngest?
    (1) Ramesh, (2) Rakesh, (3) Krushna
17. Which word is different from others?
    (1) Bird, (2) Parrot, (3) Mayna, (4) Pigeon, (5) Rabbit
18. Meaning of shouting is—
    (1) Regulation, (2) Loadn, (3) Utter loudly, (4) Jump.
19. 14, 13, 12, 11, 10, ... write the next number—
    (1) 15, (2) 16, (3) 8, (4) 11, (5) 9
20. Cat : Mew : : Dog : ?
    (1) Mother (2) Bark, (3) Brite, (4) Cat
    (Time is short, Be quick is answering from Q. No. 21 in page-2)
    (Write the Answers following questions in Page 2 coloumn of Answer sheet)
21. The opposite of word "Sportive" is—
    (1) Running, (2) Work, (3) Happy, (4) Quick, (5) Sorrowful
22. Playing is necessary for children, because—
    (1) It keeps healthy, (2) It gives new friends, (3) Time will not available in future, (4) It helps in reading.
23. Which word is different?
    (1) Lemon, (2) Banana, (3) Home, (4) Mango, (5) Papaya.
24. Ram is infront of Prem, Shyam is next after Prem, who is in last ?
    (1) Ram, (2) Prem, (3) Shyam
25. We have store, because—
    (1) It makes dark, (2) It is made of iron, (3) It looks nice, (4) It gives heat
26. Meaning of Season is—
    (1) Hot, (2) Shirt, (3) Rain, (4) Fruit, (5) Weather
27. Opposite of Nectar is—
    (1) Hard, (2) Sour, (3) Sweet, (4) Speed, (5) Poison.
28. 5, 8, 11, 14, 17, ... write next number in serial.
    (1) 18, (2) 16, (3) 20, (4) 22, (5) 21.
29. Electricity is profitable because—
    (1) It gives light, (2) It constructs river bond, (3) It is available everywhere, (4) People uses it.
30. Which word is different from others?
    (1) Table, (2) Gitar, (3) Flute, (4) Carrom Board, (5) Sitar

31. Puspa runs faster than Asha, Nirmala runs faster than puspa. Who runs fastest.
(1) Asha, (2) Puspa, (3) Nirmala.
32. Tree : Green : : State :?
(1) Red, (2) Yellow, (3) Black, (4) White, (5) Blue
33. Opposite of Pure is—
(1) Impure, (2) Unholy, (3) Pious, (4) Opague
34. Meaning of brave is—
(1) Win, (2) Strength, (3) Fight, (4) Coward, (5) Powerful
35. 32, 30, 28, 26, 24.... write the next serial number—
(1) 25, (2) 23, (3) 22, (4) 33, (5) 35
36. Which word is different from others?
(1) Black, (2) Yellow, (3) Blue, (4) Dark, (5) White
37. We watch cinema, because—
(1) We meet people there, (2) For use of money, (3) It makes study easy, (4) It gives entertainment.
38. Ram is shorter than Mohan, Mohan is shorter than Krushna, who is tallest?
(1) Ram, (2) Mohan, (3) Krushna
39. Man : Face : : Bird :?
(1) Feather, (2) Head, (3) Beak, (4) Fly, (5) Eat
40. Opposite of the word Power is—
(1) Patient, (2) Powerless, (3) Sorrow, (4) Soft, (5) Pain
(Write answer of following questions in Page-3, column of Answer sheet)
41. Meaning of word "citizen' means—
(1) Villagers, (2) residents of a capital, (3) Hill dwellers, (4) Votes live in a state, (5) Turban
42. 4, 14, 22, 31, 40.... write the next serial number—
(1) 46, (2) 8, (3) 49, (4) 30 (5) 58
43. Which word is different from others?
(1) Table, (2) Chiar, (3) Stove, (4) Cot, (5) Wife
44. If Cricket is more expensive than hockey, hockey is less expensive than badminton and cricket is more expensive than badminton, so which play is most expensive?
(1) Cricket, (2) Hockey, (3) Badminton.
45. One should not take wine, because—
(1) Taking wine is sin, (2) It destroyes the heart, (3) person get intoxicated, (4) It smells bad
46. Opposite of word optimistic—
(1) Pleasure, (2) Success, (3) Sorry, (4) Future, (5) Pessimistic

47. Dog : Goat : : Puppy : ?
(1) Kid, (2) Pigeon, (3) Rabbit, (4) Rat, (5) Puppy
48. Meaning of word "Pradhan"—
(1) Man, (2) Rich, (3) Road, (4) Head, (5) Right
49. 1, 3, 5, 7, 9, ... write next number in serial—
(1) 10, (2) 11, (3) 13, (4) 12, (5) 8
50. Which word is different from others?
(1) Gomati, (2) Godabari, (3) Ganga, (4) Sarojini, (5) Jamuna
51. Rama is more intelligent than prava, Sita is more intelligent than Rama, who is most intelligent?
(1) Prava, (2) Sita, (3) Rama
52. Farmer cultivates, because—
(1) He has plaugh, (2) It makes soil fertile, (3) He has seeds, (4) He is proficient in it.
53. Opposite of the word hospitality is—
(1) Ideal, (2) Disobey, (3) False, (4) Disrespectful, (5) Respect
54. Head : Cap : : Leg :
(1) Cloth, (2) Body, (3) Tape, (4) Shoe, (5) Trouser
55. The organ through which we smell is—
(1) Tongue, (2) Nose, (3) Ear, (4) Eyes, (5) Hand
56. 2, 4, 6, 8, 10, ... write the next number in serial
(1) 11, (2) 9, (3) 01, (4) 12, (5) 14
57. Which word is different from others?
(1) Jump, (2) Bind, (3) Go, (4) Walk, (5) Stand
58. If 'R' is in right of 'C' to left of 'T', which letter is in the middle?
(1) R, (2) C, (3) T
59. Children should go to school, because—
(1) They quarrel at home, (2) They can play new games in school, (3) It can change their behaviour, (4) They can read well.
60. Opposite of word male is—
(1) Son, (2) Youth, (3) Girl, (4) Female, (5) Man
(Write the Answers of following questions in Page 4 column of Answer sheet)
61. Orange : Fruit : : Potato :
(1) Cabbage, (2) Tamato, (3) Beans, (4) Vegetable
62. Meaning of word similar is—
(1) Colour, (2) Same, (3) Nice, (3) Plain, (4) Size

63. 23, 21, 19, 17, 15... write the next number in serial
(1) 14, (2) 13, (3) 22, (4) 23, (5) 32
64. Which word is different from others?
(1) Sea, (2) Stream, (3) Pond, (4) Mountain, (5) River
65. Rama's name comes before Shyam, Shyam's name comes before Krishna, Hari's names comes before Krishna, so which names comes last?
(1) Rama, (2) Shyam, (3) Hari, (4) Krishna
66. We travel in train, because—
(1) It is comfortable, (2) It runs on track, (3) It has Engine, (4) Scenic environment available to see.
67. Opposite of "instruction" is—
(1) Real, (2) Discussion, (3) Beautiful, (4) Conclusion, (5) End.
68. Eating : Water : : Hungry : ?
(1) Lemon, (2) Less, (3) Thirsty, (4) Milk, (5) Fasting
69. Meaning of the word "quarrel" is—
(1) Straight, (2) Tossle, (3) Enviousness, (4) Enemy, (5) Friend.
70. 186, 62, 54, 18, 6, ... write the next number.
(1) 7, (2) 5, (3) 2, (4) 16
71. Which word is different from others?
(1) Fish, (2) Crocodile, (3) Lion, (4) Crab, (5) Tortoise
72. Shyam is more handsome than Suresh, Prem is more handsome than Shyam, Prem is less handsome than Ramesh, so who is least handsome?
(1) Shyam, (2) Suresh, (3) Prem, (4) Ramesh
73. Opposite of Word Ugly is—
(1) Black, (2) Beautiful, (3) White, (4) Young, (5) Attraction
74. Poet : Poetry : : Artist : ?
(1) Heart, (2) Colour, (3) Brush, (4) Art, (5) Scene
75. Meaning of the word "Surprise" is—
(1) Astonishment, (2) Experience, (3) Wasty, (4) Faithless, (5) Happy.
76. 1, 3, 9, 27, 81, ...write the next number
(1) 82, (2) 102, (3), 243, (4) 100, (5) 150
77. Which word is different from others?
(1) Sweet, (2) Salty, (3) Yellow, (4) Sour, (5) Pritter
78. Mannu's name comes before Chunnu, Puspa's name comes before mannu, Tunnu's name comes before Puspa, so whose name is in last?
(1) Munnu, (2) Chunnu, (3) Tunnu, (4) Puspa

79. Opposite of the word "Conscious" is—
(1) Dream, (2) Unconscious, (3) work, (4) Boat, (5) Sleep
80. Cloud : Thunder : : Rain ?
(1) Water, (2) Storm, (3) Lightning, (4) Sound, (5) Difficult.
(You have less time, so answer to Page-5 Quickly)
(Write the Answers of following questions in Page 5 column of Answer sheet)
81. 45, 42, 39, 36, 33, ... write the next number.
(1) 32, (2) 31, (3) 34, (4) 29, (5) 30
82. Which is different from other words?
(1) Tea, (2) Coffee, (3) Roti, (4) Milk, (5) Lassi
83. Om is lighter than Hari, Satish is heavier than Rama but lighter than Hari, Shyam is heavier than Om, but lighter than Rama. Who is lightest among all.
(1) Satish, (2) Rama, (3) Hari, (4) Shyam, (5) Om.
84. Cycle : Pedal : : Boat : ....
(1) Sea, (2) Traveler, (3) Driver, (4) Oar, (5) Sand
85. 1, 3, 6, 10, 15, ... write the next number
(1) 21, (2) 16, (3) 18, (4) 14, (5) 20
86. Which one is different from other words?
(1) Temple, (2) Mosque, (3) Church, (4) Gurudwara, (5) Dharamsala
87. Pear's Dictionary is smaller than Oxford Dictionary, Chamber's Dictionary is smaller than Bhargava Dictionary, Nalanda Dictionary is bigger than Bhargava, both Oxford and Chambers are same. Which dictionary is the biggest one?
(1) Nalanda Dictionary, (2) Oxford Dictionary, (3) Bhargava Dictionary, (4) Chambers Dictionary, (5) Pear's Dictionary
88. Diwali : Light :: Holi :?
(1) Dusserah, (2) Colour, (3) Sports, (4) Festival, (5) Holiday
89. Which word is different from others?
(1) India, (2) China, (3) Japan, (4) Delhi, (5) America
90. Sunday : March : : Monday
(1) Old, (2) April, (3) Month, (4) May, (5) February
91. Day : Night : : Wake up :
(1) Unfaithful, (2) Labour, (3) Comfort, (4) Slumber, (5) Conscious.
(If you have time, you may check your answer).

VERBAL GROUP TEST OF INTELLIGENCE (2/70)

ANSWER SHEET

Name : Class :

Date : School/College :

Age : Profession of father :

Annual income of Family : Your birth order in family :

Example Practice	
Q.	A.
1	5
2	
3	2
4	
5	4
6	
7	3
8	
9	4
10	
11	3
12	
13	5
14	

Page–1		*Page–2*		*Page–3*		*Page–4*		*Page–5*	
Q.	A.	Q.	A.	Q.	A.	Q.	A.	Q.	A.
1		21		41		61		81	
2		22		42		62		82	
3		23		43		63		83	
4		24		44		64		84	
5		25		45		65		85	
6		26		46		66		86	
7		27		47		67		87	
8		28		48		68		88	
9		29		49		69		89	
10		30		50		70		90	
11		31		51		71		91	
12		32		52		72			
13		33		53		73			
14		34		54		74			
15		35		55		75			
16		36		56		76			
17		37		57		77			
18		38		58		78			
19		39		59		79			
20		40		60		80			

APPENDIX B

VERBAL GROUP TEST ON INTELLIGENCE (2/70)

Scoring Key

Name :

Class :

Date :

School/College :

Age :

Profession of father :

Annual income of Family :

Your birth order in family :

Example Practice	
Q.	*A.*
1	5
2	
3	2
4	
5	4
6	
7	3
8	
9	4
10	
11	3
12	
13	5
14	

Page–1		*Page–2*		*Page–3*		*Page–4*		*Page–5*	
Q.	*A.*	*Q.*	*A.*	*Q.*	*A.*	*Q.*	*A.*	*Q.*	*A.*
1	3	21	5	41	5	61	4	81	5
2	4	22	1	42	3	62	1	82	3
3	3	23	3	43	5	63	2	83	5
4	3	24	3	44	1	64	4	84	2
5	4	25	4	45	3	65	2	85	1
6	1	26	5	46	5	66	1	86	5
7	3	27	5	47	1	67	4	87	1
8	4	28	3	48	4	68	3	88	2
9	2	29	4	49	2	69	2	89	4
10	4	30	4	50	3	70	3	90	4
11	3	31	3	51	3	71	3	91	3
12	4	32	3	52	2	72	1		
13	2	33	2	53	4	73	2		
14	4	34	2	54	4	74	4		
15	5	35	3	55	2	75	1		
16	1	36	4	56	4	76	3		
17	5	37	4	57	2	77	3		
18	3	38	2	58	2	78	3		
19	5	39	3	59	4	79	3		
20	2	40	2	60	3	80	3		

APPENDIX C

MEHDI'S VERBAL TEST ON CREATIVE THINKING

Confidential
Dr. BAQER MEHDI
M.A (Columbia), Ph.D. (Aligarh) **TCW**
Professor of Education
N.C.E.R.T., New Delhi-110016

T.M. No. 458715

Name : Age: Class:

School/College :

Father's/Guardian's name: Occupation:

Home address Date :

GENERAL INSTRUCTIONS

In this booklet you will find mentioned some interesting problems which will require the use of your thinking ability and imagination to solve them. The purpose is to see how quickly and imaginatively you can think under situation to solve them. The purpose is to see how quickly and imaginatively you can think under situations which require novel ways of dealing with them. Read each problem carefully and apply your best thinking in giving the responses. Write your responses either in English or in your mother tongue. Responses have to be given briefly but clearly in the space provided under each problem. Give a serial number to each of your responses. There are no right or wrong responses to any of these problems. Therefore, use your imagination to think of as many responses as you can.

The problems are divided into Four Activities. Each Activity is separately timed. Within the time-limit for each Activity you may work on the different problems according to your speed When you finish one problem, go to the next. If necessary. You may return to the previous one again for any addition you would like to make. Remember that you need not go to the next Activity until the time for the first Activity is over and you are told to proceed further.

At the end you will be given 5 minutes extra time. Which you may use for any problem of any Activity in which you want to do additional work.

Please do not omit any problem.

Activity : 1

WHAT WILL HAPPEN, IF ______________

DIRECTIONS

1. On this and the next page, you have been given some situations which will appear to you impossible. You have to think what would happen if such situations actually arise.
2. Give as many ideas as may come to your mind but try to think as many novel ideas as you possible can. Ideas which you think no one else might have thought of what would be the best. Write your response in the space provided for.
3. You will given 15 MINUTES for this activity. After every five minutes you will be told the time that you may move on to the next problem in the activity.

   An example has been given which will help you to know what you have to do.

EXAMPLE

Question : What will happen if birds and animals start speaking like man ?

Responses :
- (i) This world will change into a different kind of society.
- (ii) New leaders will emerge from amongst the animals.
- (iii) It is possible that he becomes our prime minister.
- (iv) It is possible that a donkey will become our leader.
- (v) Men may confide their secrets to their animal friends, etc.

PROBLEMS

1. What will happen if man flies like birds ?

2. What will happen if your school is put on wheels ?

3. What will happen if man does not require any food to eat ?

Activity : 2

NOVEL USES OF THINGS

DIRECTIONS

1. On this and the next page, you have been given names of certain things which could be used in many different ways. You have to think in how many different and new ways the things may be used.
2. Write as many uses as you can, but to try to think also those which are novel, that is, those which you think no one else might have thought of.
3. You will given 12 MINUTES for this activity. After every four minutes you will be told the time so that you may move on to the next item in the activity.

Below is given an example which will help you to know what you have to do.

Example : News paper

Question : (i) To read the news.

(ii) To make paper toys.

(iii) To get protection from the sun.

(iv) To wrap something.

(v) To cover a dirty place, etc.

PROBLEMS

1. Piece of stone

____

____

____

____

2. Wooden Stick

____

____

____

____

3. Water

____

____

____

____

Activity : 3

SIMILARITIES

DIRECTIONS

1. On this and the next page, you have been given pairs of words which can be related to each other in many different ways. You have to think in how many different and new ways are they related.
2. Write as many relationships as you can, but also try to think those which are novel, that is, those which you think no one esle might have thought of.
3. You will be given 15 MINUTES for this activity. After every five minutes you will be told the time so that you may move on to the next item in the activity.

Below is given an example which will help you to know what you have to do.

Example : Man and animal.
Relationship : (i) Both have life.
(ii) Both need food and water.
(iii) Both can fall ill.
(iv) Both are afraid of enemy.
(v) Both have the experience of feeling cold and hot, etc.

PROBLEMS

1. Tree and House

____

____

____

____

2. Chair and Ladder

____

____

____

____

3. Air and Water

____

____

____

____

Activity : 4

MAKING THINGS MORE INTERESTING AND USEFUL

Directions

Just keep in mind a simple model of a horse. You have to imagine in what ways you can change this simple model into an interesting and novel one for children to paly with. You may think of adding any number of parts or accessories in order to make it really interesting and fascinating for children. Do not bother about the cost of the new parts or accessories that you would like to use in order to make the toy model interesting and fascinating for children.

Write all the ideas which come to your mind in a serial order in the space given below.

You will be given 6 MINUTES for this activity.

APPENDIX D

SCORING SHEET OF MEHDI'S VERBAL TEST ON CREATIVE THINKING

SCORING SHEET TCW

ACTIVITY I

	Fluency	Flexibility	Originality
Item 1.	.....	.....	.....
Item 2.	.....	.....	.....
Item 3.	.....	.....	.....
Total	.....	.....	.....

ACTIVITY II

	Fluency	Flexibility	Originality
Item 1.	.....	.....	.....
Item 2.	.....	.....	.....
Item 3.	.....	.....	.....
Total	.....	.....	.....

ACTIVITY III

	Fluency	Flexibility	Originality
Item 1.	.....	.....	.....
Item 2.	.....	.....	.....
Item 3.	.....	.....	.....
Total	.....	.....	.....

ACTIVITY IV

	Fluency	Flexibility	Originality
Item 1.	.....	.....	.....

SCORE SUMMARY

	Fluency	Flexibility	Originality
Activity I	.....	.....	.....
Activity II	.....	.....	.....
Activity III	.....	.....	.....
Activity IV	.....	.....	.....
Grand Total	.....	.....	.....

See page 260 for further instructions regarding originality scorings.

ORIGINALITY SCORING FOR RESPONSES NOT MENTIONED IN THE RESPONSE LIST

For any novel response not mentioned in the response list given in the manual, first of all briefly note it down in the space provided below giving the number of the activity and the item to which it belongs. Then, after you have scored all the test scripts, give it a score according to the scheme given in the manual and note the score in the appropriate column in the Scoring Sheet. In all probability, there will be very few such responses.

Activity	*Item*	*Response*	*Originality Score*

APPENDIX E
A MODEL OF SUPER LEARNING LESSION

Date - 18.2.03

School - University High School, Vani Vihar

Class - IX

Subject - HISTORY

Topic - Industrial Revolution

Time - 50 minutes

Step I. Simple Relaxation (5 minutes)

Teacher : Dear students, Two students are to sit in two extreme ends of a bench. Do as I am doing here. (Teacher has to show following exercises in his action to make things easy for student)

: Take easy breaths. Sit straight. Roll your head clockwise and very slowly. (4 times)

: Stretch your both the hands forward. Raise them up squeez the fingers and open them slowly in both the positions. (2 times)

: Keep two palms in two sides of your waist. Tilt the upper part of your body to right-left and forward-backward. (2 times)

: Stretch your legs, squeez the fingers and open them (4 times) (All those activities are to be practised in open eyes and closed eyes, so that students feel each organ by themselves)

Teacher : How do you feel now ?

Student 1: Sir, I recognised my body.

Student 2: In closed eyes I feel my body better.

Student 3: I am feeling light.

Student 4: I am feeling my body as a oiling bi-cycle.

Student 5: Now I feel easy to work.

Teacher : Very good. All your feelings are interesting. If we will practise these exercises more and more you would experience more better things.

Step II. Visualization and Affirmation (7 minutes)

Teacher : Let us sit comfortably. Take deep and easy breaths. Close the eyes, take deep breaths easily. Listen the music going on in background and take breaths. Alongwith imagine-"It is an early morning. Golden rays of rising sun spreading allover. Green meadows shine calm and dazzling as if fogs washed them and soft sun rays giving a cleansing touch. You are walking in a wide road. You are going up to a hill. Hill is full of natural beauties. Green deep dense forest. As you go up you feel as if the bushes, grasses, plants and trees are welcoming you with rosy smiles. You are exchanging your laugh. You are moving forward. You entered a snowy land where the sun seems nearer to you. You see, the sun is coming nearer and nearer to you. The 'Big sun' is becoming small and getting slowly into your head through the root of your nose. You see inside your head the sun is flashing light brighter and brighter."

Teacher : Dear students if you have not seen all the above things don't feel inferior. Everything will be seen by you through practice.

Now you say to yourself the following sentences and feel:

'I am powerful'
'I can do everything'
'Success is at my hand'
'Failure would FAIL at me'
'I am full of super energy'
'I can achieve everything'

Teacher : How do you feel now ?
Student 1: "I feel delighted"
"I have lost my weakpoints".
Student 2: "I feel myself rising"
"I feel, I am floating on calm sea"
Student 3 : "I am getting my memory return"
Student 4 : "I am feeling energetic"
Student 5 : " I can do mathematics"
Student 6 : "I would never fear at snake, I can play with that"
Student 7 : "I would sing better than Tapasi"

Teacher : Many many thanks. Your are young and all energy is within you. You are full of all possibilities. What you want is only cultivation of that energy. Your feeling is very satisfactory. You can do everything. Go on thinking so.

Student 4: "Thank you sir"

Teacher : You are welcome

Student 7: "Sir, I am feeling confident"

Student 8: "I can win the first prize in long jump"

Teacher : Yes, you can.

Step III. Breathing Exercise (8 minutes)

Teacher : 'Dear students' sit silently in straight, and comfortably keeping both hands on the lap. Look at the point on the cardboard. Listen to the music, take the breath rhythmically to the count of 4 keep it for count of 4 leave the breath in counting four, take rest till counting four. Repeat the activities again and again but according to the rhythm of music. If you can, you can increase inhaling, exhale, etc. to the count of 5, 6, 7, and so on.

(Two cardboards containing deep black points are to be hanged on the wall before two rows of students)

- Feel the movement of breath within your body.
- Concentrate the point of cardboard in the root of at your nose and practise breathing with music. Continue for 5 minutes.
- How do you feel now ?

Student 1: "I feel open"

Student 2: "I feel free"

Student 3: "I have no problem. Now I can solve all mathematics".

Student 4 : "Solution of problems seem to me clearly"

Student 5 : "I feel comfort"

Teacher : Very good. All of your feelings are right. If you go on practising like this, you can feel better.

: Now you practise that concentration again for two minutes.

Step IV. Presentation of Super Learning Frame (30 minutes)

(i) Statement of Instructional Objectives

(a) Knowing the concept of Industrial Revolution, Invention, Discoveries of great persons, characteristics of industrial revolution. Contribution of nations towards it.
(b) Understanding cause and impact of industrial revolution.
(c) Inspiring students to develop such type of creative thinking and skills.
(d) Imagining the effects of invented things.

(ii) Statement of Major Themes

(a) Concept of Industrial Revolution.
(b) Factors effected of Industrial Revolution.
(c) Process of Industrial Revolution.
(d) Impact of Industrial Revolution.

(iii) Statement of Minor Themes

(a) Concept of Industrial Revolution
- a_1 : Concept of Revolution.
- a_2 : Difficulties of Mannual Labour.
- a_3 : Solution through machinery assistance.
- a_4 : Change brought through Machines and Industries is Revolution.

(b) Factors effected Industrial Revolution.
- b_1 : Capitalist and Industrialists.
- b_2 : Imperialism of Capitalists and Industrialists.
- b_3 : Demand and Supply theory-Problem.
- b_5 : England the centre of Industrial Revolution.

(c) Process of Industrial Revolution.
- c_1 : Discovery of Sea Routes.
- c_2 : Creation of New markets.
- c_3 : Invention of modern process of production.

(d) Impact of Industrial Revolution.
- d_1 : Change in lifestyle.
- d_2 : Impact on Industrial field.
- d_3 : Impact on Agriculture.

d_4 : Socio-economic life of people.
d_5 : Cultural Transmission.

(It is natural that the entire topic cannot be presented in a single class. Considering this, it was decided to transact the entire topic in four classes making students learn one major theme in a single period. Since, the proposed model is for a single period, only one major theme is presented here in synchronized form and the succeeding activities also based on this single major theme.

Though all the major and minor themes are presented here for complete knowledge on the topic, it is needless to present all in the lesson plan which is prepared for a single class. In a single lesson plan/model those themes should be presented which will be transacted within that specific class).

IV. Synchronized presentation of learning theme (15 minutes)

(a) Presentation without music

Major Theme : Factors effected Industrial Revolution.

Minor Theme No. 1 : Capitalists and Industrialists.

It was 15th century A.D. The European society gave rise to a section of rich people. Those rich people invested their money in producing articles required by others. By selling their products they get profit and become richer. As maximum of Capital was with those persons of the society, they were called CAPITALIST.

* Rich persons those become richer by business and acquire much capital were called CAPITALISTS, in Europe.
* Capitalism developed in Europe from 1500 A.D.

To get more profit with less investment, the capitalists established industries. Industries produced more goods in less time and owner get more profit. Persons, those established industries came to be known as INDUSTRIALIST.

CAPITALIST	INDUSTRIALSIT
* Has much money or capital	* Has much money or capital
* Does business to increase money	* Establishes factories/ Industries to produce required products.

* BOTH INVEST THEIR CAPITAL FOR PROFIT.

PROFIT-MOTIVES OF INDUSTRIALISTS AND CAPITALISTS HELPED INDUSTRIAL REVOLUTION

INCREASED NECESSITIES OF PEOPLE BECAME CAUSE OF DEVELOPMENT OF CAPITALISM

Minor Theme No. 2 : Imperialism of Capitalists and Industrialists.

Columbus discovered sea route to America. Vasco-da-Gama discovered sea route to India.

What could have been the impact of such discoveries ? → See the world Map and Say

Impacts of Sea Route Discovery

* Imperialism Established by Capitalists
* Big Cities and Towns established
* New Business Centres Founded
* Imperialists and Capitalists exploited the new lands.

*IMPERIALISM HELPED CAPITALISTS IN GETTING RAW-MATERIALS AT LOWEST COST.
*THEY COLLECTED HUMAN LABOUR AT LOW COST

CAPITALISTS GET NEW MARKET, NEW DEMANDS AND SET-UP NEW INDUSTRIES

CORDIAL RELATION AMONG PEOPLE OF VARIOUS COLONIES AND HOMOGENOUS STATES CREATED GOOD ATMOSPHERE FOR INDUSTRIALIZATION

Minor Theme No. 3 : Demand-Supply Problem

Teacher : What happens when people's requirement exceeds the supplied things ?

Students : People compete to take the things first.
- People search for another market.
- Some think of solving problem.

Teacher : When new colonies found, new states were discovered and route of communication established, the Businessmen took their things to the new places. In comparison to the number of people and their requirements businessmen had less product to sell. So capitalists wanted to sell more and get more profit.

* LESS SUPPLY AND MORE DEMAND INSPIRED BUSINESSMEN TO PRODUCE MORE

* TO PRODUCE MORE WAS TO REPLACE MANUAL LABOUR BY MACHINE

Minor Theme No. 4 : Imagination to solve Demand-Supply Problem.

Teacher : What do you do when you face a problem ?
Student 1 : "I try to solve that"
Student 2 : "I take help of elders and friends"
Student 3 : "I remember the related problem I faced before"
Student 4 : "I sit and think the way to solve"
Student 5 : "I try, I fail, I again try and solve"
Student 6 : "I leave the task, go to play and try to solve after sometime"
Studnet 7 : "I never leave the problem unsolved"

Student 8: "I think when I face the problem".

Teacher : Very good. Actually these are the ways to solve the problem and some Europeans also thought of the means to replace the manual labour. They imagined and invented different power machines which could able to produce more things in less time.

NECESSITY IS THE
MOTHER OF INVENTION

* IMAGINATION BRINGS SOLUTION EASILY.
* IMAGINATION IS THE ROOT OF EVERY CREATION.

Minor Theme No. 5 : England—The centre of Industrial Revolution.

Teacher : Among all countries of Europe England was atop industrial revolution, Why ?

Student 1: "People of England were very intelligent and Creative"

Student 2: "They were educated"

Student 3: "They were businessmen, They knew the process"

Student 4: "England had an empire where sun never sets"

Student 5: "England was taking everything from India at no cost and was producing different things."

Teacher : You all are absolutely right. England had a large number of colonies all over the world. That commercial race had a large market and demand. English people were collecting raw-materials from their colonies without payment They had wide sea routes and ships for voyage and transportation. So England led the Industrial revolution, in Europe.

England led Industrial Revolution in Europe because—

* It had maximum number of colonies
* It had a wide market with high demand
* It had viable sea route and ships for transport
* England was collecting raw materials from her colonies without payment and labourers at low cost.

ENGLAND WAS THE CENTRE OF THE INDUSTRIAL REVOLUTION IN EUROPE

CAUSES OF INDUSTRIAL REVOLUTION

* Capitalists and industrialists invested in business of profit.
* There was high demand and low supply of goods.
* Imperialism brought the raw materials and labourer to easy reach of capitalists.
* Opening of sea routes, new cities and Towns increased people's access and demand.
* Shortage of supply made entreprenuers to think of new means.
* Necessity is the mother of Inventions.
* Wide-spread British imperialism excelled industrial revolutions.

(b) Presentation with music

The informations those were given in blocks are to be presented before the students in cardboards. Then those things were presented again before the students with rhythmic pace of the super learning music.

V. Memorisation of Learned Maters with Music (7 minutes)

Teacher : Dear Students, raise the point of your difficulty. We will present them again. But try to listen them attentively and in calm.

Student 1 : Sir, I could not remember the similarity between capitalists and industrialist.

Teacher : (Showing the cardboard containing similarity between capitalists and industrialist) both have money and both are interested to invest money for profit. Increased necessities made both more interested to invest money in business and industry.

Student 2 : Sir, Who discovered sea route to India ?
Teacher : Who can say ?
Student 1 : Sir, Vasco-da-gama.
Teacher : Good, you are absolutely correct.
Student 3 : I could not member the last point of Impact of sea route discovery.
Teacher : Who can tell that ?
Student 4 : "Imperialists exploited the new lands".
Student 5 : "Capitalist looted the new-land".
Teacher : You both are correct. But see it again. What it reads ?
"Imperialists and capitalists exploited the new lands".
Student 6 : "Why capitalists were interested in setting new industries ?"
Student 7 : Sir, Can I say ?
Teacher : Yes, you are welcome.
Student 7 : "New market and high demand inspired them to set-up industries"
Teacher : Good, You are absolutely correct.
Student 8 : What is Industrial Revolution ?
Teacher : "You can speak".
Student 8 : "It it the spread of machine power and industry to meet people's demand ?"
Student 9 : "No, Sir, it is the replacement of manual labour by machine to bring more products".
Teacher : You both are correct. Primarily there was manual labour to produce things. By industrial revolution people depend more on machines than on hand. And spread of industry brought spectacular change in economic, social, cultural and agricultural life of Europe. So it was called industrial revolution. Have you.
: "Have you any other problem" ?
Student : "No Sir".
Teacher : Thanks.

VI. Evaluation and Feedback (5 minutes)

Teacher : Dear Students, I am giving you all an evaluation sheet containing some questions. You are to answer the questions within 5 minutes and handover that to me.

Q. 1. Answer in a word or two:

(a) When did capitalism developed in Europe ?

(b) Who first established the imperialism ?

(c) Who discovered Sea route to India ?

Q. 2. (a) How Industrial revolution is helped by sea route discovery ?

(b) Why England spearheaded the industrial revolution ?

Q. 3. "Necessity is the mother of Invention". Explain in context of Industrial Revolution in Europe.

Q. 4. What are the causes of Industrial Revolution ?

(The collected evaluation sheets will be scrutinized later on and the student's achievement will be judged. On the performance of students they will be provided proper guidance and feedback thereof).

APPENDIX F
SCATTERGRAM CORRELATION BETWEEN ACHIEVEMENT GAIN SCORE AND CREATIVE THINKING GAIN SCORE

AGS/ CTGS	*-39 to -44*	*-33 to -38*	*-27 to -31*	*-21 to -26*	*-15 to -20*	*-9 to -14*	*-3 to -8*	*3 to -2*	*9 to 4*	*15 to 10*	*21 to 16*	*27 to 22*	*32 to 28*	*f*	*y*	*fy*	*fy²*	*fxy*
-8 to -22	1 7						2 2	1 0	1 -1					5	-1	-5	5	8
7 to -7			1 0		4 0	5 0	9 0	15 0	3 0	1 0				38	0	0	0	0
22 to 8						2 -4	1 '-1	2 0						5	1	5	5	-5
37 to 23									1 2	1 4	1 6			3	2	6	12	12
52 to 38									3 9	3 18	3 27	2 24	1 15	12	3	36	108	93
67 to 53										5 40	1 12	2 32	3 48	11	4	44	176	132
82 to 68									1 5	6 60	3 45	1 20		11	5	55	275	130
97 to 83											2 36			2	6	12	72	36
102 to 98											2 42			2	7	14	98	42
117 to 103										2 32	2 43			4	8	32	256	80
122 to 118									1 9					1	9	9	81	9
137 to 123									1 10					1	10	10	100	10
142 to 138														0	11	00	00	0
157 to 143										1 24				1	12	12	144	24
t	1	0	1	0	4	7	12	18	11	19	14	5	4	96		230	1332	571
x	-7	-6	-5	-4	-3	-2	-1	0	1	2	3	4	5					
fx	-7	0	-5	0	-12	-14	-12	0	11	38	42	20	20	81				
fx²	49	0	25	0	36	28	12	0	11	76	126	80	100	543				
fxy	7	0	0	0	0	-4	1	0	34	178	216	76	63	571				

AGS = Achievement Gain Score. CTGS = Creative Thinking Gain Score.

BIBLIOGRAPHY

Abhedanada S. (1999). *Yoga Psychology*, Calcutta : Ramakrishna Vedanta Matha.

Abney, C.W. (1970). A Comparative study of creative thinking ability in three student groups at the University of Arkansas as measured by the Remote Associates Test. *Dissertion Abstracts International*, 30, 7, 2717-A.

Abrezol, R. (1988). *Winning ! Sporology*, New York : Super Learning INC

Abrezol, R. (1987). *Adventuring With Brain*. New York : Super Learning INC.

Acharyula, S.T.V.G. (1977). *A study of the relationship among creative thinking, intelligence and school achievement*. Unpublished doctoral dissertation, Utkal University, Orissa.

Adaman, J.E. and Blaney, P.H. (1995). The effects of musical mood induction on creativity. *The Journal of Creative Behaviour, 29* (2), 95-108.

Adamson, C. (1990). *Suggestopedia*. New York : Chiron.

Aggarwal, Y.P. (1990). *Statistical Methods—Concepts, Applications and Computation*. New Delhi : Sterling Publishers Pvt. Ltd.

Ajaya, S. (1983). *Psychotherapy East and West : A unifying paradigm*. Honedale, Pennsylvania : The Himalayan International Institute of Yoga Science and Philosophy of the USA.

Ali, H., Boorstein, S., Dass, R., Goldstein, J., Goleman, D., Hall, R., Kornfield, J., Mc Donald, M., Salzberg, S., Vaughan, F.

and Walsh, R. (1988). Psychotherapy and Meditation. *Inquiring Mind, 5*(1), 1-9.

Anastati, A., and Schaefer, C.S. (1971). Note on the concepts of creativity and intelligence. *The Journal of Creative Behaviour. 5* (2), 113-16.

Arieti, S. (1976). *Creativity : The Magic Synthesis*. New York : Basic Books.

Asha, C.B. (1980). Creativity and academic achievement among secondary school children. *Asian Journal of Psychology and Education, 6,* 1-4.

Ashman, A.F., Write, S.K., and Conway, R.N.F. (1995). Developing the metacognitive skills of academically gifted students in mainstream classroom. *Psychological Abstracts, 81*, 8, 3595.

Ausubel, D.P. (1963). *Psychology of meaningful verbal learning : An introduction to school learning*. New York : Grace and Stratton Inc.

Bagchi, S. (2004). Headed for a heart attack. *The Telegraph—Weekend,* Feb. 28.

———, (2004). Memory pills. *The Telegraph Know-how*. Monday, March 1st.

Bandler, R. (1985). *Using Your Brain—For a Change*. Mob UT : Real People Press.

Banerjee, S. (2004), Healing Touch. *The Telegraph—Weekend,* Saturday, 21 Feb.

Barber, T.X. (1970). *LSD, marijuna, yoga and hypnosis*. Chicago : Aldine Publishing Company.

Baska, J.V. (1997). Response to varieties of intellectual talent. *The Journal of Creative Behavior. 31*(2), 125-50.

Basu, A.N. (1947). *Education in Modern India,* Calcutta : Orient Book Company.

Bay, E. (1984). *Maximizing performance*. Toronto : Relaxation Response.

———, (1983). *Progressive Relaxation and Basis Autogenics*. Toronto : Relaxation Response.

Behera, A.P. (1993). Sex Difference in Creativity : A Study in Navodaya Vidyalayas. *Journal of Indian Education, 19*(2), 46-48.

Benson, H. (1975). *The Relaxation Response*. New York : Morrow.

Best, J.W. and Khan, J.V. (1991). *Research in education*. New Delhi: Prentice Hall of India Pvt. Ltd.

Bhajanananda, S. (1980a). Concentration and meditation-I. *Prabudha Bharata, 85*, 7, 282-88.

———, (1980b). Concentration and Meditation-II. *Prabudha Bharata, 85*, 8, 322-29.

———, (1980c). Concentration and Meditation-III. *Prabudha Bharata, 85*, 9, 362-68.

———, (1980d). Concentration and Meditation-IV. *Prabudha Bharata, 85*, 10, 402-09.

———, (1980e). Concentration and Meditation-V. *Prabudha Bharata, 85*, 11, 442-49.

———, (1981a). Types of meditation-I. *Prabudha Bharata, 86*, 5, 202-07.

———, (1981b). Upasana—A unified descipline. *Prabudha Bharata. 86*, 7, 282-89.

———, (1983). Three highways of meditation. *Prabudha Bharata, 88*, 9, 162-70.

Bhatia, S. (2004). The art of living well, *The Telegraph—Weekend*, Saturday 14. February.

———, (2004). At full stretch. *The Telgraph—Graphiti*, Sunday, May 9.

Bhowmik, S. (2004). On a high. *The Telegraph—Weekend*. Saturday, March 13.

Bloom, B.S. (1956). *Taxonomy of educational objectives : Cognitive domain, Book I*. New York : Mc Kay.

Bochow, P., and Wagner, H. (1986). *Suggestopedie Superlearning*. Sp eyer, Ger : Gabal.

Bono, E.D. (1986). *CoRt Thinking Teacher's Notes 1-6*. Oxford : pergamon Press.

Borg, W.R., and Gall, M.D. (1989). *Educational Research : An Introduction*. New Delhi : Longman.

Bower, G.H., and Hilgard, E.R. (1986). *Theories of Learning*. New Jersy : Prentice-Hall International Inc.

Brandt, R. (1984). Overview : Teaching of Thinking, for Thinking, about Thinking. *Educational Leadership, 42*(1), 3.

Brown, D.R. (1977). A Model for the Levels of Concentration Meditation. *International Journal of Clinical and Experimental Hypnosis*. 25, 266-73.

Brown, D.P. (1986). The Stages of Meditation in Cross Cultural Perspective. In K. Wilber; J. Engler and D.P. Brown, *Transformations of Consciousness : Conventional and Contemplative Perspectives on Development* (pp. 17-52). Shambala, Boston and London : New Science Library.

Brown, D.P. and Engler, J. (1980). The Stages of Mindfulness Meditation : A Validation Study. *The Journal of Transpersonal Psychology. 12,* 2, 143-92.

Bruce, J., and Weil, M. (1992). *Models of Teaching*. New Delhi : Prentice-Hall of Indian Pvt. Ltd.

Bruch, C.B. (1988). Metacreativity : Awareness of thoughts and feelings during creative experiences. *The Journal of Creative Behavior,* 22 (2), 112-21.

Broks, P. (2004). Innerself. *The Telegraph—Knowhow, Monday*. 1st December.

Buch, M.B. (ed.) (1985). *Third All India Survey on Educational Research*. New Delhi : National Council of Educational Research and Training.

———, (ed.) (1993). *Fourth All India Survey on Educational Research*. New Delhi : NCERT.

———, (ed.) (1998) *Fifth All India Survey on Educational Research*. New Delhi : NCERT.

Burns, M.T. (1988). Music as a Tool for Enhancing Creativity. *The Journal of Creative Behavior, 22*(1), 62-69.

Buyer, L.S. (1988). Creative Problem-solving : A Comparison of Performance under Different Instuctions. *The Journal of Creative Behaviour. 22*(1), 55-61.

Camp, G.C. (1995). A Longitudinal Study of Correlates of Creativity. *Psychological Abstructs, 82*(3), 1417.

Carroll, J. and Howieson, N. (1992). Recognizing Creative Thinking Talent in the Classroom. *Roeper Review, 14*(4), 209-21

Carson, P.P., and Carson, K.D. (1993). Managing Creativity Enhancement through Goal Setting and Feedback. *The Journal of Creative Behavior, 27* (1), 36-45.

Chadha, N.K. and Chandna, S. (1990). Creativity, Intelligence and Scholastic Achievement : A Residual Study. *Indian Educational Review, 25*(3), 81-85.

Chaudhury, H.C. (1975). *Yoga Psychology*. In C.T. Tart (ed.) Transpersonal Psychologies. San Francisco : Harper and Row.

Chandhury, K.P. (1953). *Contents of History in Indian Schools.* New Delhi : Ministry of Education. Govt. of India.

———, (1954). *Audio-visual Aids in Teaching Indian History.* Delhi: Atmaram and Sons.

———, (1975). *Effective Teaching of History in India—A Handbook for History Teachers.* New Delhi. NCERT.

Chaudhury, P. (2003). Powerful chemicals combat stress at cellular level. *The Telegraph—Knowhow,* Monday, 17, November.

Chakrabarty, B.D. (1992). *Education of the Creative Children.* New Delhi : Konark Publishers Pvt. Ltd.

Cheng, S.K. (1999). East-West difference in views on creativity : Is Howard Gardner correct ? Yes or No. *The Journal of Creative Behavior, 33(2),* 112-25.

Chetanananda, S. (ed.) (2003). *Meditation and Its Methods.* New York : Vedanta Press, Hollywood.

Chopra, P. (Ed.) (2003). Yoga returns. *Life Positive, 7(12).*

———, (2003). Memory to improve it. *Life Positive. 8(5).*

Chopra, P. (Ed.) (2003). Memory to improve it. *Life Positive. 8(7).*

Chumaceiro, C.D. (1995). Serendipity or Pseudoserendipity ? Unexpected *versus* Desired Results. The *Journal of Creative Behaviour. 29(2),* 143-47.

Cline, V.B., Richards, J.M., and Needham, W.E. (1963). Creativity Tests and Achievement in High School Science. *Journal of Applied Psychology. 47(3),* 184-89.

Cole, D.G., Sugioka, H.L., and Lynch, L.C.Y. (1999). Supportive Classroom Environments for Creativity in Higher Education. *The Journal of Creative Behavior. 33(4),* 277-93.

Cronish, I.M. (1989). The Relationship beween Convergence-Divergence and Free Recall of Discourse. *British Journal of Educationl Psychology, 52*(2), 258-61.

Crawford, R.P. (1954). *The Teachniques of Creative Thinking.* New York : Howthorn Books Inc.

Clurtis, L. (1989). *How to Turn Stress into Energy with Seven Minutes Stress Breakers.* New York : Super borning Inc.

Dasgupta, S.N. (1927). *Hindu Mysticism.* Delhi : Motilal Banarasidass.

———, (1930). *Yoga Philosophy.* Delhi : Motilal Banarasidass.

Davidow, J.R. (1995). The Aims of Intervention. *Psychology in the Schools, 31* (4), 305-08.

Davis, G.A., Kogan, N., and Soliman, A.M. (1999). The Qutar Creativity conference : Research and Recommendations for School, Family and Society. *The Journal of Creative Behavior, 33* (3), 151-66.

Davrou, J. and Lecerg, F. (1982). *Sophotherapy : Psychotherapeutic Application of Sporology.* Paris : Retz.

Dececco, J.P., and Crawford, W.R. (1988). *The Psychology of Learning and Instruciton.* New Jersy : Prentice Hall Pvt. Ltd.

De Kieffer, R., and Lee, W.C. (1995). *Manual of Audio-Visual Teachniques.* New Jersy : Prentice-Hall Pvt. Ltd.

De Haan, R.F., and Havinghurst, R.J. (1957). *Educating Gifted Children.* Chicago : Chicago University Press.

Delmonte, M.M. (1987). Contemporary Theoretical Approaches to Meditation. In M.A. West (Ed.), *On the Psychology of Meditation.* Oxford, England : Clarendon Press.

Deneen, J. (1998). Super Learning : Relaxation, Baroque Musio Key to New Teaching. *The Toronto Star,* 22.

Devananda, S.V. (2001). *Meditation and Mantras.* Delhi : Motilal Banarasidass Publishers Pvt. Ltd.

Devananda, S.V. (1986). *A Complete Illustration of Yoga.* New York: Advaita Ashram.

Dewing, K. (1970). Some Correlates of Creativity Test Performance in Seventh Grade Children. *American Journal of Psychology, 22* (3), 269-76.

Drevadahl, E.J. (1962). Educational Etiology of Creativity. *The Gifted Child Quarterly, 6,* 91-94.

Edward, M.P., and Tylor, L.E. (1965). Intelligence, Creativity and Achievement in a Non-selective Public Junior High School. *Journal of Educational Psychology, 56* (2), 96-99.

Engler, J. (1986). Therapeutic Aims in Psychotherapy and Meditation. In K. Wilber, J. Engler and Brown, D.P., *Transformation of Consciousness : Conventional and Contemplative Perspectives on Development* (pp. 17-52). Boston: New Science Library.

Feldhusen, J.F., and Clinkenbeard, P.R. (1986). Creativity Instructional Materials : A Review of Researh. *The Journal of Creative Behavior, 20* (3), 153-81.

Feldhusen, J.F., (1995). Creativity : A Knowledge base, Metacognitive Skills and Personality Factors. *The Journal of Creative Behavior, 29* (4), 255-67.

Feuerstein, G. (2002). The Yoga Tradition—Its History, Literature, Philosophy and Practice, Bhavana Books and Prints N.D.

Findlay, I.J. (1923). *History and It's Place in Education.* London : University of London Press.

Foshay, W.R., and Foshay, A.W. (1981). Curriculum Development and Instructional Development. *Educational Leadership,* 38(8), 621-25.

Frasier, M.M. (1987). Creativity. In Cecil R. Reynolds (Ed.). Aging in the 1980s : *Encyclopedia of Special Education, 1,* (pp. 422-24). New York : John Wiley and Sons.

Freeman, F. S. (1962). *Theory and Practice of Psychological Testing.* New Delhi : Oxford and IBH Publishing Co.

Freeman, J., Butcher, H.J., and Christie, T. (1971). *Creativity—A Selective Review of Research* (Second Ed.). Monograph 5. London : Society for Research into Higher Education Ltd.

Freeman, J. (1995). Gifted School Performance and Creativity. *Psychological Abstracts, 82,* 3, 1417.

Freud, S. (1964). *An Outline of Psychoanalysis.* London : Hograth Press.

Fryling, V. (1983). *Autogenics and Success Strategies.* New York : Superlearning Inc.

———, (1982). *Stressfree Learning and Super Perforamce.* New York: Superlearning Inc.

Gakhar, S.C. (1985). Intelligence, Creativity and Achievement in Mathematics : A Regression Analysis. *Journal of the Institute of Educational Research, 9* (3), 17-20.

Gaekwad, A., Nautiol, S., Pai, S., and Paremu, B. (1994). The Effect of Brainstorming on the Creativity Scores of Institutionalized and Non-institutionalized Girls. *Indian Journal of Psychology, 69* (1&2), 51-56.

Garrett, H.E. (1966). *Statistics in Psychology and Education.* Bombay : Vakils, Feffer and Simons Pvt. Ltd.

Gawain, S. (1978). *Creative Visualization.* San Ratael CA : New World Library.

Gay, L.R. (1990). *Educational Research : Competencies for Analysis and Application,* Singapore : Maxwell Maxmillan Publishing Pvt. Ltd.

Gehlbach, R.D. (1991). Play, Piaget and creativity : The promise of design. *The Journal of Creative Behavior, 25* (2), 137-44.

Gelade, G. (1995). Creative Style and Divergent Production. *The Journal of Creative Behavior, 26* (1), 36.53.

Getzels, J.W., and Jackson, P.W. (1962). *Creativity and Intelligence—Exploraton with Gifted Students*. New York : John wiley and Sons.

Ghate, V.D. (1953). *Suggestions for Teaching of History*. Bombay : Oxford University Press.

Ghose, K.D. (1951). *Creative Teaching of History*. London : Oxford University Press.

Gilgen, A.R., and Cho, J.H. (1980). Eastern and Western Perspectives in Transpersonal Belief Systems. *Psychological Reports, 47*, 1344-46.

Gill, A.S., and Viswakarma, M. (2004). Beat it. *The Telegraph-Fitness*, 11, Monday, 16th February.

Goldberg, C. (1986). The Interpersonal aim of Creative Endeavor. *The Journal of Creative Behavior, 21* (1), 35-48.

Goleman, D. (1977). *The Varieties of Meditative Experiences*. New York : Dutton.

Goleman, D. (1978). Meditation : Aspects of Research and Practice. *The Journal of Interpersonal Psychology, 10* (2), 113-33.

Golub, S., and Hann, K.S. (1983). Training Creative Thinking in the Open and Traditional Classroom. *The Journal of Creative Behavior, 17* (3), 217-18.

Goode, E. (2003). Critical Purpose. *The Telegraph—Knowhow. Health. Monday*, 1st December.

Gowan, J.C. (1977). Some New thoughts on the Development of Creativity. *The Journal of Creative Behavior, 11* (2), 77-90.

Gnaneswarananda, S. (2001). *Yoga for Beginners*. Chennai: Sri Ramkrishna Math.

Greeley, L. (1986). The Bumper Effect Dynamic in the Creative Process : The Philosophical, Psychological and Neuropsychological Link. *The Journal of Creative Behavior. 20* (4), 261-74.

Grigsby, C.E., and Harshaman, H.W. (1984). Learning to Relax: A Self-directed Method for Enhancing Creative Behavior. *The Journal of Creative Behavior, 18* (4), 275.

Grossman, S. and Wiseman, E.E. (1993). Seven Operating Principles for Enhanced Creative Problem-solving Training. *The Journal of Creative Behavior, 27* (1), 01-17.

Guilford, J.P. (1950). Creativity. *The American Psychologist*. 5, 444-54.

———, (1956). *Fundamental Statistics* in *Psychology and Education*. (Third Edition), New York : Mc Graw Hill Pvt. Ltd.

———, (1959). Three faces of intellect. *American Psychologist, 14*; 469-79.

———, (1967). *The Nature of Human Intelligence*. New York : Mc Graw Hill.

———, (1983). Transformation Abilities or Functions. *The Journal of Creative Behavior, 17* (2), 75-83.

Gulati, S. (2000). Teaching for Creative Edeavour. *Journal of Indian Education, XXVI* (3), 01-21.

Gupta, A.K. (1974). Creativity Research in India-Its Past and future. *Creativity News letter, 3* (1), 18-24.

Gupta, P.K. (1990). Development and Evaluation of Creative Training Programme for Sixth Grade Children. *Indian Educational Review, 25* (1), 95-99.

Gupta, R. (1972). Creativity : Its Relation with Intelligence. *Creativity Newsletter, 1*, 1.

Hall, C.S. and Lindzey, G. (1985). *Theories of Personality*. New Delhi : Wiley Eastern Ltd.

Hampden-Turner, C. (1981). *Maps of the Mind : Charts and Concepts of Mind and its Labyrinths* : New York : Macmillan Publishing Co.

Heiman, B. (1964). *The Facets of Indian Thought*. England : George Allen and Unwin Ltd.

Holmes, D. (1984). Meditation and Somatic Arousal. *American Psychologist, 39* (1), 1-10.

Holland, J.L. (1961). Creative and Academic Performance among Talented Adolescents. *Journal of Educational Psyhcology, 52* (3), 136-47.

Hooda, R.C. and Jarial, G.S. (1986). Effect of Teaching through Mastery Learning Strategy on the Creativity of Students. *The Journal of Creative Behavior, 20* (2), 143.

Hota, A.K. (1993). Creative Potential, Achievement Motivation and Self-concept of Urban, Rural and Tribal Adolescents of Western Orissa. *Indian Educational Review, 28* (2, 3 and 4), 106-10.

Hullfish, G., and Smith, P.G. (1964). *Reflective Thinking, The Method of Education*. New Delhi : Do DD, MEAD and Co.

Isaksen, S.G., Puccio, G.J., and Treffinger. (1993). An Ecological Approach to Creativity Research : Profiling for Creative Problem-solving. *The Journal of Creative Behavior, 27* (3), 149-70.

Isaksen, S.G., and Parnes, S.J. (1985). Curriculum Planning for Creative Thinking and Problem-solving. *The Journal of Creative Behavior, 19* (1), 1-29.

Jacobson, M.A. (1966). The Relationship of Creative Thinking Ability, Intelligence and School Performance. *Dissertation Abstracts International, 26* (12), 7157.

Jampole, E.S. (1993). Effects of Imagery Training of the Creative Writing of Academically Gifted Elementary Students. *Psychological Abstracts, 80* (1), 424.

Jampole, E.S., Mathews, F.N. and Konopack, B.C. (1994). Academically Gifted Students' Use Imagery for Creative Writing. *The Journal of Creative Behavior, 28* (1), 1-20.

Kaha, C.W. (1983). The Creative Mind : Form and Process. *The Journal of Creative Behavior, 17* (2), 84-94.

Kaile, H.S. (1983). *Intelligence and Creativity as Predictors of Scholastic Achievement in Mother Tongue and Foreign Language at different Levels of Socio-ecnomic Status.* Unpublished Doctoral Dissertation in Education, Punjab University, India.

Katiyar, P.C., and Jarial, G.S. (1985). Programme for Developing Creativity in School Children. *The Journal of Creative Behavior. 19* (3), 219-20.

Kaur, P., and Kharb, D. (1993). Creativity in Children : The Impact of School and Home Environment. *Journal of Indian Education, 18* (6), 46-49.

Khandwalla, P.N. (1995). *Fourth Eye-Excellence Through Creativity.* New Delhi : Wheeler and Co. Ltd.

Khanna, O.P. (2004). Solitude Nurtures Creativity. *The Competition Master,* Feb., 622.

Kiran Kumar, S.K. (2002). *Psychology of Meditation: A Conceptual Approach.* New Delhi : Concept Publishing Company.

Kochhar, S.K. (1990). *Methods and Techniques of Teaching.* New Delhi : Sterling Publishers Pvt. Ltd.

———, (1988). Teaching of History. New Delhi : Sterling Publishers Pvt. Ltd.

Kornfield, J. (1979). Intensive Insight Meditation : A Phenomenological Study. *The Journal of Transperosonal Psychology, 11* (1), 41-59.

Krathwohl, D.R., Bloom, B.S., and Masia, B.B. (1964). *Taxonomy of Educational Objectives—The Classification of Educational Goals. Handbook-II : Affective Domain*. New York : David Mc Kay Company, Inc.

Krishnamurthi, A. (2004). Go ahead, Treat Yourself. *The Telegraph—Weekend, Saturday*, 29th May.

Kuppuswamy, B. (1985). *Element of Ancient Indian Psychology*. New Delhi : Vikas Publishing House.

Kutz, I., Borysenko, J.Z., and Benson, H. (1985). Meditation and Psychotherapy : A Rationale for the Integration of Dynamic Psychotherapy : The Relaxation Response and Mindfulness Meditation. *American Journal of Psychiatry, 14* (2), 1-8.

Lang, D. (1984). *Charisma*. London : Blond and Briggs Ltd.

Lenz, L. (1986). It's Superlearning Era Here. *Chicago Sun Times*, November 30.

Lesner, W.J. and Hillman, D. (1983). A Developmental Schema of Creativity. *The Journal of Creative Behavior, 17* (2), 103-14.

Lewis, E.M. (1960). *Teaching of History in Secondary Schools*. London : Evans Brothers Limited.

Lifton, R. (1971). *Maps of Consciousness*. New York : Collier Books.

Lindquist, E.F. (1953). *Design and Analysis of Experiments in Psychology and Education*. New York : Houghton Mifflin Co.

Lobuts, J.F. and Pennwill, C.L. (1984). Do we dare restructure the classroom environment. *The Journal of Creative Behavior, 18* (4), 237-246.

Locke, R.H., and Kelly, E.F. (1986). *A preliminary model for the cross-cultural analysis of altered states of consciousness*. Ethos.

Loomba, S., and Verma, S. (1990). Learning abilities as a function of creativity and attention span in children. *Indian Educational Review, 25* (4), 74-83.

Lozanov, G. (1971). *Problems of Suggestology*. Bulgaria : Sofia.

———, (1978). *Suggestology and Outlines of Suggestopedy*. New York : Golden Breach.

Lutzer, V.D. (1991). Gender Differnces in pre-schoolers ability to interpret common metaphors, *The Journal of Creative Behaviour, 25* (1), 69-74.

Mahaney, T. (1989). *Change Your Mind.* Santa Barbara : Super Learning Press.

Mangal, S.K. (1993). *Advanced Educational Psychology.* New Delhi: Prentice-Hall of India Pvt. Ltd.

Mann, C. (1994). New Technology and Gifted Education. *Psychological Abstracts, 81* (8), 3796.

Matson, J.V. (1991), Failure 101 : Rewarding Failure in the Classroom to Stimulate Creative Behaviour. *The Journal of Creative Behavior, 25* (1), 82-85.

May, R. (1959). The Nature of Creativity. In Anderson, H.H. (Ed.). *Creativity and its Cultivation.* New York : Haper and Brothers.

Mc Ghee, S.D., and Davis, G.A. (1994). The Imagery Creativity Connection. *The Journal of Creative Behaviour. 28* (3), 151-73.

Mc Cabe, M.P. (1991). Influence of Creativity and Intelligence on Academic Performance. *The Journal of Ceative Behavior, 25*(2), 116-22.

Mcnemar, Q. (1964). Lost : Our Intelligence, Why ? *American Psychologist, 19,* 871-82.

Mednick, M.T., and Andrew's, F.M. (1967). Creative Thinking and Level of Intelligence. *The Journal of Creative Behavior, 1*(4), 428-31.

Meha, D.G., and Shaver, P.A. (1996). Goal Structures in Creative Motivaiton, *The Journal of Creative Behavior, 30* (2), 77-104.

Mehdi, B. (1973). Creativity and Intelligence : The Evidence of Present Research. *The Educational Trends. 8* (1-4), 150-56.

Mehdi, B. (1985). *Manual of Verbal Test of Creative Thinking (Rev. ed.).* Agra : Natioanl Psychological Corporation.

Mellou, E. (1996). The Two Conditions View of Creativity. *The Journal of Creative Behavior, 30* (2), 126-43.

Ministry of Education, Government of India (1986). *National Policy on Education-1986.* New Delhi: Shastri Bhawan. Government of India.

Ministry of Education, Government of India (1992). *Revised Formulation of Natioanl Policy on Education-1992,* New Delhi: Shastri Bhawan. Govt. of India.

Mishra, B.C. (1986). Relationship between Creativity and Problem-solving Ability at different Levels of Intelligence. *Indian Educational Review, 21* (4), 112-18.

Mitchell, B.M., and Wilkens, R.F. (1986). Changes in Hemispheric Functioning through Direct Training in Creative Thinking. *The Journal of Creative Behavior, 20* (2), 144-45.

Mitra, S.K. (1986). *An Introduction to Philosophy of Sri Aurobindo.* Pondicherry : Sri Aurobindo Ashram.

Mohanty, J. (1980). Growth of Creativity—Nature *versus* Nurtune. *Progressive Educational Herald, 2* (4), 81-84.

———, (1989). Creativity : Meaning, Nature and Identification. *Journal of Indian Educaiton, 14* (6), 8-12.

Mookerji, R.K. (1989). *Ancient Indian Education.* New Delhi : Motilal Banarasidass.

Morris, C. (1956). *Varieties of Human Values.* Chicago : Chicago University Press.

Motamedi, K. (1982). Extending the Concept of Creativity. *The Journal of Creative Behavior, 16* (2), 75-88.

Moukwa, M. (1995). A Structure to Foster Creativity : An Industrial experience. *The Journal of Creative Behavior. 29* (1), 54-63.

Mukherji, S.N. (1964). *Education in India—Today and Tomorrow.* Baroda : Acharya Book Depot.

Murphy, M., and Donovan, S. (1997). *The Physical and Psychological Effects of Meditation.* Sausalito, CA : Institute of Noetic Sciences.

Murti, K. (2003). The Life Force. *The Telegraph-Fitness,* P-II, Monday, 8th December

———, (2003). The Life Force, *The Telegraph-Fitness,* P-II, Monday, 8th December.

———, (2004). Unite the body with mind. *The Telegraph-Fitness,* P-II, Monday, 8th MARCH.

———, (2004). Breath well for an energy boost. *The Telegraph-Fitness,* P-II, Monday, 10th May.

Nanak, Y. (2004). *Dehypnotic Meditation.* New Delhi : Pustak Mahal.

Nanda, S.K. (1982). *Indian Education and Its Problems Today.* New Delhi : Kalyani Publishers.

Naranjo, C., and Ornstein, R.E. (1971). *On the Psychology of Meditation.* New York : Viking Press.

NCERT. (1970). *Teaching History in Secondary Schools.* New Delhi: NCERT.

Neill, S., and Shallcross, D. (1994). Sensational Thinking—A Teaching/Learning Model for Creativity. *The Journal of Creative Behavior, 28* (2), 75-88.

Nelson, W. (1989). Experimentation with Lozonov method in Teaching Word Retention to Children with Learning Disability, *SALT Journal*, No. 4.

Narullah, S. and Naik, J.P. (1989). *A Students History of Education in India*. Bombay: Mc Millan Publishing Company.

Ochse, A. (1991). Why there were relatively few eminent women creators ? *The Journal of Creative Behavior, 25* (4), 334-42.

Ornstein, R.E. (1973). *The Nature of Human Consciousness : A Book of Readings*. San Francisco : W.H. Freeman and Co.

Osborn, A. (1957). *Applied Imagination*. New York : Charles Scribner and Sons.

Osis, K., Bokert, E., and Carlson, M.L. (1973). Dimension of the meditative experience. *The Journal of Transpersonal Psychology, 5* (2), 109-35.

Ostrander, S., Ostrander, N. and Schroeder, L. (1997). *Superlearning-2000*. New York: Dell Publishing Co.

———, and Shroeder, L. (1979). *Super Learning*. New York : Dell Publishing Co.

Ostrander, N. (1983). *Superlearning Guided Imagery for Children*. New York : Superlearning Inc.

Ostrander, S. and Schroeder, L. (1970). *Psychic Discoveries Behind the Iron Curtain*. New Jersy : Prentice Hall Pvt. Ltd.

———, (1984). *Superlearning*. New York : Random House Audio.

Ostrander, S., and Schroeder, L. (1990). *Learn How to Learn*. Los Angeles : Audio Renaissance.

———, (1991). *Supermemory*. New York : Carro II and Graf.

Padhi, J.S. (2000), Promotion of Creativity through Subject-related Creative Activities. *Journal of Indian Educaiton, XXVI* (3), 50-56.

———, (1995). Influence of Creativity on Academic Performance. *Journal of Indian Educaiton. 20* (6), 46-51.

Pal, Y. (1996). Interdomain Relationship between Creativity and Intelligence by Canonical Analysis. *Indian Educational Review, 26* (1), 20-27.

Parkhurst, H.B. (1999). Confusion, Lack of Consensus and the Definition of Creativity as a Construct. *The Journal of Creative Behavior, 33* (1), 1-21.

Parmananda, S. (2002) *Concentration and Meditation*. Madras : Sri Ramakrishna Math.

Paramjeet, D. and Saxena, S. (1995). Are Values Denote Creativity? *The Progress of Education, LXIX* (7), 124-26.

Passi, B.K. (1972). *An Explorating Study of Creativity and its Relationship with Intelligence and Achievement in School Subjects at Higher Secondary Stage*. Unpublished Doctoral Dissertation, Punjab University, India.

Passi, B.K. and Prabhu, S.R. (1997). Stressfree Superlearning. *The Progress of Education, LXXI* (7), 152-59.

Pesut, D.J. (1990). Creative Thinking as a Self-regulatory Metacognitive Process—A Model for Education, Training and further Research. *The Journal of Creative Behavior, 24* (3), 105-10.

Pickard, E. (1990). Towards a Theory of Creative Potential. *The Journal of Creative Behavior, 24* (1), 01-09.

Prabhupada, A.C.B.S. (1998). *The Path of Yoga*. Bombay : Bhakti Vedanta Trust.

Prabhupada, A.C.B.S. (1980). *Discourse on Srimad Bhagabat Gita*. Bombay : Bhakti Vedanta Trust.

Prichard, A., and Taylor, J. (1980). *Accelterated Learning* Novato, CA : Academic. Therapy Publications.

Prichard, A. (1981). Adapting the Lozanov Method for Remedial Reading Instruction. *SALT Journal, 1* (2).

Powel, M.C. (1994). On Creativity and Social Change. *The Journal of Creative Behavior, 28* (1), 21-32

Prusty, P.K. (2001). Relationship between Intelligence and Creativity. *The Educational Review, 44* (b).

———, (2001). Relationship between Intelligence and Creativity. *The Educational Review, 44*(6).

———, (2002). Influence of SEX and SES on Creative Thinking. *The Educational Review, 45*(8), 2002.

———, (2004). Effect of Creative Method of Teaching English (CMTE) on Development of Creative Thinking of Secondary School Students. *Global Peace, 3*(3), 25-30.

Rednitzki, G. (1968). *Contemporany Schools of Metascience*. Goteborg : Academiforlaget.

Raina, M.K. (1969). A Study of Sex Difference in Creativity in India. *The Journal of Creative Behavior, 3* (2), 111-14.

———, (Ed.). (1980). *Creativity Research in International Perspective*. New Delhi : NCERT.

Raina, M.K. (1991). *Talant in Perspective*. New Delhi : NCERT.

Rama, D. (1990). *Journey of Awakening : A Meditator's Guide Book*. New York : Bantam Books.

Rao, K.R. (1989). Meditation : Sacred and Secular—A review and assesment of some recent research. *Journal of Indian Academy of Applied Psychology, 15* (2), 51-74.

Reich, R. (1993). Reclaiming our Age. *Working Woman*, September, 1993.

Renzulli, J.S. (1993). A general theory for the development of creative productivity through the persuit of ideal act of learning, *Psychological Abstracts*, 80(b), 2834.

Ricouer, P. (1970). Freud. New Haven : Yale University Press.

Robbins, A. (1991). *Awaken the Giant Within*. New York : Summit Books.

Rose, C. (1985). *Accelerated Learning*. New York : Dell Publishing Co.

Rossi, E. (1988). *Psychobiology of Mind-Body Healing*. New York : Norton and Co.

Roy, A. (2004). Tantra is the Mantra. *The Telegraph-look Women*, Sunday, 29th February.

Rubenstein, D.J. (2000). Stimulating Students' Creativity and Curiosity : Does Content and Medium Matter ? *The Journal of Creative Behavior, 34* (1), 1-15.

Russel, S. (1995). Effect of Creativity Training upon Concept map Complexity : SLD, Gifted and Regular Education 5th, 6th and 7th Grade Students. *Dissertation Abstracts International, 7-8* (1 and 2), 1-10.

Sandhu, T.S. (1979). Relationship of Creativity with Academic Achievement in Science Subjects. *Creativity Newsletter, 7-8* (1 and 2), 1-10.

Sarnoff, D.P., and Cole, H.P. (1983). Creativity and Personal Growth. *The Journal of Creative Behavior, 17* (2), 95-102.

Seki, H. (1983). Influence of Music on Memory and Education. *International Journal of Acupuncture and Research. 8* (1), 1-16.

Sennett, J.B., and Ceci, S.J. (1996). Clue Efficiency and insight : Unvelling the Mystry of Inductive Leaps. *The Journal of Creative Behavior, 30* (3) 153-72.

Setia, R. (1984). *Intelligence, Creativity and Achievement in Mathematics : A Regression Analysis*. Unpublished M.Ed. Thesis, Panjab University, India.

Shan, H.R. (1992). Effectiveness of Certain Curricular Activities in Development of Creative Thinking of High School Students of Backward Hilly Region of Jammu. *Indian Educational Review, 27* (2), 68-72.

Shapiro, D.H. (1978). Meditation : Aspects of Research and Practice. *The Journal of Transpersonal Psychology, 10* (2), 113-33.

———, (1982). Overview : Clinical and Physiological Comparison of Meditation with Other Self-control Strategies. *American Journal of Psychiatry, 139* (3), 267-74.

———, (1990). Meditation, Self-control and Control by a Benevolent Other : Issues of Content and Context. In Maurits G.T. Kwee (Ed.). *Psychotherapy, Meditation and Health : A Cognitive—Behavioral Perspective*. London : East-West Publication.

———, (1994). Examining the Content and Context of Meditation : A Challenge of Psychology in the Areas of Stress Management, Psychotherapy and Religion or Values. *Journal of Humanistic Psychology. 34* (4) 101-35.

———, and Walsh, R. (Eds.), (1984). *Meditation : Classic and Contemporany Prospectives*. New York : Aldine and Co.

Sharma, V.P. (2000). *Creativity—Potentials and Prospects*. Agra : H.P. Bhargava Book House.

Sri Aurobindo (1918). *Light for Students. Pondicherry* : Sri Aurobindo Ashram.

Sharma, R.A. and Bharatiya, A. (1988). Mathematical Performance of Convergent and Divergent Thinkers. *Indian Educational Review, 23* (1), 116-21.

Shaw, J., and Cliatt, M.J.P. (1986). A Model for Training Teachers to Encourage Divergent Thinking on Young Children. *The Journal of Creative Behavior, 20* (2), 81-88.

Siau, K.L. (1995). Group Creativity and Technology. *The Journal of Creative Behavior, 29* (3), 201-16.

Simonton, D.K. (1998). Donald Campbell's Model of the Creative Process : Creativity as Blind Variation and Selective Retention. *The Journal of Creative Behavior, 32* (3), 153-58.

Singer, E. (1992). Teacher Consultation to Develop Students' Higher-level Thinking Skills. *Dissertation Abstracts International, 52* (7), 2476.

Singh, A. (1986). Sex difference in Verbal Creativity of Science Teachers. *Indian Educational Review, 21* (3), 113-15.

Singh, B. (1988). Mathematical Ceativity and some Socio-psychological Factros of Hindus and Muslims. *Indian Educational Review, 23* (4), 121-29.

Singh, J. (2002). Creative Thinking, Examination Stress and Eduction. *Parenting,* March. 41-61.

Sivananda, S. (1999). *Tripple Yoga*. Gharwal : Divine Life Society.

Sivananda, S. (1989). *Yoga Vasistha,* Gharwal : Devine Life Society.

Stein, M.I. (1983). Creativity in genesis. *The Journal of Creative Behavior, 17* (1), 1-8.

Stockley, D. (1993). Being Productive, being Cleaver : The Enhanced Forest of Intellectual Property. *Australian Journal of Education, 37* (1), 96-111.

Strauss, A., and Corbin, J. (1990). *Basics of Qualitative Research : Grounded Theory Procedures and Techniques*. Newbusy Park. CA : Sage Publication.

Tapasyananda, S. (2000). *Four Yogas of Swami Vivekananda*. Mayavati : Advaita Ashram.

Tast, C.T. (1969). *Altered States of Consciousness*. New York : Wiley.

Tart, C.T. (1975). *States of Consciousness*. New York : Dutton.

Tart, C.T. (1989). *Open Mind, Discriminating Mind : Reflections on Human Possibilities*. San Françisco : Harper and Row.

Tart, C.T., and Young, S. (1989). Meditation and Psychology : A Dialogue. In C.T. Tart. *Open Mind, Discriminating Mind : Reflections of Human Possibilities*. San Francisco : Harper and Row.

Thaleourne, M.A. (2000). Transliminality and Creativity. *The Journal of Creative Behavior, 34* (3), 193-200.

Thorstad, H., and Garry, W. (1977). *Suggestopedia, An Advanced Simulation Technique*. Norfolk VA : Atlantic Fleet Training Centre.

Tiwari, R.S. (2004). *The Yoga of Gita*. New Delhi : Pustak Mahal.

Toffler, A. (1982). *The Third Wave*. New York : Bantam Books.

Tohei, K. (1979). *Co-ordinating Mind and Body in Daily Life*. New York : Japan Publications.

Tomatis, A. (1988). *Sleep Learning : Its Theory, Application and Technique*. New York : Sleep Learning Research Assosiation.

Torrance, E.P. (1959). *Exploration in Creative Thinking in Early School Years (VIII) IQ and Creativity in School Achievement.* Minneapollis : Bureau of Educational Research; University of Minnesota.

Torrance, E.P. (1961). Factors Affecting Creative Thinking in Children. An Interim Report. *Merill Palmer Quarterly, 7,* 171-80

Torrance, E.P. (1962). *Guiding Creative Talent.* New Jersy : Prentice Hall Pvt. Ltd.

Torrance, E.P., and Myers, R.E. (1970). *Creative Learning and Teaching,* New York : Dodd, Mead and Co.

Torrance, E.P. and Safter, H.T. (1986). Are Children Becoming more Creative ? *The Journal of Creative Behavior, 20* (1), 01-13.

Treffinger, D.J., Isaksen, S.G., and Firestein, R.L. (1983). Theoretical Prerspectives on Creative Learning and its Facilitation : An Overview. *The Journal of Creative Behavior, 17* (1), 9-17.

Tripathy, S.N. (1996). *Talent and Creativity.* Agra : National Psychological Corporation.

Tylor, C.W. (Ed.). (1972), *Climate for Creativity-Report of the Seventh National Research Conferance on Creativity.* New York : Pergamon Press.

Vannon, P.E. (1964). Creativity and intelligence. *Educational Research, VI* (3).

Vivekananda, S. (1923). *Raja Yoga.* Kolkata : Advaita Ashram.

———, (1928). *Six lessons on Raja Yoga.* Kolkota : Advaita Ashram.

Vajreswari, R. (1973), *A Handbook for History Teachers,* New Delhi: Allied Publishers.

Varkey, C.J. (1940). *The Wardha Scheme.* London : Oxford University Press.

Vigne, J. (1997). Meditation and Mental Health. *Indian Journal of Clinical Psychology. 24* (1), 46-51.

Volinn, E. (1985). Eastern Meditation Groups : Why Join ? *Sociological Analysis, 46* (2), 147-56.

Von, E.R. (1989). Maps of the Mind : The Cartography of Consciousness. In R.C. Valle and R. Von (Eds.) *Metaphors of Consciousness.* New York : Plenum Press.

Wade, J. (1987). *Accelerative Learning*. Aus : Community Education.

———, (1990). *Super Study*. Lyons. Aus : Dellasta.

———, (1992). *Teaching Without Text Books*. Carlfon Victoria. Aus: CIS Educational.

Wagner, W. (1993) *Beyond Teaching and Learning*. East Aurora. NY: United Educational Service.

———, (1991). *How to be a Better Teacher, Today*. Gaitherburg. MD: Project Renaissance.

———, (1994). A Proposal to Measure Effects of Image Streaming upon Intelligence, Performance and Proficiency. *Journal SALT, 9* (1).

Wallaach, M.A. and Kogan, N. (1965). A New Look at the Creativity-Intelligence Distinction. *Journal of Personality. 33* (3).

Walsh, R. (1983). Meditation Practice and research. *Journal of Humanstic Psychology. 23* (1), 18-50.

Ward, T.B. and Sifonis, C.M. (1997). Task Demands and Generative Thinking : What Changes and What Remains the Same ? *The Journal of Creative Beavior, 31* (4), 245-59.

Weisborg, R.W. (1992). *Creativity-Beyond the Myth of Genius*. New York : W.H. Freeman and Company.

West, M.A. (1986). *Meditation : Psychology and Human Experience*. London : Wisdom Publications.

———, (1987). *On the Psychology of Meditation*. Oxford. England : Clarendon Press.

Wertheimer, M. (1959). *Productive Thinking*. New York : Harper and Row Publishers.

Westberg, K.L. (1996). The effects of Teaching students how to invent. *The Journal of Creative Behavior, 30* (4), 249-67.

Woodman, M. (1990). *Chaos or Creativity* ? Pacific Grove CA : Oral Tradition Archive.

Wexu, M. (1975), *The Ear : Galewa to Balancing Body—A Modern Guide to Ear Acupuncture*. Santa fe : Aurora Press.

Wilson, R.A. (1977). *Cosmic Trigger*. New York : Pocket Books.

Wonder, J., and Donovan, P. (1984). *Whole Brain Thinking*. New York : Ballantine Books.

Yadav, R.S. (1986). A Study of correlation among intelligence, academic achievement and creativity. *Progress of Education, LXI* (3), 50-53.

Yamamoto, K. (1964). Threshold of Intelligence in Academic Achievement of Highly Creative Students. *The Journal of Experimental Education. 32*, 4.

———, (1964). Creative Thinking : Some Thoughts on Research. *Exceptional Children, 30* (a) 403-10.

Yates, F. (1966). *The Art of Memory,* Chicago : Chicago University Press.

Yepsen, R.J. (1987). *How to Boost your Brain Power, Achieving Peak Intelligence, Memory and Creativity*. Emaus, Pa : Rodale Press.

Young, J.G. (1985). What is Creativity. *The Journal of Creative Behaviour, 19* (2), 77-87.

Super Learning on the Web

1. Superlearning.com
2. Nancy @ Superleaning.ca.
3. Superlearning Inc. Home Page-http://www.Superlearning-inc.com
4. http://www Health-O-Rama.org/Superlearning/
5. http://www. lucent.com/Superlearning/

INDEX